关博萃珍

中国海关博物馆展藏精选

中国海关博物馆 编著

科学出版社
北京

内容简介

海关作为国家主权的象征，始终与国家同呼吸、与民族共命运，3000多年的中国海关发展史揭示出“国盛则关兴、国弱则关衰”的历史规律。中国海关博物馆认真贯彻落实习近平总书记“让文物活起来”系列重要指示精神，倾力为社会奉献优秀文化作品，满足新时代人民群众不断增长的精神文化需求。本书收录了本馆近300件最具代表性实物的精美图片和文字说明，并配以展厅中重要场景照片，采用多视角、图文并茂的形式阐释了中国海关的发展历程和建设成就。

本书可作为海关史、外贸史和海关业务研究人员的参考资料，也可供历史学、文博爱好者鉴赏、交流。

图书在版编目（CIP）数据

关博萃珍：中国海关博物馆展藏精选 / 中国海关博物馆编著. —北京：科学出版社，2020.11

ISBN 978-7-03-066375-7

Ⅰ. ①关… Ⅱ. ①中… Ⅲ. ①海关—博物馆—历史文物—介绍—中国 Ⅳ. ①K872.714

中国版本图书馆CIP数据核字(2020)第197815号

责任编辑：任晓刚 / 责任校对：韩 杨
责任印制：师艳茹 / 封面设计：黄华斌

联系电话：010-64011837
E-mail:yangjing@mail.sciencep.com

科学出版社 出版
北京东黄城根北街16号
邮政编码：100717
http：//www.sciencep.com

北京九天鸿程印刷有限责任公司 印刷
科学出版社发行 各地新华书店经销
*
2020年11月第 一 版 开本：880 × 1230 1/16
2020年11月第一次印刷 印张：15 3/4 插页：10
字数：280 000

定价：298.00元

（如有印装质量问题，我社负责调换）

序

中华文明灿烂辉煌，中国海关源远流长。作为进出境监督管理机关，海关因国家而生、应外贸而兴。西周时期，侧重于军事防卫功能的关“执禁以讥”“讥而不征”，距今已有3000多年历史。春秋晚期至战国时期，出现了“关市之征”“关市之赋”，关津具有监管、查私和征税等事权。此后，历代中央政府均在陆路交通要道、水路渡口设置具有海关事权的专门机构——关津。

汉武帝时期，张骞凿空西域，“列四郡，据两关”；路博德、杨仆等率兵平定南越（今中国岭南及今越南北部地区），设立苍梧、合浦等七郡，陆上、海上丝绸之路兴起并发展，位于西北陆路边境的阳关、玉门关以及海上丝绸之路始发港的合浦（《汉书·地理志》曰：“有关”）、徐闻所设之关拥有了对进出口贸易货物、人员进行监督管理和征税的职权。隋代于边境州府设置掌管与周边各族及外国商人贸易的“交市监”，唐初改为“互市监”。

唐开元年间，在安南、广州设市舶使，“籍其名物，纳舶脚，禁珍异，蕃商有以欺诈入牢狱者”，与地方长官共同管理市舶事务，包括奏报、检阅（检查蕃船及其所载货物）、款待、舶脚（征收关税）、收市（政府优先垄断蕃舶珍贵商品的交易）、进奉（向皇帝进贡珍异物品）、作法（制订某些有关蕃舶管理的政策法令）等。宋、元、明三代，在东南沿海港口设市舶司，集海关、外贸和外事职能于一体。明朝“隆庆开关”，“准贩东西二洋”，在漳州月港设督饷馆管理海外贸易并首开征收外贸货币税的先河。清康熙年间收复台湾后，开海贸易、开洋设关，闽、粤、江、浙四海关设立，“海关”之名始现。

鸦片战争后，外国人担任总税务司、税务司的“洋关”“新关”在全国各地陆续出现，统管征税、监管、缉私、统计，以及新式邮政、海务港务、经理内外债及赔款、“业余外交”、代购军舰、参加世博会、商标挂号、管理同文馆等事务，涉足中国政治、经济、文化、军事、外交等领域，成为英美法等西方列强“对华关系的基石”。由于关税自主权、海关行政管理权、海关税款收支保管权相继丧失，随着民族意识的崛起和中国共产党的诞生，党领导中国人民为收回关权进行了长期不懈的斗争。

1949年10月，中华人民共和国成立，“中国人民从此站起来了”，揭开了中国历史的新篇章。自此，中国“掌握了国家大门的钥匙”，实行独立自主的关税制度，废除外籍税务司制度。全国海关推行集中统一的垂直管理体制，为维护国家的主权和利益、促进对外经济贸易发展和科技文化交往、保障社会主义现代化建设做出了突出贡献。沐浴着改革开放的春风，中国海关恢复了生机和活力，服务党和国家大局的作用日益凸显。特别是党的十八大以来，在以习近平同志为核心的党中央集中统一领导下，中国海关扎实推进“政治建关、改革强关、依法把关、科技兴关、从严治关”，全力打造“让党中央放心、让人民群众满意”的新时代中国特色社会主义新海关和国际上最具竞争力的海关监管体制机制，更好服务于高水平开放、推动高质量发展，为决胜全面建成小康社会，实现中华民族伟大复兴的中国梦做出更大贡献。

为系统收集保护海关文物、全面展现中国海关的历史文化与建设成就，海关总署党组于2002年决定筹建中国海关博物馆。经过十多年的深入调研、精心筹备以及征地拆迁建设，海关总署直属国家级行业博物馆——中国海关博物馆于2014年3月正式开馆。开馆以来，中国海关博物馆认真贯彻落实习近平总书记“让文物活起来”系列重要指示批示精神，致力于满足人民群众日益增长的对美好生活的新期待，努力发挥全国海关和文博行业两种资源优势，主动围绕中心、服务大局，成为收藏海关文物的中心、展示海关文化的平台、研究海关历史的阵地、宣传海关使命担当的窗口、开展爱国主义和海关职业素质教育的基地、中国海关的“金色名片”和“第二会客厅”，为赓续海关文脉、传承海关精神、弘扬中华优秀传统文化和社会主义核心价值观发挥了积极作用，并先后荣获“第十二届（2014年度）全国博物馆十大陈列展览精品奖”“北京市中小学生社会大课堂资源单位”“北京市第一次全国可移动文物普查工作先进集体”，以及全国、中央国家机关、北京市、东城区爱国主义教育（示范）基地等荣誉。

在筹建过程中，我们先后编纂出版了《中国海关文物集萃》《中国海关博物馆》。为进一步展现新时代中国特色社会主义新海关建设成果、弘扬海关文化，我们组织人力编著了这本浓缩中国海关博物馆近年文物征藏、展览展示、学术研究成果的《关博萃珍——中国海关博物馆展藏精选》。本书从馆藏30000余件文物以及展品、复仿制品中，精选最具有代表性的近300件实物并配以展厅中重要场景，按照海关建制、典章制度、近代人事、近代兼办、人民海关、海关监管、税收征管、查缉走私、海关统计、检验检疫10个部分组织而成，以图文并茂的形式从不同侧面、不同视角生动形象地反映了中国海关的发展历程与建设成就。

3000多年来，中国海关与国家同呼吸、与民族共命运，共同走过了跌宕起伏的不平凡历程，谱写了可歌可泣的英雄赞歌，成为透视国家命运的一扇窗口。为此，我们衷心希望广大读者朋友从中国海关博物馆丰富的馆藏、精美的文物中，发现中国海关的悠久历史、辉煌成就，探究海关与老百姓血浓于水的紧密联系，感悟“国盛则关兴、国弱则关衰”的历史规律，了解中国海关捍卫国家主权利益、维护人民群众身体健康和生命安全的过去与现在、今天与明天、使命与担当、作用与贡献。

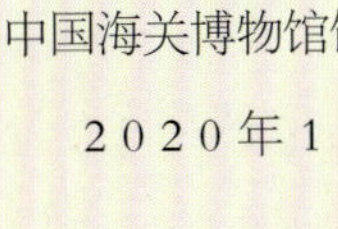

中国海关博物馆馆长

2020年11月

Preface

China Customs has a long history and splendid civilization. As an inward and outward supervisory and administrative organ, China Customs originated from the state and has thrived along with foreign trade. Early in the Western Zhou Dynasty over 3,000 years ago, although mainly focused on military defense, passes already took the responsibility on travelers examination. Starting from the late Spring and Autumn Period to the Warring States Period, "customs, and market duties and taxes" were adopted, during which passes were in charge of supervision, inspection and tax levy. Since then, central governments in successive dynasties set up professional passes in charge of customs affairs at vital land transportation routes and waterway ferries.

During the reign of Emperor Wu of the Western Han Dynasty, Zhang Qian led his missions to open the trade routes between the East and the West, with four prefectures (Wuwei, Zhangye, Jiuquan and Dunhuang) and two passes (Yumen Pass and Yang Pass) being set up. During this period, military leaders Lu Bode and Yang Pu led their armies to conquer Nanyue and established seven prefectures including Cangwu and Hepu. Therefore, land and maritime Silk Roads sprang up and enjoyed development. Since then, these passes were authorized to be in charge of supervision and administration over imported and exported goods and travelers, as well as tax levy. In the Sui Dynasty, *jiaoshijian* (supervisory office of border trade) was set up.

During the Kaiyuan period of the Tang Dynasty, superintendents of maritime trade (*shiboshi*) were set up in Annan and Guangzhou, and in charge of maritime trade affairs together with local governors, with duties such as reporting, inspection (inspecting foreign ships and the goods), reception, anchorage tax levy (customs collection), monopoly of rare goods trade by the government, tribute payment and formulation of management policies and decrees on foreign ships. In the Song, Yuan and Ming Dynasties, "maritime trade supervisory organizations" (*shibosi*) were set up at southeast coastal ports, which integrated the functions of customs affairs, foreign trade and diplomatic affairs. In the Ming Dynasty, maritime trade between the West and the East was allowed by Emperor Longqing, *Duxiangguan* (Tariff Supervising Bureau) was set up at Yuegang in Zhangzhou taking responsibility for overseas trade. This was the first time to collect foreign trade tax in cash. After the recovery of Taiwan region during the Kangxi period in the Qing Dynasty, maritime trade reopened, and Fuzhou, Guangzhou, Shanghai and Ningbo customs were set up, since then the name *haiguan* (the Chinese name of customs) came into being.

After the Opium War, foreign customs with foreigners as the inspector generals appeared nationwide to be in general charge of taxation, supervision, anti-smuggling, statistics, modern postal service, coast and harbor affairs, debt handling, diplomatic affairs, agent purchasing of warships, participation in world exhibitions, trademark registration and management of School of Combined Learning (*Tungwen Guan*). They intervened in China's political, economic, cultural, military and diplomatic affairs and became the "footstone for Western powers' relations with China." As a result, China lost tariff autonomy, customs administration right, as well as the right to customs revenue custody. With the rise of national consciousness and the birth of the Communist Party of China (the CPC), Chinese people had long-term and unremitting struggles to recover the sovereignty of customs.

In October 1949, the People's Republic of China was founded. Since then, China Customs implemented an independent tariff system, carried out centralized and unified vertical management system nationwide, made outstanding contributions to protect national sovereignty and interests, promoted the development of foreign economic trade, technological and cultural exchanges and safeguarded socialist modernization. With the reform and opening-up, China Customs has been revitalized and it has played an increasingly prominent role in serving the overall initiatives of the Party and the country. Since the 18th National Congress of the CPC, in particular, under the centralized and unified leadership of the CPC Central Committee taking Xi Jinping as the core, China Customs has made solid progress in "managing Customs under political governance, strengthening Customs through reforms, safeguarding Customs according to law, making Customs with science and technology, and governing customs based on strict accountability." China Customs is also striving to build socialist customs with Chinese characteristics for the new era which is trustworthy to both the CPC Central Committee and the people, and build the most internationally competitive customs supervision system and mechanism, in order to better serve the high-level opening-up and high-quality development, as well as making greater contributions to securing a decisive victory in building a moderately prosperous society in all aspects and realizing the Chinese dream of national rejuvenation.

For the purpose of systematically collecting and protecting customs-related cultural relics and comprehensively presenting the history, culture and construction of China Customs, the CPC leadership group of GACC decided on the preparation and construction of China Customs Museum in 2002. After more than ten years of in-depth survey, elaborate preparations and land requisition, demolation and construction, China Customs Museum officially opened in March 2014 as a nation-level specialized museum directly under GACC. Since its opening, China Customs Museum has carefully implemented General Secretary Xi Jinping's important instructions of "bringing cultural relics back to life" and engaged itself in meeting the general public's increasing hope for a beautiful life. Leveraging its resource advantages both in customs and in the museum sector, the Museum actively serves the central task as well as the overall interests of the country, building itself into a center that collects customs-related cultural relics, a platform demonstrating customs culture, a front to study customs history, a window to publicize the mission and responsibilities of China Customs, a base to carry out education on patriotism and professional qualities of customs, and finally the "golden name card" and the second reception room of China Customs. It has played an active role in continuing the customs culture, inheriting the customs spirit and carrying forward fine Chinese culture and the socialist core values. It has won a number of honors including the "12th (2014) National Top Ten Exhibitions Award of Museums", "Resources Unit for the Social Classroom of Primary and Secondary School Students in Beijing", "Advanced Group in the 1st National Survey of Movable Cultural Relics in Beijing" as well as the Patriotism Education Base for the whole country, organs of the CPC Central Committee and the state, Beijing Municipality and Dongcheng District, etc.

During the preparation and construction of the Museum, we successively compiled and published *Fine Cultural Relics Collection of China Customs* and *China Customs Museum*. In order to further show the achievements in building socialist new customs with Chinese characteristics in the new era and carry forward the customs culture, we hereby compiled the *Treasures from China Customs Museum*, a compendium of collections, exhibitions and academic research findings of China Customs Museum in recent years. This book covers nearly 300 most representative material objects and scenes of the exhibition hall. The material objects are selected from over 30,000 pieces of cultural relics as well as exhibits, copies collected in the Museum, which constitute such ten parts as Organizational System of Customs, Decrees and Regulations, Modern Personnel Management, Modern Additional Services, People's Customs, Customs Supervision and Control, Taxation, Anti-smuggling, Customs Statistics, as well as Inspection and Quarantine. The book vividly reflects the development and achievements of China Customs from different aspects and angles in an illustrated manner.

Over 3,000 years, China Customs has always shared the outlook and destiny with the country, and experienced an extraordinary journey with heroic acts full of ups and downs, making itself a showcase of the country's past. To this end, we sincerely hope that from the rich collections and exquisite cultural relics, our readers can learn about the long history and brilliant achievements of China Customs, discover its close connection with civilians, comprehend the historical law that the vicissitude of a country's customs is closely linked with that of the country, and understand how China Customs has safeguarded national sovereignty and interests and protected the people's life and health and will continue to fulfill its mission in the future.

Fan Kun

Director of China Customs Museum

November 2020

目　录

序

第一部分　海关建制　001

第二部分　典章制度　013

第三部分　近代人事　025

人员管理　026

用具用品　034

人才培养　046

第四部分　近代兼办　053

代办邮政　054

海务港务　060

商标注册　066

世界博览会　070

其他兼办　074

第五部分　人民海关　079

队伍建设　080

争取关权　094

边关精神　110

海关荣誉　116

第六部分　海关监管　123

第七部分　税收征管　147

第八部分　查缉走私　163

第九部分　海关统计　195

第十部分　检验检疫　203

国境卫生检疫　204

出入境动植物检疫　210

进出口食品安全　218

进出口商品检验　222

展厅实景

后记

Contents

Preface

Part Ⅰ Organizational System of Customs 001

Part Ⅱ Decrees and Regulations 013

Part Ⅲ Modern Personnel Management 025

Staff Management 026

Appliances and Articles 034

Personnel Recruitment and Training 046

Part Ⅳ Modern Additional Services 053

Agent Postal Services 054

Coast and Harbor Affairs 060

Trademark Registration 066

World Exposition 070

Other Additional Services 074

Part Ⅴ People's Customs 079

Team Construction 080

Struggle for Customs Sovereignty 094

Border Safeguarding Spirit 110

Customs Honor 116

Part Ⅵ Customs Supervision and Control 123

Part Ⅶ Taxation 147

Part Ⅷ Anti-smuggling 163

Part Ⅸ Customs Statistics 195

Part Ⅹ Inspection and Quarantine 203

Frontier Health Quarantine 204

Entry-Exit Animal and Plant Quarantine 210

Import and Export Food Safety 218

Import and Export Commodity Inspection 222

Photos of Exhibition Hall

Postscript

海关建制

Organizational System of Customs

The long history of customs in China can date back to the Western Zhou Dynasty when passes were set up for military defense. From the late Spring and Autumn Period to the Warring States Period, passes were in charge of supervision, smuggling inspection and tax levy. Afterwards, regimes of all dynasties set up passes and ferries to be in charge of cross-region trade, border trade and foreign trade; *Shiboshi* or *Shibosi* were set up during the Tang, Song, Yuan and Ming Dynasties integrating customs, foreign trade and foreign affairs. *Duxiangguan* was set up for the first time in the middle and late Ming Dynasty to collect foreign trade tax in cash; during the Kangxi period in the Qing Dynasty, Fuzhou, Guangzhou, Shanghai and Ningbo Customs were set up, since then the name *haiguan* began to be used by China's entry-exit supervision authorities; in mid-nineteenth century, foreign customs were set up successively at various trading ports (generally called "customs" later) to supervise foreign or foreign-style ships, and the original organizations in charge of domestic and coastal ships were renamed "native customs," forming a situation of long-term coexistence of foreign and native customs.

我国设关历史悠久，西周时期出现用于军事防御的关、塞，春秋晚期至战国时期关津具有监管、查私、征税等海关事权，故有“关者，诸侯之陬隧也，而外财之门户也，万人之道行也”之谓。其后各政权在陆路、水路交通要道（含边境要塞）设置“关津”“交市监（互市监）”“榷署”“茶马司”等管理跨区域商贸或边境贸易、对外贸易的专门机构；唐代始设集海关、外贸和外事职能于一体的市舶使，宋元明三代从之；明代中后期设“督饷馆”，始征对外贸易货币税；清康熙年间设置闽、粤、江、浙四海关，我国进出境监督管理机关开始启用“海关”之名；近代各通商口岸陆续设立“新关”“洋关”（后统称“海关”）监管洋船或洋式船只，原设监管国内和近海船舶机构改称“老关”“旧关”“大关”（后统称“常关”），形成海关与常关长期并存的局面。

“关”字瓦当

“Guan” Character Eaves Tile

西汉

函谷关始建于春秋战国时期，为出入关中的门户，原址位于今河南省灵宝市以北15公里处。因其紧靠黄河岸边，关在谷中，深险如函，故得名。我国第一个在史籍上留下姓名的关令尹喜即任职于此。张骞凿空西域后，函谷关成为丝绸之路上的重要关卡。后因将军杨仆“耻为关外侯”，也为了加强对东部的控制，汉武帝将函谷关东移至今河南省新安县境内。带有“关”字的瓦当仅见于汉代函谷关遗址及其窑址中，成为古关起源的有力证物。

“九江关”青花碗

Blue-and-white Porcelain Bowl with Design of Jiujiang Customs

清代

明清时期，运河、长江水运商道多设关征税，称为钞关或户关。这件青花瓷碗产自景德镇，描绘了悬挂“九江关”幡旗的两层官衙建筑场景。九江钞关始设于明景泰元年（1450年），是景德镇御窑厂瓷器进京的转运枢纽，并监管外销瓷出口事务。清代九江关监督一般由内务府派员外郎出任，同理关务和景德镇窑务。雍正、乾隆年间，唐英曾任九江关监督兼景德镇督陶官近三十年。

闽海关涵江口地契

Title Deeds of Hanjiang Port of Fuzhou Customs

1838年

闽海关涵江口在莆田买地的地契。1684年，清政府开海设关，闽、粤、江、浙四海关相继设立，负责管理对外贸易，监管进出境的货物并征税，“海关”正式成为进出境监督管理机构名称，并形成了一套海关业务管理制度。乾隆二十二年（1757年），清政府施行广州“一口通商”制度，即一般情况下欧美商船只准停靠广州贸易；闽、江、浙海关只办理本国商船沿海贸易及东亚、东南亚、南亚商船贸易手续。鸦片战争后，关权旁落，福州、厦门先后辟为通商口岸并设立闽海新关、厦门新关，实行片面协定关税。原闽海关改称“常关”仅征收常关税。

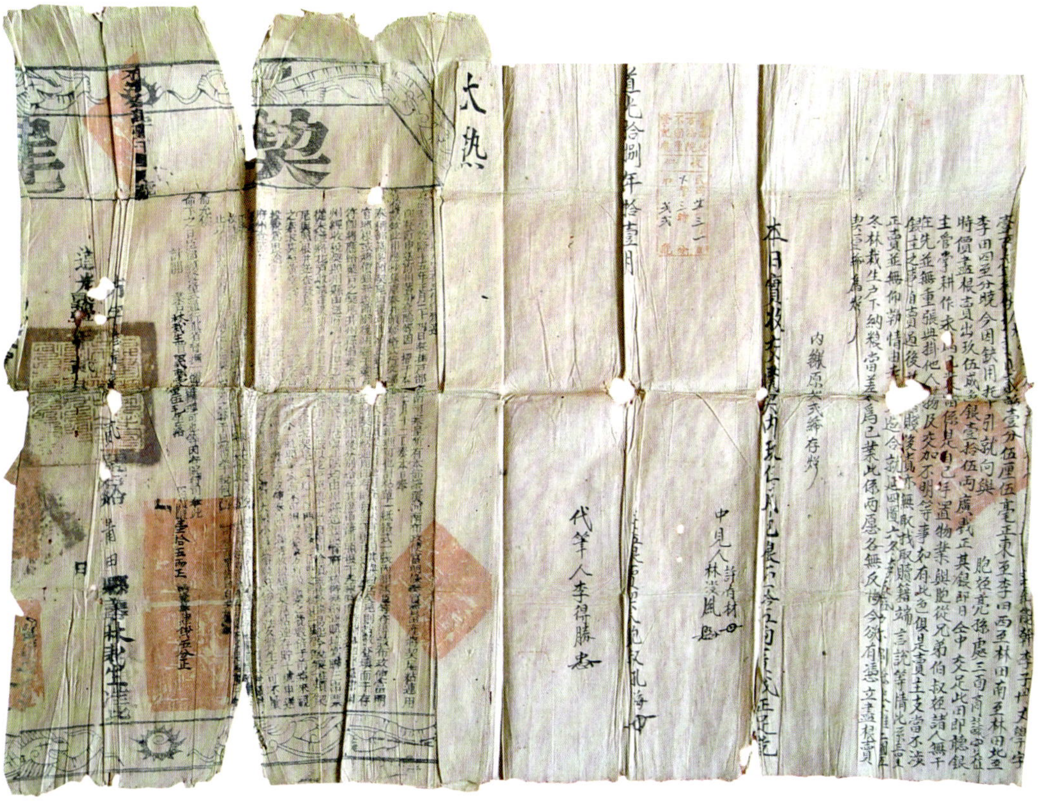

总税务司署上海办事处储金股印章

Stamp of the Pensions Chief Accountant's Office, Inspectorate General, Shanghai

民国时期

1858年，《通商章程善后条约》规定任凭总理大臣邀请洋人"帮办税务，并严查漏税"。1859年，李泰国开始行使"各通商口岸海关总税务司"职权并将江海关税务监督改为江海关税务司，税务司制度形成。1861年，总税务司署设立，1865年迁至北京。1927年4月，国民政府定都南京后令"总税务司署移京设置"，但代理总税务司易纨士（A.H.Edwards）以南京没有可资利用的办公地点为由，获批设总税务司署上海办事处，实际为真正的总税务司署。1941年底太平洋战争爆发后，日伪劫夺了上海的总税务司署，国民政府在重庆另立总税务司署，抗日战争胜利后迁回上海，1949年底随国民政府逃往台北。

官衙式江海北关铜版

Copper Plate of the Chinese-style Architecture of Shanghai Customs

民国时期

江海北关建筑印刷铜版。上海于1843年11月17日正式对外开埠，与广州、厦门、福州、宁波相继成为第一次鸦片战争后被迫对外开放的五个通商口岸。江海关在洋泾浜北路（今上海市延安东路外滩）设盘验所办理外商进出口申报和纳税手续。1846年在上海北门外头坝设江海北关，清初设立的江海关被称为"江海大关"，两关并存。1857年，江海北关迁至汉口路外滩（今上海市中山东一路13号），建成官衙式关署。

教堂式江海关铜版

Copper Plate of the Church Style Architecture of Shanghai Customs

民国时期

江海关建筑印刷铜版。1893年，原官衙式江海北关被翻建为教堂式建筑，该建筑是当时规模最大、式样最新的西式建筑，配有33米高钟楼，其作用有三：一是充当黄浦江上的航标和灯塔；二是为市民提供准点报时服务；三是在以天数征收船舶吨税时，避免因船舶自备时钟误差而引起争议。此后建成的粤海关、潮海关、江汉关等大楼也都安装了大钟。

江海关大楼建筑设计图

Picture of Shanghai Customs

民国时期

1927年原教堂式江海关再次翻建，该建筑本体共8层，另配有3层高的钟楼，共78.2米，是当时亚洲第一、世界第三高的钟楼，成为外滩的标志性建筑并一直沿用至今。1996年作为外滩建筑群组成部分被列入全国重点文物保护单位。

“潮海关”碑

Stele of Chao Haiguan(Swatow Customs)

1889年

潮海关（潮州新关）成立于1860年1月，选址汕头妈屿岛，后于1865年经总税务司署批准迁至汕头市区。1889年，潮海关在礐石岛购地建造帮办公寓（1901年改为副税务司公馆）时所立的界碑，2002年汕头海关实地踏勘时发现。

“潮海关税务司”印章

“潮海关税务司关防”印章

潮海关印章

Seals of Swatow Customs

民国时期

20世纪上半叶潮海关税务司使用的各类印章。潮海关（潮州新关）成立后，直接受总税务司管辖，专责管理外轮货物稽查征税，并兼管港内外灯塔、浮筒等助航设备，也负责气象测录、码头仓库管理和船舶检疫等。

“潮海关税务司放行货物专用关防”印章

“文华殿大学士”

“津海新关”匾

Board of Tientsin Maritime Customs

1888年

1861年3月，津海新关正式开关，办公地点在天津市内东浮桥附近（今天津市古文化街北门口一带）。光绪十四年（1888年），迁至紫竹林地区英法租界交界处（今天津市营口道2号）。时任直隶总督兼北洋大臣的李鸿章应邀为津海关扩建办公楼题写了“津海新关”四个字，被制作成匾额悬挂。

“厦门常关”碑

Stele of Amoy Native Customs (in Shima, Zhangzhou)

1913年

1989年厦门海关所属漳州海关驻石码办事处拆除旧楼时发现。清同治元年（1862年），厦门新关成立，直属总税务司管理。原闽海关厦门口及其所辖各口改称老关、旧关或大关（后统一改称“常关”）。是时，厦门常关领辖有石码、刘五店分口及本港海沧、排头门、厦门港、鼓浪屿分卡。1912年6月，常关机构人员并入厦门关相应部门。石码常关于次年兴建办公楼，该石碑即为其奠基石。1931年6月1日，厦门常关全部裁撤。

“九龙关公署”铜牌
Copper Plaque of the Office of Kowloon Customs
1887年

九龙关是深圳海关的前身，1887年为防止不法商人以香港为基地向中国内地走私鸦片而设，因当时九龙半岛新界部分尚未被英国侵占，故名“九龙关”，1949年九龙关起义后，为彰显对香港的主权，仍名“九龙海关”，直至1997年香港回归后更名为“深圳海关”。九龙关总关位于香港维多利亚城皇后大道，先后历经66位税务司，均为英国人。九龙关建立后，在九龙界限街附近设置鸦片趸船征收鸦片税费，并在香港外围设置多个关卡、成立武装关勇队，专司缉私工作。九龙关还对民船贸易的进出口货物及进出境旅客进行监管、征收关税，但业务量较小。

“九龙新关大铲厂界”碑

Stele of Dachan Office Boundary
of Kowloon Maritime Customs

1899年

清光绪二十五年（1899年）九龙关在大铲岛所立，是深圳海洋文化历史地标的重要证物，发现于20世纪80年代。光绪二十四年（1898年），清政府被迫与英国政府签订《展拓香港界址专条》，将九龙半岛北部地区及附近岛屿和海域租借给英国。1899年，九龙关下属关卡逐步后撤。九龙关改称九龙新关，并对设在沿海和边境的关卡，均树立“九龙新关”界碑。大铲即是关卡后移后九龙关在新的海陆边界设立的五个海上税收关卡之一，是海上防御和反走私的咽喉之地。

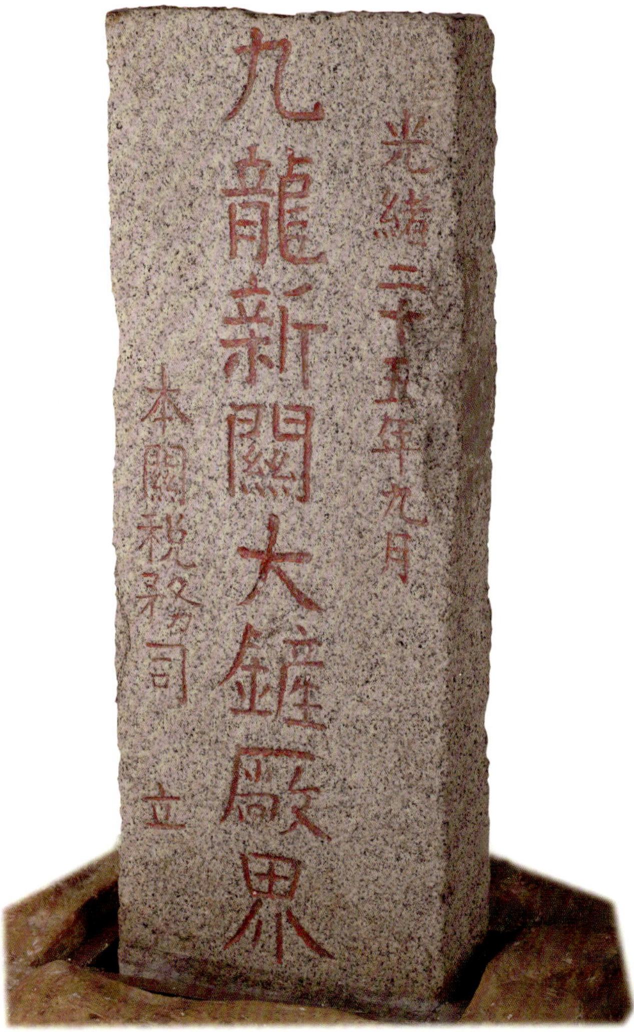

九龙关印章

Seal of Kowloon Customs

民国时期

民国时期九龙关使用的关印。1899年，九龙关下属关卡相继后撤，辖区交通不断改善，进出境贸易及人员往来不断增加，九龙关业务工作日益繁忙。但由于所处地理位置特殊，与其他口岸海关开展业务有所不同，未承揽海务、港务、检疫、邮政等事务。

九龙关钢印

“九龙新关税务司印（洋药）”印章

“九龙新关税务司印”印章

中華人民共和國暫行海關法

典章制度

Decrees and Regulations

The development and evolution of China Customs has experienced several historical periods including the slave, feudal, semi-feudal and semi-colonial, as well as socialist societies, during which the policy orientations and management systems of politics, economy and foreign affairs of the regimes of all dynasties varied and the codes and norms of conduct of the organizations performing customs-related functions also kept changing. From the extant earliest management system record of passes in the early Western Han Dynasty, to the legal provisions on passes, borders and other fields in the Tang Dynasty, to the extant earliest management system record of foreign trade in the Yuan Dynasty, to each regulation of various periods for different customs affairs, all customs decrees and regulations reflected the social environment in different periods and the development of the legal system of customs, which also provided reference for the issuing of the first independent *Customs Import and Export Tariffs* and *Provisional Customs Law* of China.

中国海关的发展演变，相继经历了奴隶社会、封建社会、半殖民地半封建社会、社会主义社会四个历史阶段。其间，我国历代政权的政治、经济、外事外贸等政策导向、管理制度各不相同，行使海关事权机构的行为规范准则也在不断变化。从现存最早的关津管理制度——西汉初期《津关令》，到唐代关于皇室、宫廷警卫和州县、城戍、关津要塞保卫的法律规定——《卫禁律》，到现存最早的外贸管理制度——元代至元年间《整治市舶司条律》，再到各时期《税则》以及晚清时期《会讯船货入官章程》、1934年《海关缉私条例》，乃至中华苏维埃共和国颁布的《关税条例》《关税征收细则》等，历代海关典章制度反映了其所处时代的社会环境和海关法制发展进程，也在一定程度上为我国第一部独立自主的《中华人民共和国进出口税则》和《中华人民共和国暂行海关法》提供了参考借鉴。

张家山汉简《津关令》

Pass (Jinguan) Decree Bamboo Slip

西汉早期

张家山汉简《二年律令》1984年出土于湖北江陵张家山第247号汉墓，其中包含颁布于汉吕后二年（前186 年）的《津关令》共37 枚，原件现存荆州博物馆。

《津关令》是以制诏形式颁发的法律之一，是中国现存最早、比较系统记载关津制度的文物。根据《津关令》记载，汉代关津设于水陆交通要塞，设关都尉等负责关津的日常管理，在检查行人和违禁物品、征收关税、缉拿罪犯、军事防御等方面起着重要作用。

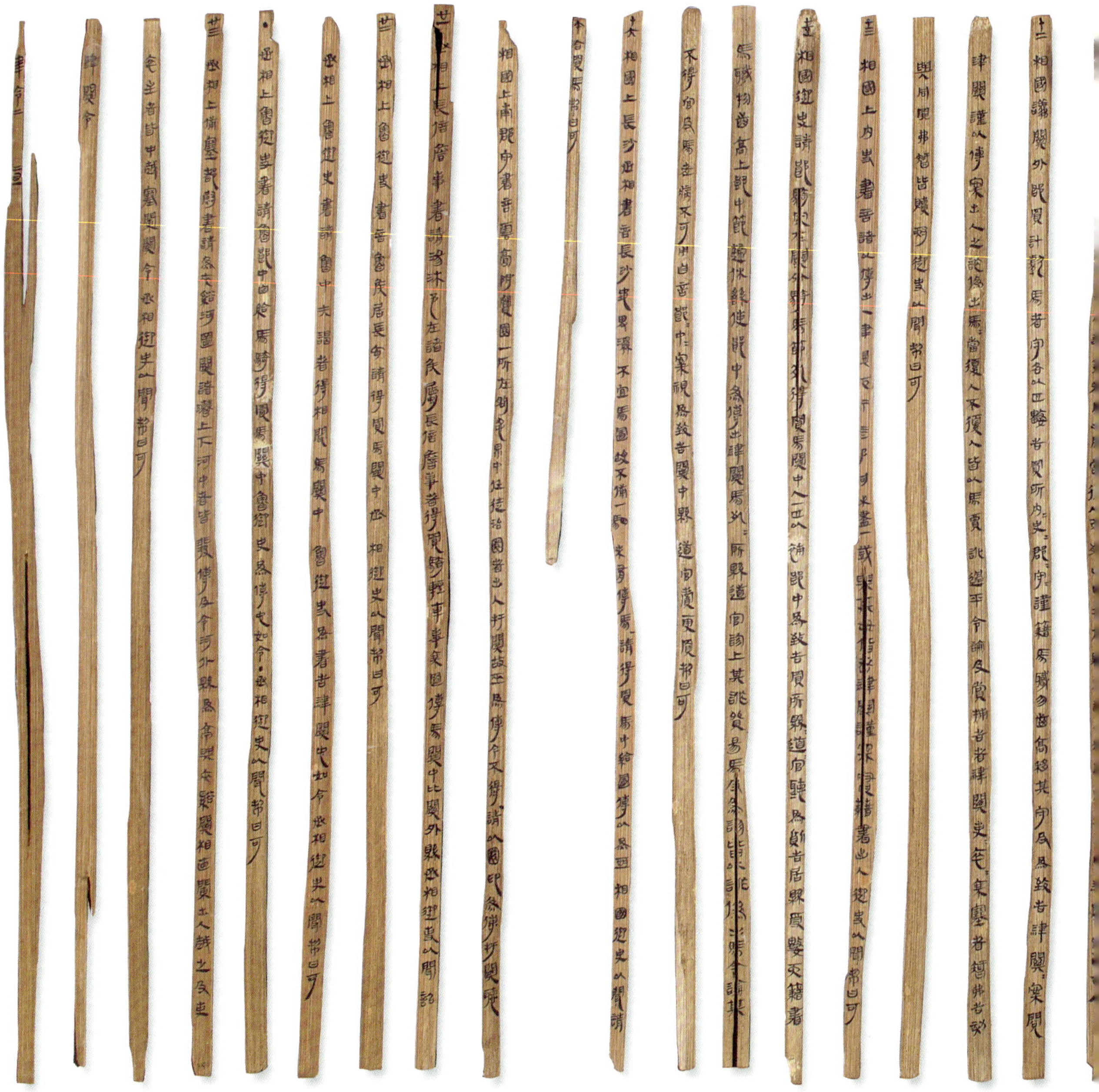

汉代实行严格的通关管理制度，吏民出入关津须携带“符”“传”等有效证件，否则不予放行；对“阑出入关塞”（即走私），诈伪符传，偷运马匹、黄金、铜铁等禁限物品的行为予以相应刑罚，并明确界定了守关吏卒失职、渎职的行为及其处罚。当时还重点通过武关、函谷关、临晋关等关隘与沿黄河渡口构筑起由南而北的军事屏障拱卫关中地区，确保长安作为全国政治、经济、军事中心的安全。

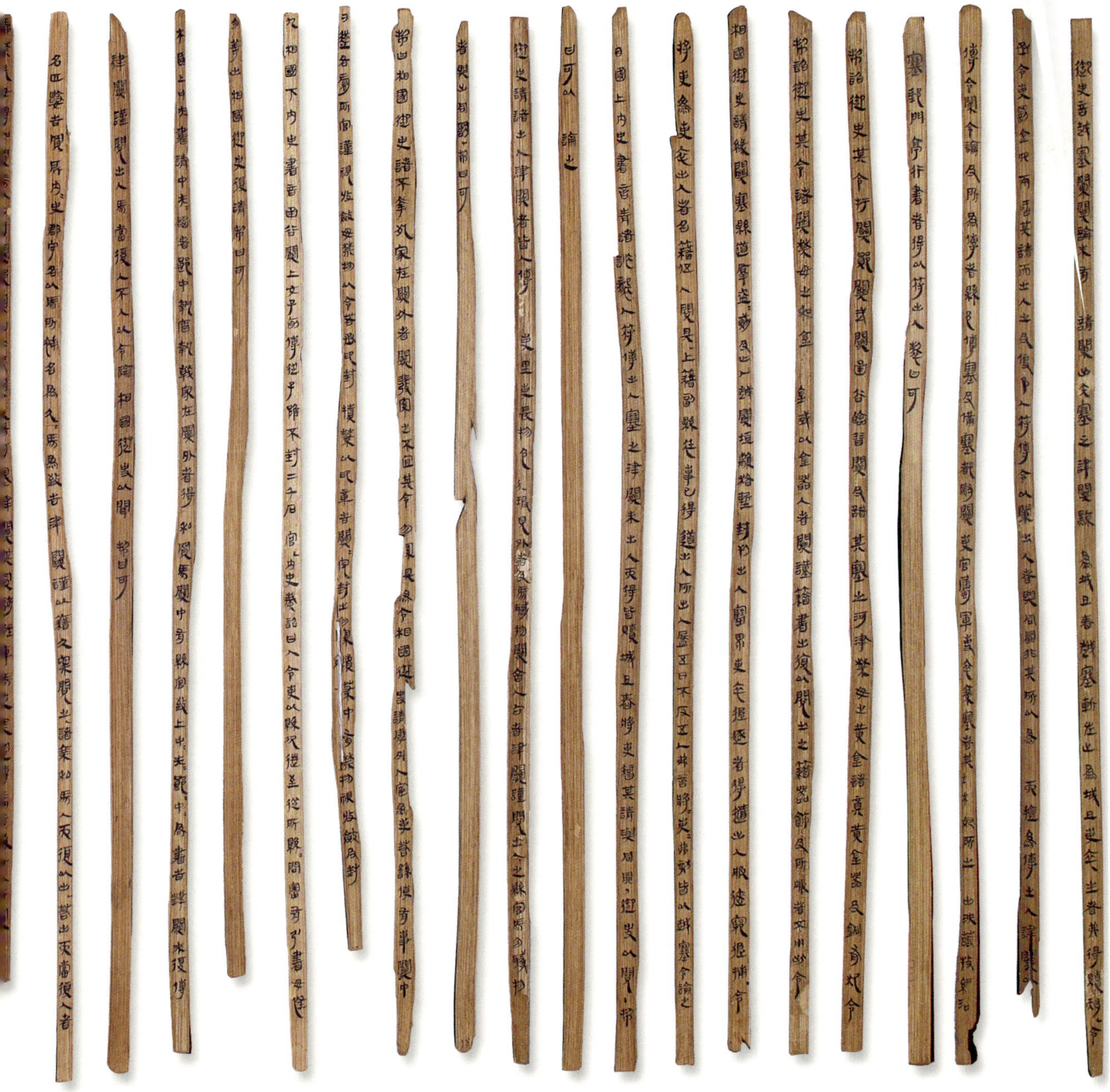

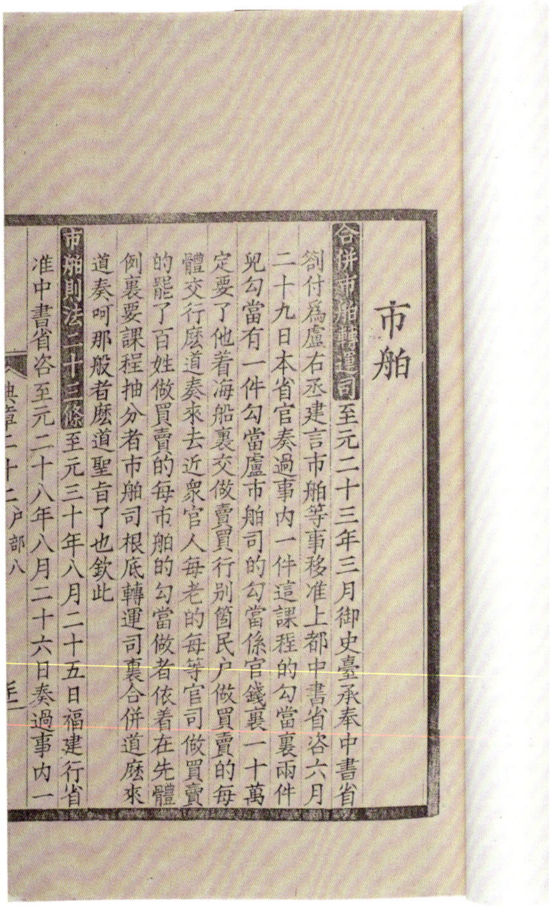
市舶
合併市舶轉運司至元二十三年三月御史臺承奉中書省劄付爲盧右丞建言市舶等事移准上都中書省咨六月二十九日本省官奏過事內一件這課程的勾當裏兩件兒勾當有一件勾當盧市舶司的勾當係官錢裏一十萬定要了他着海船裏交做賣買行别箇民户做買賣的每體交行麽道奏來去近衆官人每老的每等官司做買賣的罷了百姓做買賣的每市舶的勾當做者依着在先體例裏要課程抽分者市舶司根底轉運司裏合併道麽來道奏呵那般者麽道聖旨了也欽此
市舶則法二十三條至元三十年八月二十五日福建行省准中書省咨至元二十八年八月二十六日奏過事內一
典章二十二　戶部八

至元《整治市舶司条律》

The Law of Shibosi of the Zhiyuan

1293年

至元《整治市舶司条律》颁布于元至元三十年（1293年），原名《整治市舶司勾当》，又称《市舶抽分杂禁》，全文录于《元典章·户部·市舶》，为现存最早、最完整的市舶管理法则，共22条。原件现存上海图书馆。

我国古代管理海外贸易的市舶制度始自唐代。元灭宋后沿袭宋制，在东南沿海主要港口继续设立市舶机构，核发贸易凭证、查缉走私、抽分征税。为更好监管对外贸易，元世祖忽必烈在总结以往海外贸易管理经验的基础上，参考借鉴北宋《元丰广州市舶条法》，制定颁布了《整治市舶司条律》，对市舶司的职责范围、舶商出海手续、检查办法、抽分抽税比例、禁止出口的货物种类、外船与外商来元的处置办法等做了详细的规定。

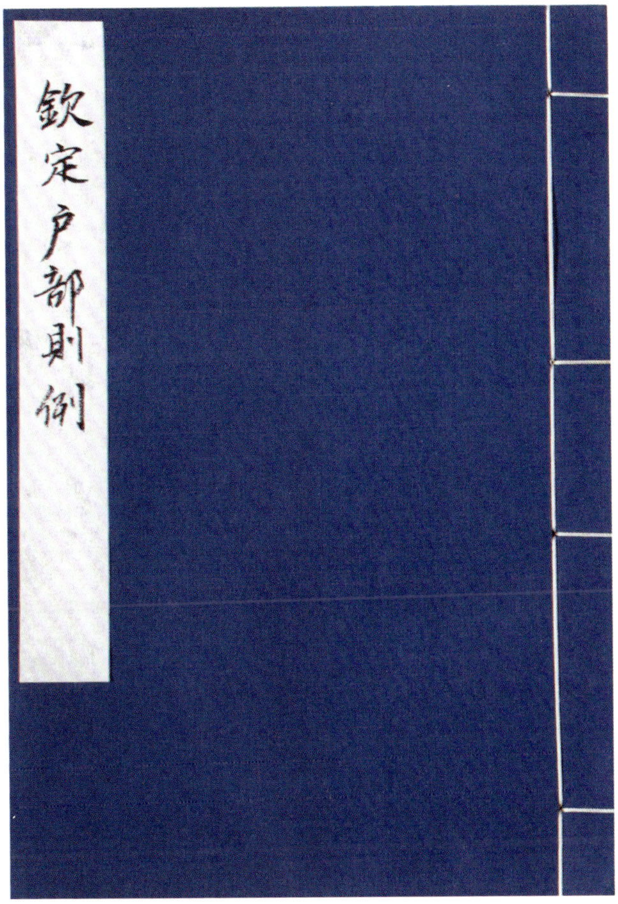

《钦定户部则例》

Imperial-sanctioned Regulations of the Ministry of Revenue (Qin Ding Hoppo Ze Li)

1776年

清朝乾隆四十一年（1776年）编撰，原件现存上海图书馆。户部是清政府总理全国户籍、钱粮的部门。《钦定户部则例》所载内容翔实，除规定户部职掌外，还设立户口、田赋、库藏、仓庾、漕运、盐法、参课、钱法、关税、廪禄、兵饷、蠲恤、杂支等门类，类似经济法规。其中“关税”项下收录了闽、粤、江、浙海关税则，是清初四海关征税准绳，也是研究清代海关及税收制度的重要依据。

《会讯船货入官章程》

the Joint Investigation Rules

1868年

同治七年（1868年），清政府总理衙门批准时任总税务司赫德推行至所有通商口岸的缉私处理章程，共八条，在1866年《上海海关扣留案件条款》基础上扩充而成，虽只冠“入官”之名，但也涵盖了惩罚措施。章程规定由税务司、外国驻华领事和海关监督组成会讯公堂，海关监督主持没收案件，领事主持罚款案件，税务司和委员（监督代表）可在堂指正。章程的颁布在一定程度上对商人的违法行为起到了约束作用，但实际是外国势力对中国海关处理走私违章管辖权的掠夺。

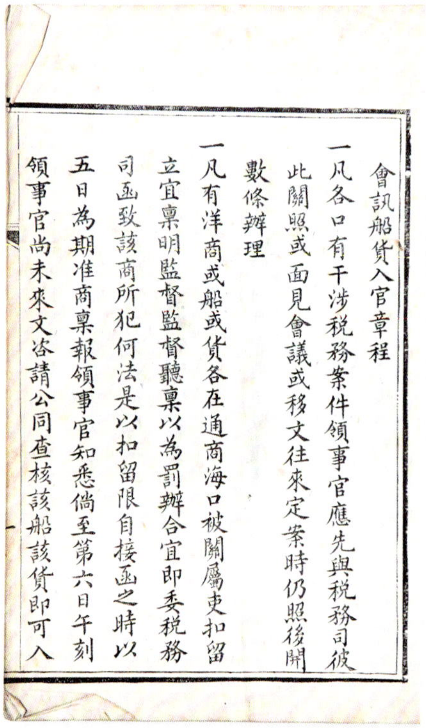
會訊船貨入官章程
一凡各口有干涉稅務案件領事官應先與稅務司彼此關照或面見會議或移文往來定案時仍照後開數條辦理
一凡有洋商或船或貨各在通商海口被關屬吏扣留立宜稟明監督監督聽稟以為罰辦合宜即委稅務司函致該商所犯何法是以扣留限自接函之時以五日為期准商稟報領事官知悉倘至第六日午刻領事官尚未來文咨請公同查核該船該貨即可入

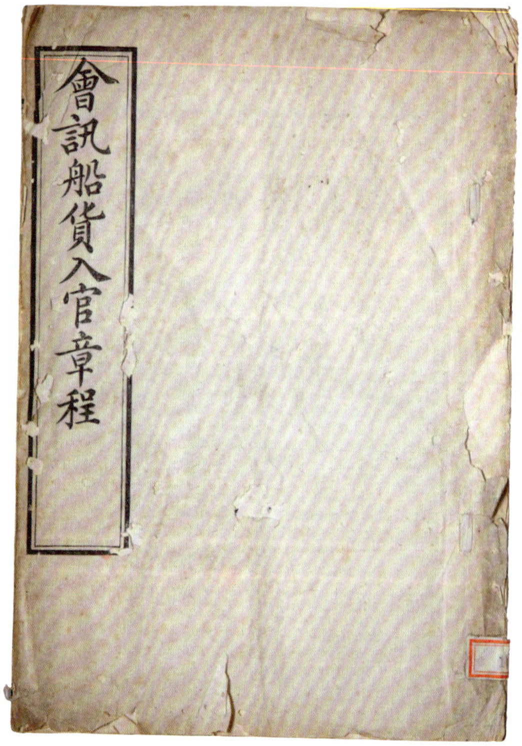

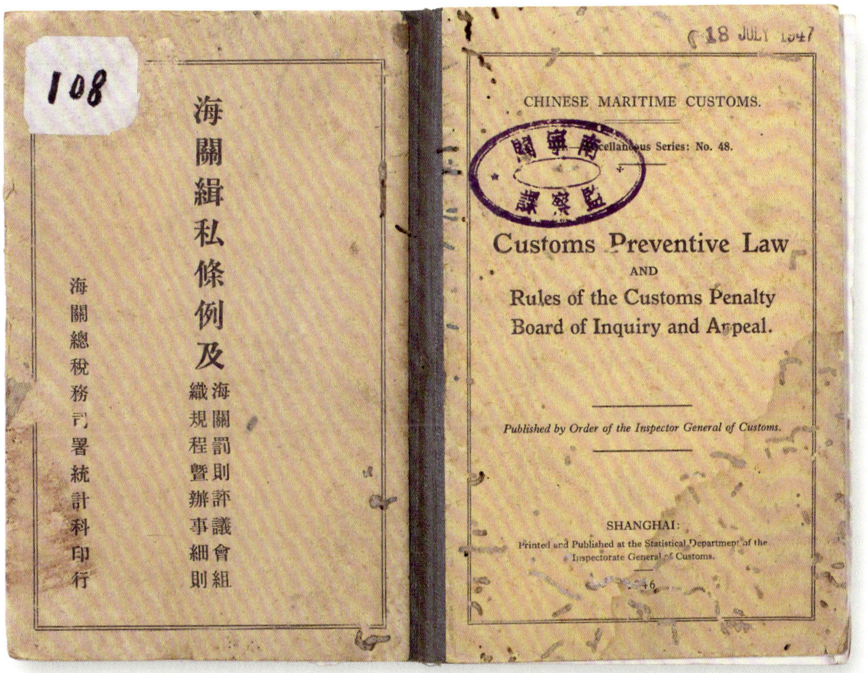

《海关缉私条例及海关罚则评议会章程暨办事细则》

Customs Preventive Law and Rules of the Customs Penalty Board of Inquiry and Appeal

1934年

《海关缉私条例》共7章53条，为1934年国民政府颁布的中国海关第一部较完整的缉私法规。《海关缉私条例》规定了海关查缉、扣押、罚则、处分程序与执行等方面的内容。根据《海关缉私条例》，财政部关务署于同年成立海关罚则评议会，颁布《海关罚则评议会办事细则》，规定海关罚则评议会直属关务署，没收或罚款案件均收归海关罚则评议会审理，摆脱了领事对走私违章处置的干预，收回了“会讯”制度下被掠夺的海关缉私管辖权。其局限在于行政处罚重经济制裁，未涉及追究涉案人员刑事责任。

《咸丰戊午通商出口税则》

Export Tariff for the Trade of China
(General Tariff of 1858)

1931年

民国二十年（1931年）第9次重印的《咸丰戊午通商出口税则》，初版颁布于清咸丰八年（1858年）。第二次鸦片战争后，清政府被迫与英、美、法、俄四国分别签订《天津条约》，并按条约规定与列强议定新税则。该税则草案由李泰国（1861年起正式任中国海关第一任总税务司）草拟，将海关税则分为进口及出口两大类，按从量税计征关税，除出口茶、丝外，一律按“值百抽五”的从价税率标准折算。

1858年经修订的税则随附于《通商章程善后条约》，并正式公布实施。该税则不仅损害了中国关税自主权，而且严重阻碍了中国社会经济的发展。

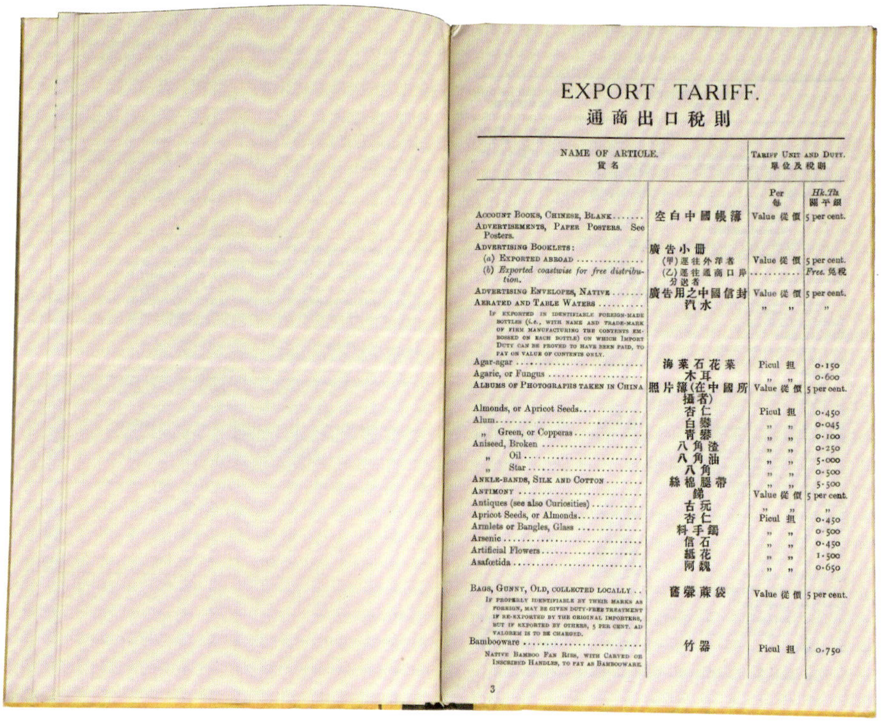

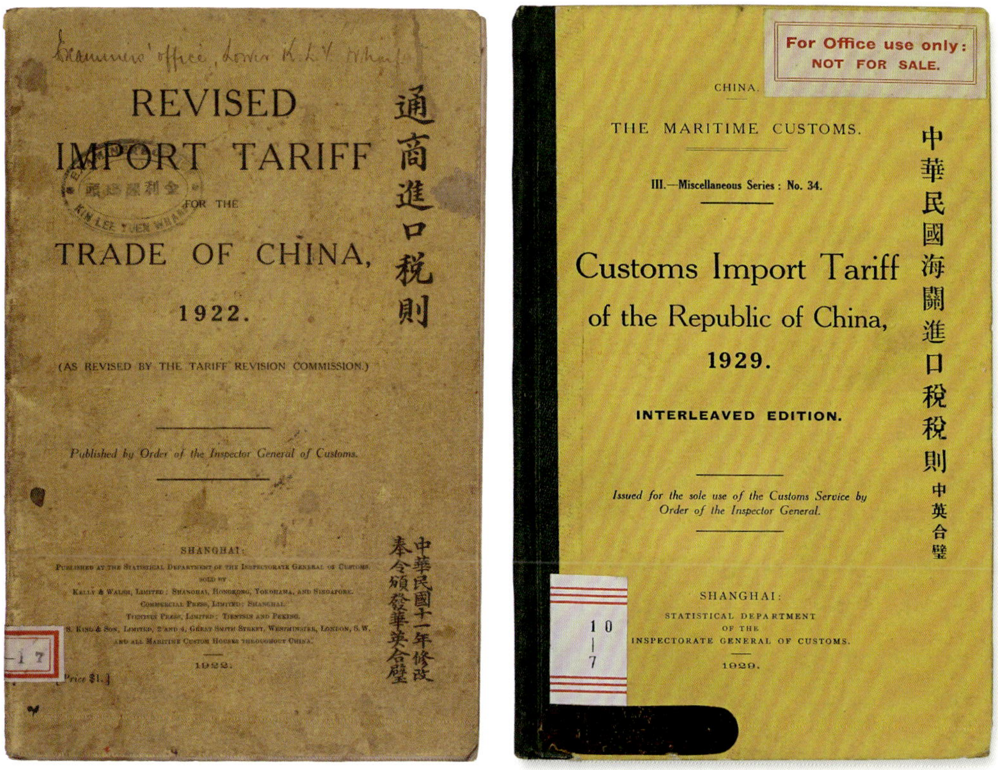

民国时期进出口税则

Customs Import and Export Tariff of the Republic of China

民国时期

1922、1929年由北洋政府和民国政府颁布的两部税则。1922年，北洋政府颁布的通商进口税则，为华盛顿会议及其后税则修订会议谈判成果，未对提高税率方法予以确定。1929年，南京国民政府开始施行的《中华民国海关进口税税则》，废除了对洋、土货所征收的子口税和对转口土货所征收的复进口税，同时规定进出口货物的关税税率为7.15%～27.15%，标志着1858年以来实行的“值百抽五”税率被废除，中国部分收回了关税自主权。该税则因此被称为“国定进口税则”。

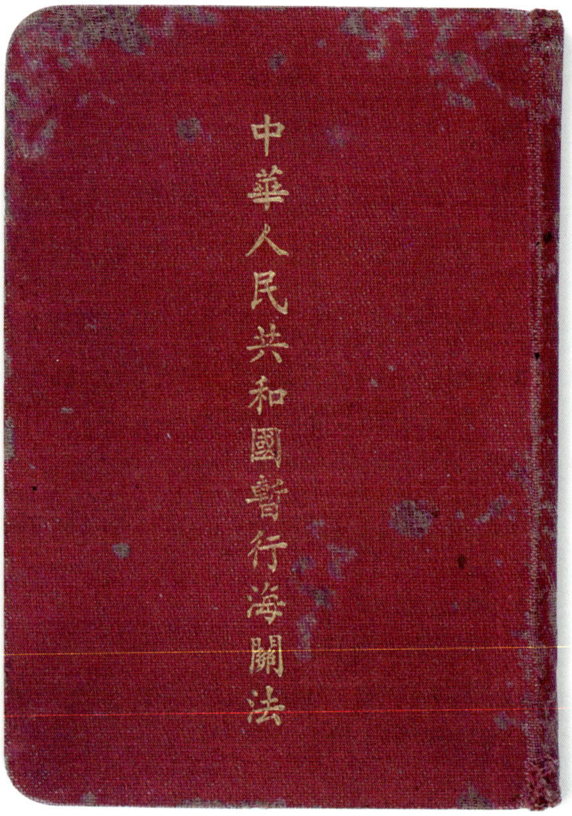

《中华人民共和国暂行海关法》

Provisional Customs Law of the People's Republic of China

1951年

《中华人民共和国暂行海关法》于1951年4月18日经周恩来总理签署、以政务院命令颁布，并自同年5月1日起施行，是中华人民共和国第一部海关基本大法，是建设中华人民共和国海关制度的法律基础和具体纲领。

《中华人民共和国暂行海关法》分为8篇、19章、217条，明确了中华人民共和国海关的组织、任务、职权、进出口货物监管、进出口货物的海关手续、进出境行李和邮递物品监管，以及走私与违章案件的处理方式。

《中华人民共和国海关进出口税则》

Customs Import and Export Tariff of the People's Republic of China

1951年

《中华人民共和国海关进出口税则》经中央人民政府政务院命令公布，自1951年5月16日起施行，是中华人民共和国颁布的第一部独立自主的进出口税则，与同年中央人民政府政务院批准颁布的《海关进出口税则暂行实施条例》及《中华人民共和国暂行海关法》共同确立了中华人民共和国海关法律制度的基础。该税则的颁布，标志着海关税收成为保护和促进国内产业健康发展的重要屏障、中央财政收入的重要来源、国家宏观调控的重要工具。

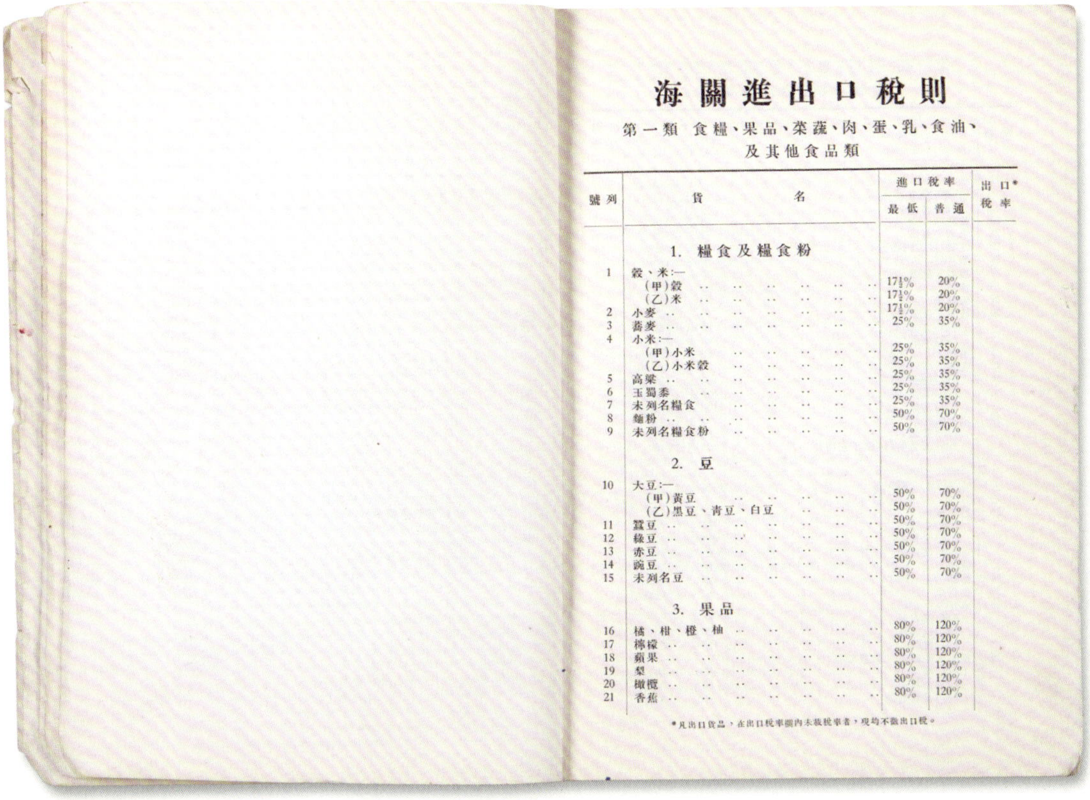

海關進出口稅則

第一類 食糧、果品、菜蔬、肉、蛋、乳、食油、及其他食品類

號列	貨名	進口稅率 最低	進口稅率 普通	出口* 稅率
	1. 糧食及糧食粉			
1	穀、米:—			
	(甲)穀	17½%	20%	
	(乙)米	17½%	20%	
2	小麥	17½%	20%	
3	蕎麥	25%	35%	
4	小米:—			
	(甲)小米	25%	35%	
	(乙)小米穀	25%	35%	
5	高粱	25%	35%	
6	玉蜀黍	25%	35%	
7	未列名糧食	25%	35%	
8	麵粉	50%	70%	
9	未列名糧食粉	50%	70%	
	2. 豆			
10	大豆:—			
	(甲)黃豆	50%	70%	
	(乙)黑豆、青豆、白豆	50%	70%	
11	蠶豆	50%	70%	
12	綠豆	50%	70%	
13	赤豆	50%	70%	
14	豌豆	50%	70%	
15	未列名豆	50%	70%	
	3. 果品			
16	橘、柑、橙、柚	80%	120%	
17	檸檬	80%	120%	
18	蘋果	80%	120%	
19	梨	80%	120%	
20	橄欖	80%	120%	
21	香蕉	80%	120%	

*凡出口貨品，在出口稅率欄內未載稅率者，現均不徵出口稅。

海關
CHINESE MARITIME CUSTOMS

近代人事

Modern Personnel Management

After the Opium Wars, China lost tariff autonomy, customs administration right, custodian right of customs revenue. At the time, foreign taxation and tariff system was adopted, the foreign inspector generals were in charge of Chinese Maritime Customs, the management mode of foreign staff restraining native staff and indoor staff restraining outdoor staff was implemented and the Western personnel management system was introduced. It formed a relatively complete personnel system, which adopted vertical leadership and hierarchy management system. Provisions on personnel management in aspects including employment, appointment, salary, promotion, exchange, education, training, resignation, reward, punishment, vacation and welfare were formulated respectively according to the levels of the staff. In addition, the principle of "high salary for a clean government" was implemented, which was particularly true for the high salary of foreign staff at customs.

鸦片战争后，我国相继丧失了关税自主权、海关行政管理权和海关税款收支保管权。当时，海关实施外籍税务司制度，外籍总税务司控制中国近代海关管理权，推行以洋员制华员、以内班制外班的管理模式，并引进西方人事管理制度，创建了一套较为完整的人事管理体系，实行垂直领导与等级管理制度，并根据人员等级分别制订录用、任命、薪俸、晋升、迁调（交流）、教育、培训、退职、奖惩、休假、福利等方面的人事管理规定，推行“高薪养廉”，尤以海关洋员的高薪丰酬为甚。

人员管理
Staff Management

《天津条约》补充条款《通商章程善后条约》于1858年签订后，税务司制度逐步形成。其间共有五位外籍（前四任英籍、末任美籍）总税务司，其中第二任总税务司赫德先后起草并经清政府批准颁布《海关募用外国人帮办税务章程》《大清国海关管理章程》，并引进英国海关管理模式，建立了以总税务司为首脑、各国洋员为骨干的近代海关人事管理制度。南京国民政府实施“关制改革”，对海关部分体制进行调整，推行降低洋员人数比例、缩小华洋员薪金差距、提供华洋员同等晋升机会、培训华员等改革措施，但仍继续任用外籍总税务司管理各地海关。

After the signing of the *Treaty on the Aftermath of the Articles of Commerce* in 1858, the supplemental clauses of the *Treaty of Tientsin*, the foreign taxation and tariff system was gradually formed. During that period, there were in total five foreign inspector generals (the first four were British and the last one was American), among which the second Inspector General Robert Hart successively drafted and issued the *Regulations on Recruiting Foreigners to Assist in Handling Tax Affairs at Customs* and the *Statutes of Customs Management of the Great Qing Dynasty* upon the approval of the Qing government, and introduced the British model of customs management to establish the modern customs personnel management system with the inspector general as the head and foreign staff of various countries as the backbone. The Nanjing National Government carried out customs reforms and adjusted part of the customs organization by reducing the proportion of foreign staff, narrowing the salary gap between native and foreign staff, providing them with equal promotion prospects and training Chinese staff, but continued to appoint foreign inspector generals.

海关内班职员照片集

Photographs of Indoor Staff

1874年至1937年

近代海关聘请英、美、法、德、俄、日等20多个国家的洋员担任中高级管理职务，由外籍总税务司统一管理全国各地海关。从1872年起，经选察入职内班、外班者，须提交个人登记照片，按入关时间顺序排列汇集成册，以备管理。从照片集中可以看出，早期海关内班税务司、帮办等职员均为外籍人员。

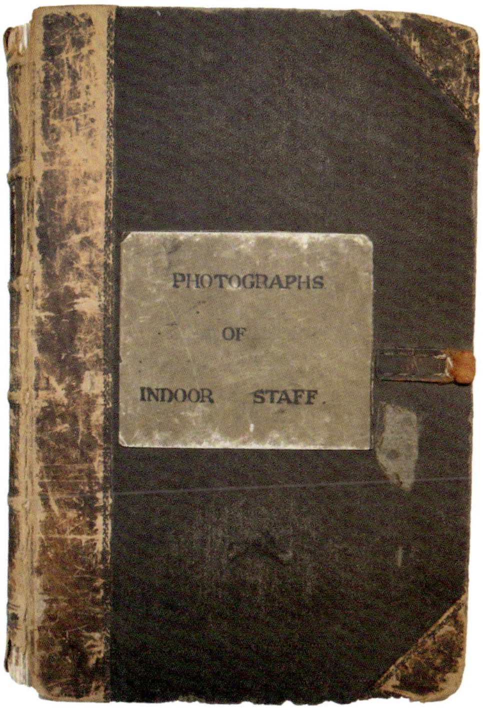

《投考海关指南大全》

A Complete Guide to Customs Examinations

1925年

光绪三十二年（1906年）税务处统管海关后即要求更多使用华员、提高华员职位职级和待遇。尤其是第一次世界大战爆发后，洋员回国参战，海关人员短缺，各关开始陆续招募华员承担过去洋员的工作。为便于报考人员了解情况，《投考海关指南大全》出版，内容包括各类职位如何申请、考试科目、往年试题、岗位职责等。

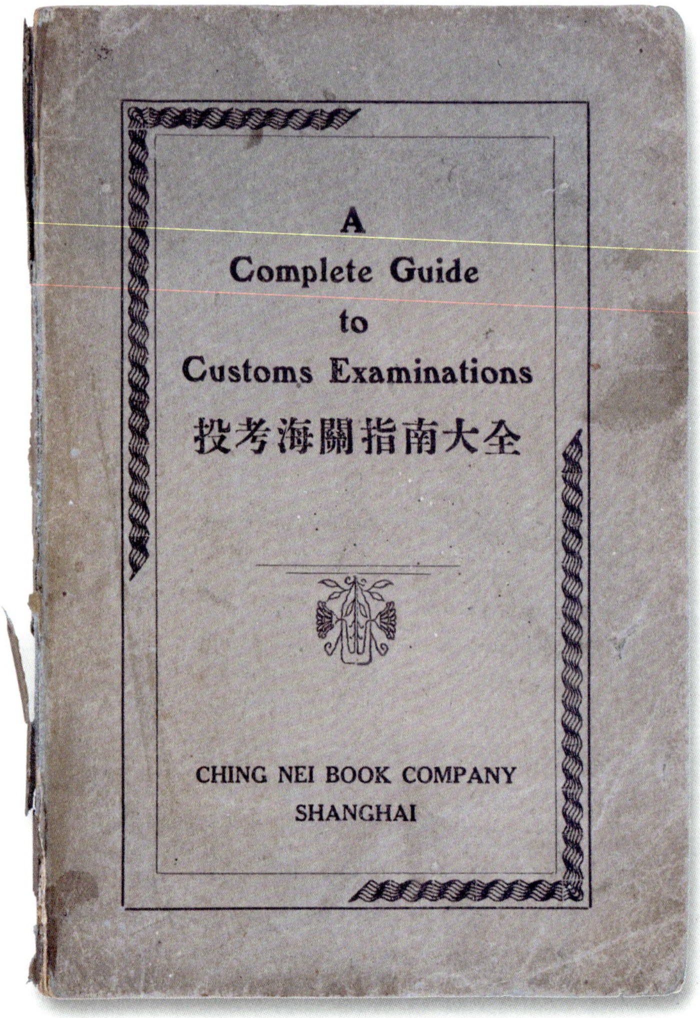

《海关职员俸给表》

Salary Scale of Customs Staff

20世纪20年代

1922年6月，总税务司署制定海关人员薪俸章程，规定总税务司月俸4000两、税务司月俸900～1250两、外籍副税务司月俸700两、华人副税务司月俸500两、外籍帮办月俸175～700两、华人帮办月俸100～400两（均为关平银）。《海关职员俸给表》记录当时各级、各职关员的薪俸待遇。晚清、民国时期，海关职员薪酬包括薪俸、酬劳金（退休津贴）、养老金、抚恤金、医药生育丧葬补助费、遣散费，以及加班费、节假日劳动津贴、住房补贴、带薪假等，洋员还享受在勤俸（侨居津贴），在当时属于绝对的“金饭碗”。但当时海关员工有华洋之分，在任职、薪俸和福利等方面均存在华洋职员不平等的现象。

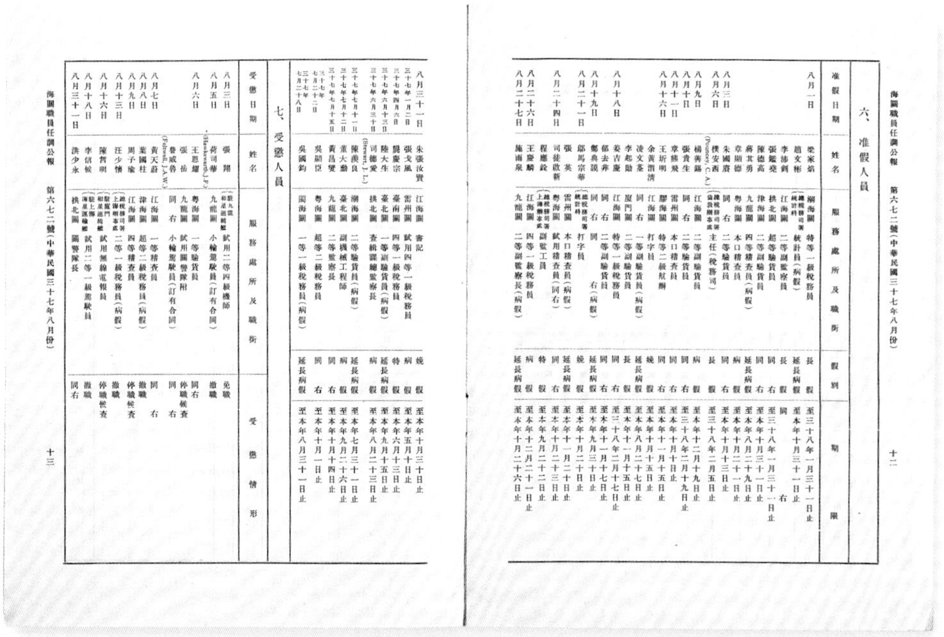

《海关职员任调公报》

Service Movements in the Gazette

1948年

晚清、民国时期，为培养海关关员业务能力、防止贪腐，海关实行工作轮换制度和“调口”制度。根据《大清国海关管理章程》及南京国民政府《关员迁调章程》等规定，海关会根据全国各口岸人力配置需要和关员个人情况，定期将内、外班华洋职员调往其他口岸，并发给调口差旅费、搬家费。民国时期，总税务司署数次下发通令明确执行迁调（调口）制度的有关要求，勒令关员顺应海关工作需要随时服从调遣，对无正当理由拒不服从迁调命令的关员予以免职或辞退。

中华民国海关奖章

The Chinese Maritime Customs Service Medal

1945年

1945年颁发的中华民国海关奖章。近代海关对任职年限长、勤劳卓著或有特殊功绩的关员颁发奖章，以资奖励。民国时期分为财政奖章和海关奖章两种，财政奖章分为三等九级；海关奖章分为金质、银质和铜质三等，关员服务满25年且勤劳卓著者方可颁给，有特殊功绩者服务未满25年由总税务司特别呈请亦可颁给。

赫德像铜版

Copper Plate Statue of Robert Hart

民国时期

赫德病逝后上海中外人士集资树立的铜像的印刷铜版。该铜像1914年落成，1943年为侵华日军拆毁熔铸武器。赫德（Robert Hart），英国北爱尔兰人，1863年11月至1911年9月任中国海关第二任总税务司。铜像基座北面镌刻一幅墨丘利（罗马神话中为众神传递信件并兼管商业道路之神）行走于地球之上的图像，代表赫德创办的海关邮政；南面为一位手执圆灯、赤足立于岸边为行船导航的女神，象征赫德管理的海务港务事业；正面铭刻哈佛大学校长艾里奥（C.W.Eliot）撰写评价赫德功绩的铭文；背面铸有赫德历年所受荣典表。

上海赫德铜像旧影

《梅乐和总税务司荣膺爵位及任职三周年纪念册》

Album on the Commemoration of the Knighthood and the Third Anniversary of Frederick Maze as Inspector General

1932年

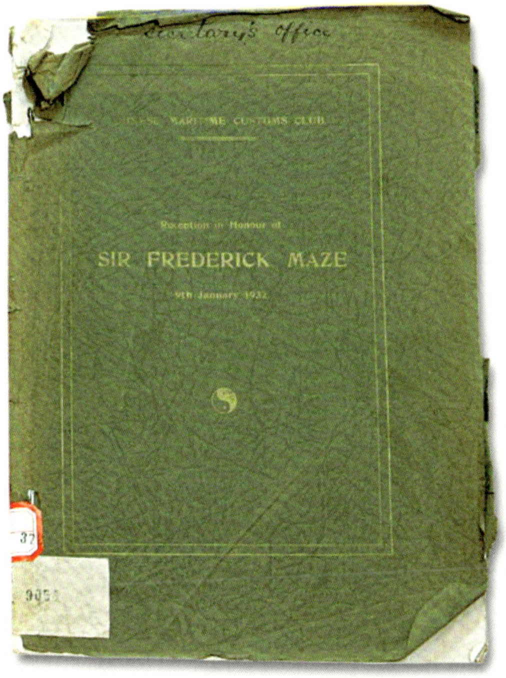

梅乐和（F.W.Maze），英国人，1929年1月至1943年任中国海关第四任总税务司，并被英国国王乔治五世授予勋爵。任职期间，他曾向国民政府提议加强缉私管理、成立缉私科、组建海关缉私舰队，将原存于汇丰银行的税款改存于上海中央银行，极力维护海关“完整性”，保障华员开展“护关运动”正当权益。1941年12月，日军占领上海公共租界，梅乐和被拘禁；1943年初获释后辗转到重庆，恢复其总税务司职务，5月辞职回到英国。

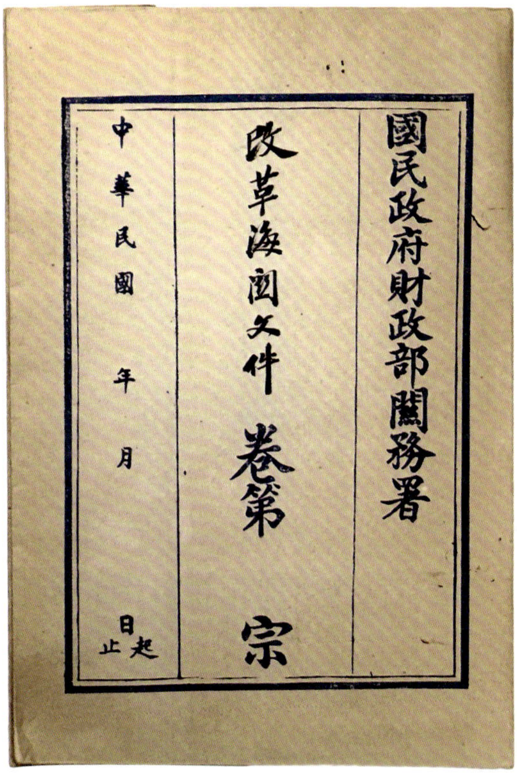

张福运海关改革文件夹

File with Fuyun Chang’s Handwriting

民国时期

张福运，山东福山（今烟台）人，毕业于美国哈佛大学并获文学学士、法学学士学位，曾任南京国民政府财政部关务署署长、国定税则委员会委员长。任职期间，组织实施恢复关税自主权和改革海关行政管理体制的工作，其中“停止招录外籍职员”“中外职员在权利和义务上享有均等机会”“中外职员同工同酬”等改革措施为中国人逐步掌握海关行政管理权打下基础。

用具用品
Appliances and Articles

因中国近代海关地位特殊、经费来源稳定、各国“洋员” 众多，且在伦敦设办事处负责采购各类物品，其办公用具和生活用品多为西方进口或符合外国审美标准的中式或中西结合产物，质量上乘、做工精良，反映出近代海关工作性质与特点。

Due to the special status of Chinese Maritime Customs, stable fund sources, large number of foreign staff and the office set up in London, most of the customs office appliances and articles of daily use were imported from the West. Those appliances and articles of Chinese style or an integration of both Chinese and Western styles that met the esthetic standard of foreigners, were of high quality, reflecting the characteristics of modern customs and the nature of the work.

近代海关制服及标志

Uniform and Badges of the Chinese Maritime Customs Service

民国时期

中国近代海关制服及纽扣、帽徽。近代海关内班、外班、关警及常关关员的制服与标志各成体系，反映出当时海关独特的队伍构成和业务特点。

近代海关外班冬季制服

Winter Uniform of the Chinese Maritime Customs Service

中国近代海关自1869年开始为外班关员定制制服，1917年为华籍巡役配发洋式制服，1947年起为女检查员配发制服。其中冬季制服为藏青色哔叽布。

近代制服纽扣

Uniform Button of the Chinese Maritime Customs Service

“财政部粤海关”胸章

“财政部重庆关”徽章

1940年抗战时期海关胸章

Badge of the Chinese Maritime Customs Service in 1940

抗日战争期间，总税务司署向地方海关统一制配的徽章。

1941年制服帽及布质帽徽
Cap of the Chinese Maritime Customs Service in 1941

1941年铜质帽徽
Cap Badge of the Chinese Maritime Customs Service in 1941

1945年海关关警领章

Collar Badge of the Chinese Maritime Police Service in 1945

关警是民国时期海关陆上缉私的专业武装人员，在查缉走私工作中发挥了积极的作用。1945年关警队着军服，佩戴领章、胸章、臂章。其中，领章为绿底黄叉上印“海关”和“关警”字样，佩带于军服领口，左右各一。同时期还配发有手写姓名、阶层、所属部队之番号，以及加盖税务司官章的胸章、白布绿边黄底内印绿色中英文海关关警字样的臂章等。

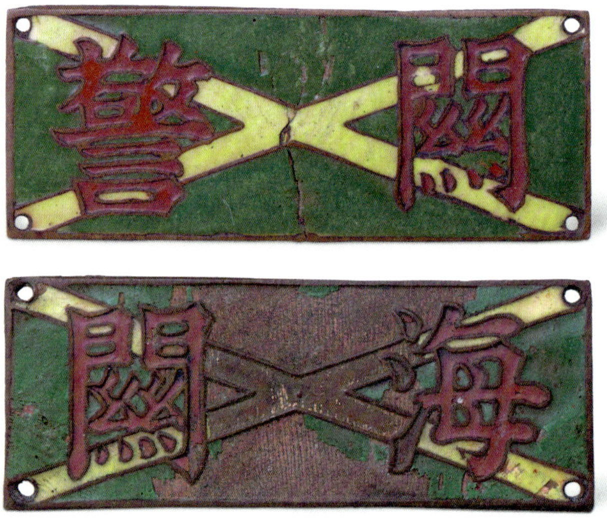

单人办公桌

Single Office Desk of Shanghai Customs

民国时期

江海关缉私课税务司使用过的办公桌。

法式书柜
A French-style Bookcase
民国时期

蒙自海关使用过的书柜。

素三彩镂空长鼓形花架

Hollow Flower Stand

民国时期

近代海关办公楼摆放花卉的支架。

铜座绿玻璃罩台灯

Desk Lamp with Copper Seat

20世纪30年代

江海关税务司用过的台灯。税务司、副税务司、帮办等办公桌上专用台灯，一般由英国进口。

报警钟

Alarm Bell

晚清时期

厦门关遭遇火情时报警使用。

青花印油盒

Blue-and-white Ink Container

晚清时期

近代海关的办公用品。

子母钟

Primary-secondary Clock

1927年

1927年竣工的江海关大楼在税务司、副税务司、帮办以及重要办公室共装有36只子钟、1只母钟。母钟每隔一定时间发送一次脉冲电流给所有子钟，使子钟的指针系统同步运转，以达到计时统一、精准。

广彩开光人物花卉纹碗

Porcelain Bowl with Design of Figures and Flowers

晚清时期

晚清时期海关关员聚餐调制潘趣酒的餐具，直径40厘米。潘趣（Punch）酒是一种果汁鸡尾酒，调制原料多样并能够自由组合，通常作为宴会、派对的主要饮品。

银质象牙柄西餐餐具

Silver Knife and Fork with Ivory Handles

民国时期

近代海关高级职员使用的餐具，中华人民共和国成立后变卖给海关关员。关员无偿捐给中国海关博物馆。

金属咖啡壶

Coffee Pot

民国时期

近代海关高级职员在办公场所喝咖啡的餐具。

餐盘

Plate of Swatow Customs

民国时期

潮海关高级职员使用的餐具。

海关西洋乐队乐器

Western Musical Instruments of Canton Customs

民国时期

粤海关西洋乐队使用过的乐器。海关总税务司署搬迁至北京后，赫德招募了一批年轻华人组建西洋铜管乐队，主要为在华洋人家庭舞会和一些外交活动演奏。乐队的部分乐手后来被袁世凯军乐队、北大音乐传习所管弦乐队等吸纳，成为“西乐中播”的使者。后来江海关、粤海关等也分别建立了西洋铜管乐队。中华人民共和国成立后变卖给海关关员。关员无偿捐给中国海关博物馆。

人才培养

Personnel Recruitment and Training

1908年，清政府在北京开设“税务学堂”，主要培养本国海关管理人才，为接管海关行政管理权作准备。1913年更名为“税务专门学校”，1935年迁往上海。抗战时期先后迁往香港、重庆，1946年2月迁回上海，1949年7月停办，共培养学生约2700人。

In 1908, the Qing Government set up the Customs College in Beijing to cultivate domestic customs management personnel and prepare for taking over the customs executive power. It moved to Shanghai in 1935, and to Hong Kong and Chongqing during the Anti-Japanese War, and moved back to Shanghai in February 1946, finally closed down in July 1949. A total of about 2,700 students were cultivated there.

税务专门学校校徽

School Badge of the Customs College

1946年

1913年，税务学堂更名为税务专门学校，1949年7月停办，共计办学41年。税务专门学校前期隶属于税务处，后改隶财政部关务署，由总税务司署协助管理，以培养海关华员人才为宗旨。先后开办过内勤、外勤、海事等班，并曾专门为在职海关华员开办了验估班、验货班。

税务专门学校影集

Photograph Album of the Customs College

20世纪20年代

南京国民政府成立后，实施“关制改革”，决定停止聘用洋员，税务专门学校成为输送专业华员的重要渠道。1913年至1935年，税务专门学校（北平）共招收税务专门班22期，培养了大批人才，其中毕业生丁贵堂主持建立了迪化（今新疆）关，1943年任副总税务司、代理总税务司，成为中国近代海关史上职务最高的华员。

税务学校廿年纪念册

Twenty-year Anniversary of Customs College

1929年

纪念册收录了在校及已毕业全体同学录和教职员表，以及《关税自主之重要与我国应采之政策》《收回海关行政主权之我见》《关税自主与经济解放》等文章20余篇，旨在使民众“更了然于关税完全自主及收回海关行政之重要……求其早日实现”。

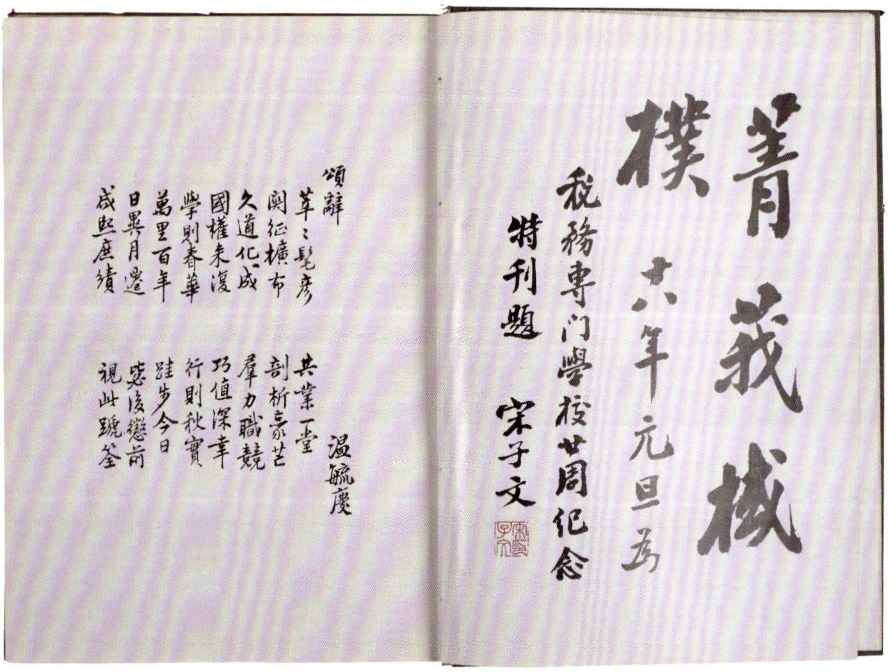

税务专门学校学籍证、毕业证书

Certificate of Student's Status and Graduation of Customs College

20世纪40年代

税务专门学校第十期海事班学生龚定鑫的学籍证及毕业证书。海事班学制3年，毕业后派关实习2年。1935年，税务专门学校南迁上海后，海事班设有国文、英文、科学原理、实用驾驶学、船艺、海图应用法、水道测量学、应用力学、无线电学、微积分、轮机常识、造船学概要、引港学、气象学、罗经学、普通信号、船员职务、船舶管理、货物装运、行船避碰章程、普通急救医术、海商法、操舵游泳实习、枪炮操练、体育和军事学等课程。

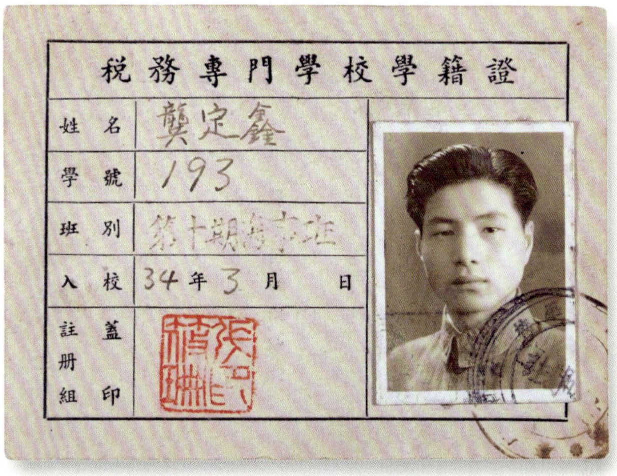

税務專門學校學籍證

姓名	龔定鑫
學號	193
班別	第十期海事班
入校	34年3月　日
註冊組蓋印	

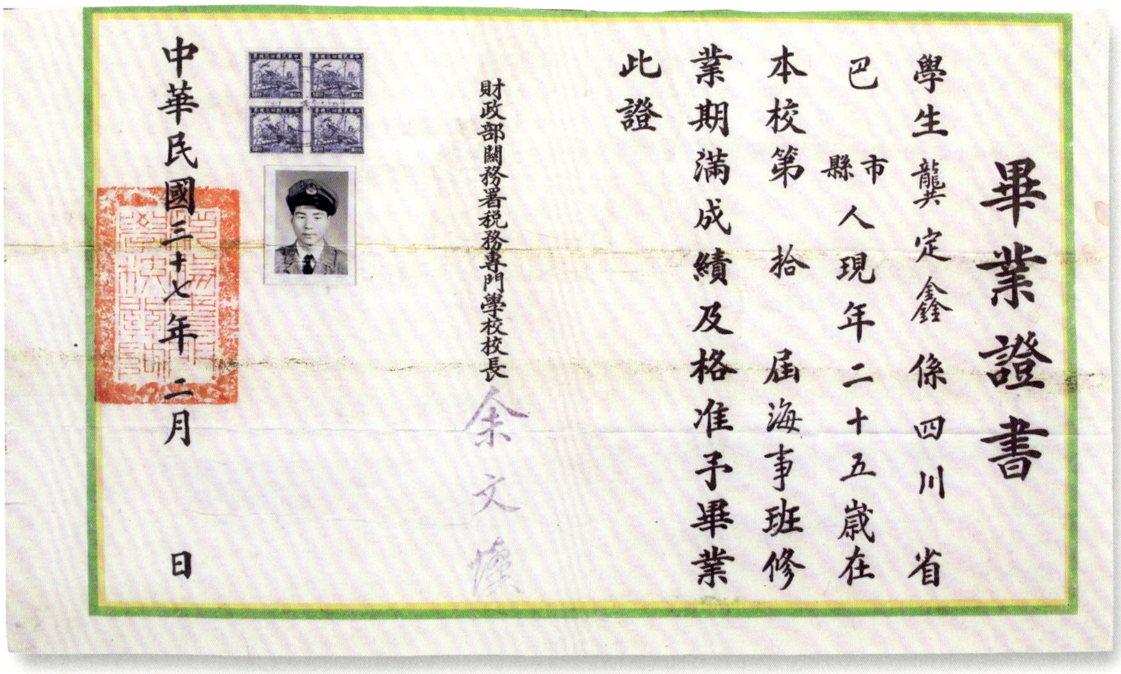

畢業證書

學生龔定鑫係四川省巴縣市人現年二十五歲在本校第拾屆海事班修業期滿成績及格准予畢業此證

財政部關務署稅務專門學校校長 余文懷

中華民國三十七年二月　日

上海税务专门学校招生简章

Admission Brochure of the Customs College

1946年

税务专门学校迁回上海后印制的招生简章。1908年税务学堂首次招生，主要面向16至22岁满汉学生招考；1929年税务专门学校在上海设立海事班和外勤班面向高中毕业生招考；抗战后迁回上海，税务专门班停办，开设内勤训练班。对于考生资格，税务专门学校有严格规定：内勤训练班招收大学本科毕业生、海事班招收高级中学或同等学校17至22岁符合身体状况要求的毕业生、外勤训练班招收普通高中毕业生。

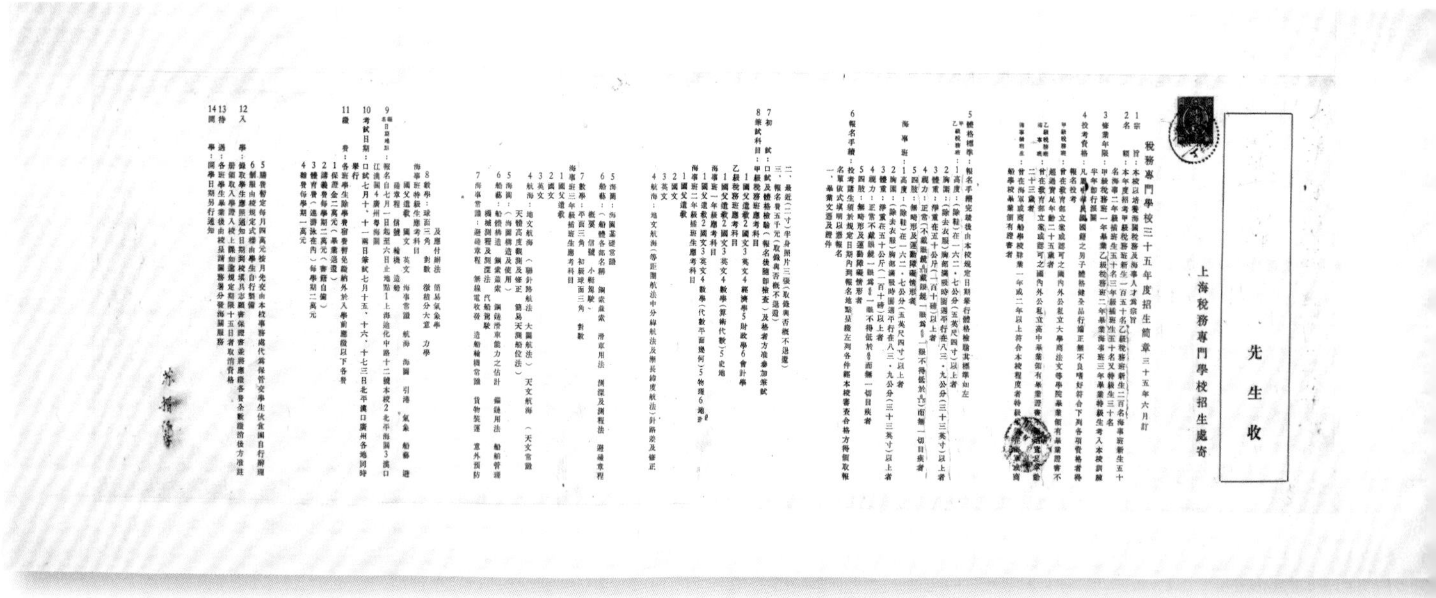

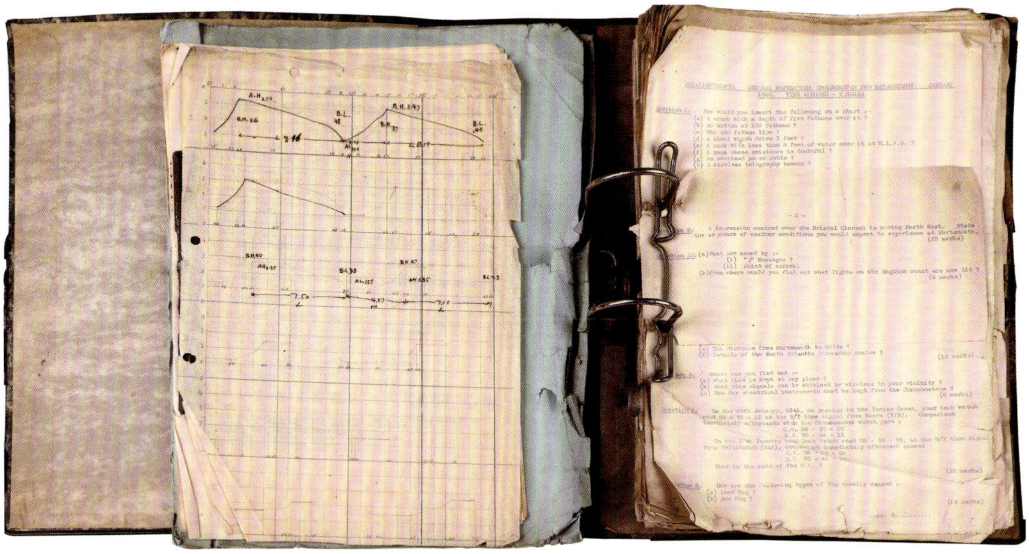

税务专门学校考试题

Examination Question of Customs College

民国时期

税务学堂及税务专门学校均根据课程设置组织期中和期末考试，以及毕业考试。税务专门学校学生在学年结束时，如单科考试低于60分，须自行补习并参加补考，补考仍不及格者作退学处理。此外，学年总平均分90分以上为优等，70分以上为中等，70分以下为不及格。

近代兼办

Modern Additional Services

When it came to the late Qing Dynasty and the period of the Republic of China, customs services covered a wide and complicated range, which, in addition to handling supervision, tax collection, anti-smuggling, statistics and other traditional customs services, also included additional affairs like coast and harbor affairs, meteorological observation, seaport quarantine, modern postal service, handling debt indemnity, *Tungwen Guan* management, agent purchasing of warships, trademark registration and participation in world expositions. It even intervened in diplomatic negotiations, directly controlled the key branches of economy of the old China and extensively intervened in China's domestic, military and diplomatic affairs.

晚清、民国时期，海关的业务范围非常庞杂，除经办监管、征税、查私、统计业务等传统海关业务外，还根据不平等条约规定或政府授权先后兼办代办了海务港务、气象观测、海港检疫、新式邮政、经理内外债赔款、管理同文馆、代购军舰、商标注册、组织参加博览会等事务，甚至染指外交谈判。列强不仅直接控制了旧中国的经济命脉，还广泛插手中国的内政、军事、外交等。

代办邮政

Agent Postal Services

1866年，总理衙门授权海关办理使馆外交邮件和海关官函邮件的邮递业务，海关设邮寄处所（亦称海关书信馆）具体负责邮件的封、发、分、送；从1878年起，海关制定邮政章程、发行首套邮票，并在北京、牛庄（今营口）、天津、烟台、上海开办华洋书信馆（1879年改称“海关拨驷达局”），从事中文信函的收寄、投递业务；1896年3月20日，经光绪皇帝御批，总理衙门颁布《邮政开办章程》，正式开办国家邮政，由海关代办，拨驷达局一律改作邮政局。1897年加入万国邮联，凡联约各国公文函件均可由中国邮政官局代收、代查、代送。1911年5月28日被清政府邮传部接管时，共移交邮政总局、分局、支局及代办所4800余处。

In 1866, the *Zongli Yamen* (Ministry of Foreign Affairs in the Qing Dynasty) authorized the customs offices to deal with the postal delivery of diplomatic mails and official mails of customs. Hence, customs established agencies in charging of mail sealing, issuing, distribution and delivery. Since 1878, the customs formulated regulations on postal services, issued the first set of postage stamps in China, and set up post offices in Beijing, Niuzhuang, Tianjin, Yantai and Shanghai to be in charge of the receiving, sending and delivery services of Chinese mails. On March 20, 1896, the *Zongli Yamen* published the *Statutes of the Establishment of Postal Services* upon the imperial approval of Emperor Guangxu to officially establish the national postal system, with customs being commissioned to operate. In 1897, China joined the Universal Postal Union, since then the official letters of all member states could be collected, inquired and delivered by Chinese Imperial Post. On May 28, 1911, more than 4,800 sites including the general post office, branches, sub-branches and agencies were handed over to the *Youchuanbu* (Ministry of Posts and Communications) of the Qing government.

总税务司赫德专用邮袋

Robert Hart's Mail Bag

19世纪70年代

第二任总税务司、曾兼任总邮政司赫德使用过的邮袋，袋面、袋里各印有收寄信息。收寄方翻袋后即可反向投寄对方。同治改元光绪年间（约1875年），当时海关已开始办理使馆外交邮件和海关官函邮件的邮递业务，该邮袋为此期间产物。其中北京、上海间往来外交邮件，从北京到镇江之间沿大运河干道由驿站传递，镇江到上海之间通过船只水运。故邮袋一面有如下文字：“内紧要公文敬烦　镇江关税务司转请　镇江关道台立饬驿站飞马驰递　钦命总理各国事务衙门告投转交总税务司查收　光绪 年 月 日江南海关械”，另一面则有：“内要件仰祈　总理各国事务衙门立饬兵部驿站驰寄　镇江关道署恳请转递　镇江关税务司转致　江南海关税务司收拆　光绪 年 月 日由京都总税务司公署缄”，其中江南海关即江海关，反映出海关邮政与驿站的合作关系。

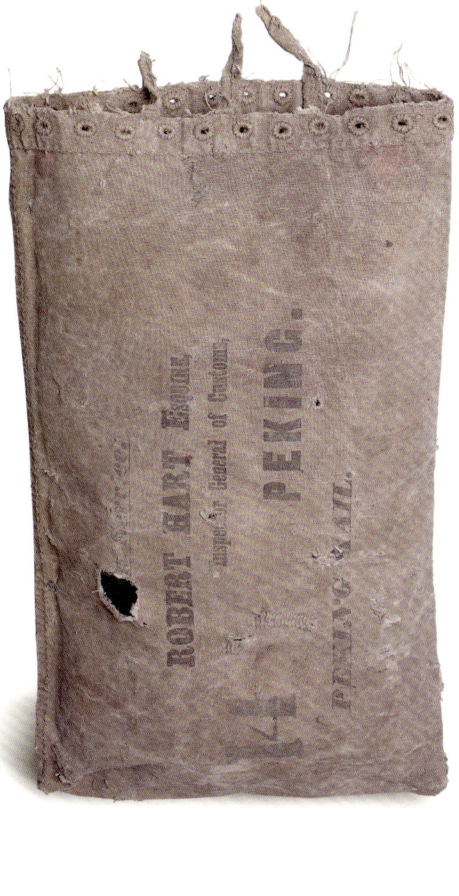

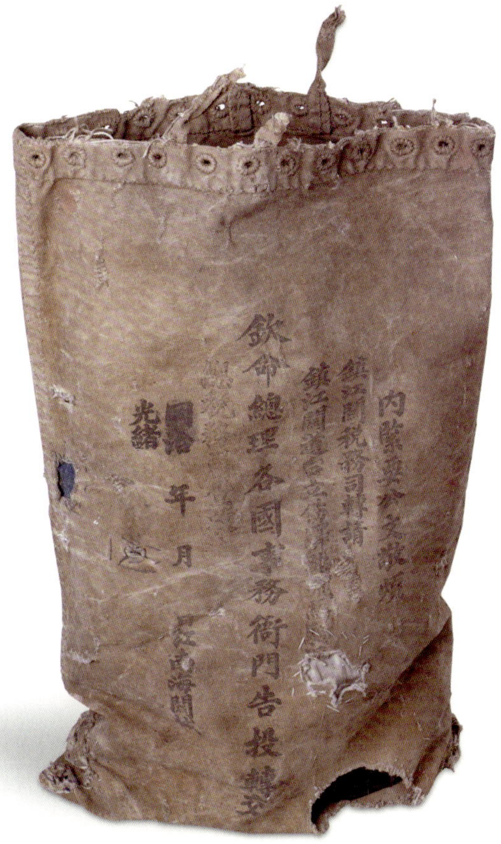

大龙邮票

Large Dragon Stamps

1878年

1878年，由海关印刷发行的中国历史上第一套邮票——大龙邮票，集邮界习惯称之为“海关大龙”，被国际邮政局长协会列入73种世界各国最早邮票之一。大龙邮票有薄纸大龙、阔边大龙和厚纸大龙三种版式，一套3枚，面值用银两计，分别是用来寄印刷品的绿色1分银、寄普通信函的红色3分银和寄挂号信函的黄色5分银。票面图案是五爪龙配以云崖海水纹，极具清皇室特色。

小龙邮票

Small Dragon Stamps

1885年

由海关发行的中国第二套邮票，每套3枚，图案为“云龙戏珠”，但规格比大龙邮票小，俗称“小龙邮票”。大龙邮票自1878年印刷发行后，因铜质印模逐渐磨损无法再用，故于1885年重新设计印制“小龙邮票”。其使用易溶解的油墨和带有“太极”水印的纸张印制，是中国第一套采用防伪技术印制的邮票。

万寿邮票

Wanshou Stamps

1894年

1894年11月19日，为庆贺慈禧太后60岁寿辰，海关发行了中国首套纪念邮票，名为“慈禧太后六旬万寿及中外通商五十周年纪念”邮票，俗称“万寿邮票”。万寿邮票全套9枚，票面共有9种图案，均为寓意福寿吉祥的字、画等，面值分别为1至6分银、9分银、12分银和2钱4分银，不同面值分别着不同颜色，是中国第一套全套异图邮票，也是第一套纪念邮票。

红印花票

Red Revenue Stamp

1897年

由于邮票数量供不应求，1896年9月18日，总税务司署指示各关将原用于复出口派司的红色印花票加盖字样充当邮票使用。红印花票面值不等，分为“当壹分”“暂作洋银贰分”“暂作洋银肆分”“当壹圆”“当伍圆”等几种。

大清邮政加紧信件大龙邮票

Express Letter Stamp Issued by the Imperial Post Office

1905年

1905年冬，大清邮政发行的 “大清邮政加紧信件” 专用邮票，即快信邮票。邮票长21厘米，宽6厘米。英国吉本斯出版公司1979年出版的《集邮图鉴》曾把它列为世界上最大的邮票之一。

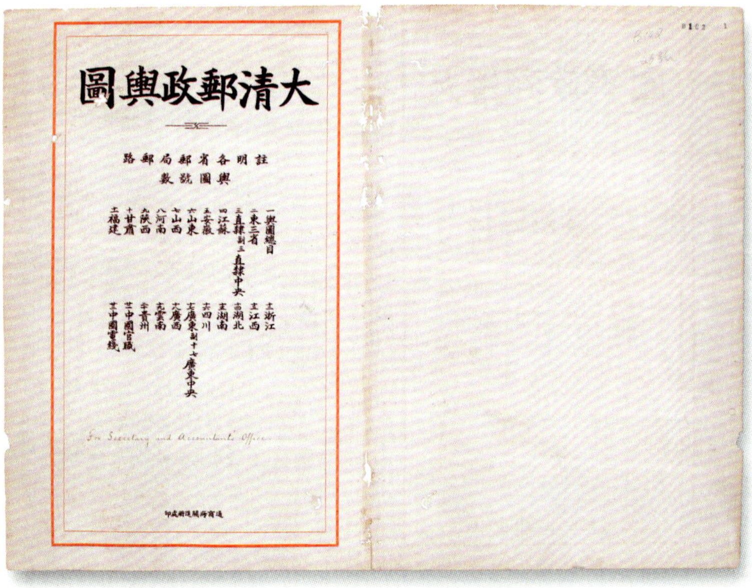

《大清邮政舆图》

Chinese Imperial Postal Map

1907年

纸质

1907年，海关造册处印制的大型地图集，共收录22幅地图，注明了各省的邮界、邮路、邮局分布，以及火汇局（设在通火车、轮船之处）、旱汇局（设在不通火车、轮船之处）、电汇局等单位，清晰详实地介绍了当时全国邮政的分布情况。邮路除铁路之外，还标明了“马差之邮路”“昼夜兼程之邮路”，有江湖水域的省份，还标明了“水道之邮路”。

“中华民国”蟠龙邮票

Panlong Stamps with the Seal of “Republic of China”

20世纪初期

蟠龙邮票发行于1897年10月，是光绪皇帝御批开办国家邮政后第一次正式发行的邮票，也是中国海关发行的第四套邮票。中华民国成立初期未印制邮票，暂将清代蟠龙邮票由海关造册处、商务印书馆和英国伦敦华德路公司分别加盖“中华民国”字样发行。其中海关造册处分别加盖黑、红色宋体字；商务印书馆加盖红色宋体字，但“国”字略大；华德路公司分别加盖蓝、黑、红色楷体字。

海务港务
Coast and Harbor Affairs

根据《通商章程善后条约》规定，近代海关负责利用征收的船钞建设助航设施。1868年，总税务司署设船钞部（1912年改称海政局，1929年改称海务科），负责沿海灯塔建造与维护、港内助航标志布设、内河航标设置、内河航道测量，以及引水、指泊、海港检疫、航道疏浚、港口治安、气象与水文观测等事务。至1948年12月，海关管理的灯塔137座、灯桩166座、灯船20艘，此外还有立标、灯浮、浮标、信号台、无线电指示标等共计1322处。

As specified in the *Treaty on the Aftermath of the Articles of Commerce*, Chinese Maritime Customs was in charge of constructing navigation aid facilities with the vessel tonnage dues collected. In 1868, the Inspectorate General set up the Marine Department to be in charge of coastal lighthouse construction and maintenance, the layout of navigation aid marks in ports, setup of navigation marks on the inland waterways, inland water course survey and the pilotage, berthing, seaport quarantine, channel dredging, public security, meteorological and hydrologic observation and other affairs. By December 1948, the various customs were in charge of 137 lighthouses, 166 light beacons and 20 lightships, as well as 1,322 standing navigation marks, light buoys, buoys, signal stations and radio direction beacon.

《海关港务章程》

Customs Harbor Regulations

晚清时期

各通商口岸的海港港务业务章程总汇。包括宁波、广州、福州、温州、龙州等多处口岸外洋船舶航行、引水、停泊、装卸货物的有关规定以及收费标准等内容。

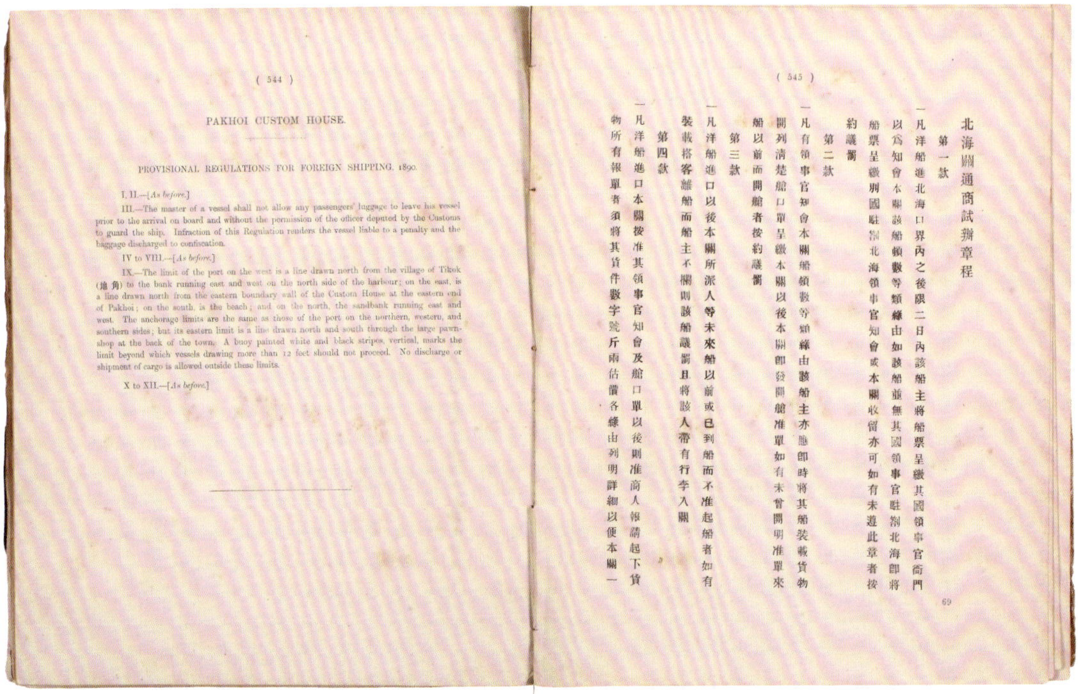

(544)

PAKHOI CUSTOM HOUSE.

PROVISIONAL REGULATIONS FOR FOREIGN SHIPPING, 1890.

I, II.—[*As before.*]

III.—The master of a vessel shall not allow any passengers' luggage to leave his vessel prior to the arrival on board and without the permission of the officer deputed by the Customs to guard the ship. Infraction of this Regulation renders the vessel liable to a penalty and the baggage discharged to confiscation.

IV to VIII.—[*As before.*]

IX.—The limit of the port on the west is a line drawn north from the village of Tikok (地角) to the bank running east and west on the north side of the harbour; on the east, is a line drawn north from the eastern boundary wall of the Custom House at the eastern end of Pakhoi; on the south, is the beach; and on the north, the sandbank running east and west. The anchorage limits are the same as those of the port on the northern, western, and southern sides; but its eastern limit is a line drawn north and south through the large pawn-shop at the back of the town. A buoy painted white and black stripes, vertical, marks the limit beyond which vessels drawing more than 12 feet should not proceed. No discharge or shipment of cargo is allowed outside these limits.

X to XII.—[*As before.*]

(545)

北海關通商試辦章程

第一款

一凡洋船進北海口界內之後限二日內該船主將船票呈繳其國領事官衙門以爲知會本關該船噸數等類緣由如該船並無其國領事官駐劄北海即將船票呈繳別國駐劄北海領事官知會或本關收留亦可如有未遵此章者按約議罰

第二款

一凡有領事官知會本關船噸數等類緣由該船主亦應即時將其船裝載貨物開列清楚艙口單呈繳本關以後本關即發開艙准單如有未曾開明准單來船以前而開艙者按約議罰

第三款

一凡洋船進口以後本關所派人等未來船以前或已到船而不准起船者如有裝載搭客離船而船主不攔則該船議罰且將該人帶有行李入關

第四款

一凡洋船進口本關按准其領事官知會及艙口單以後則准商人報請起下貨物所有報單者須將其貨件數字號斤兩估價各樣由列明詳細以便本關一

69

"琼海关1893"碑
Stele of Qiong Haiguan (Kiungchow Customs)
1893年

琼海关于1893年建造临高灯塔时所立。临高灯塔位于海南临高县临高角海边，在琼州海峡西面进口处，是海南岛西北部的重要航标。中国共有5座灯塔被列为世界100座历史文物灯塔，其中临高灯塔、舟山花鸟山灯塔、大连老铁山灯塔都是近代海关建造的。

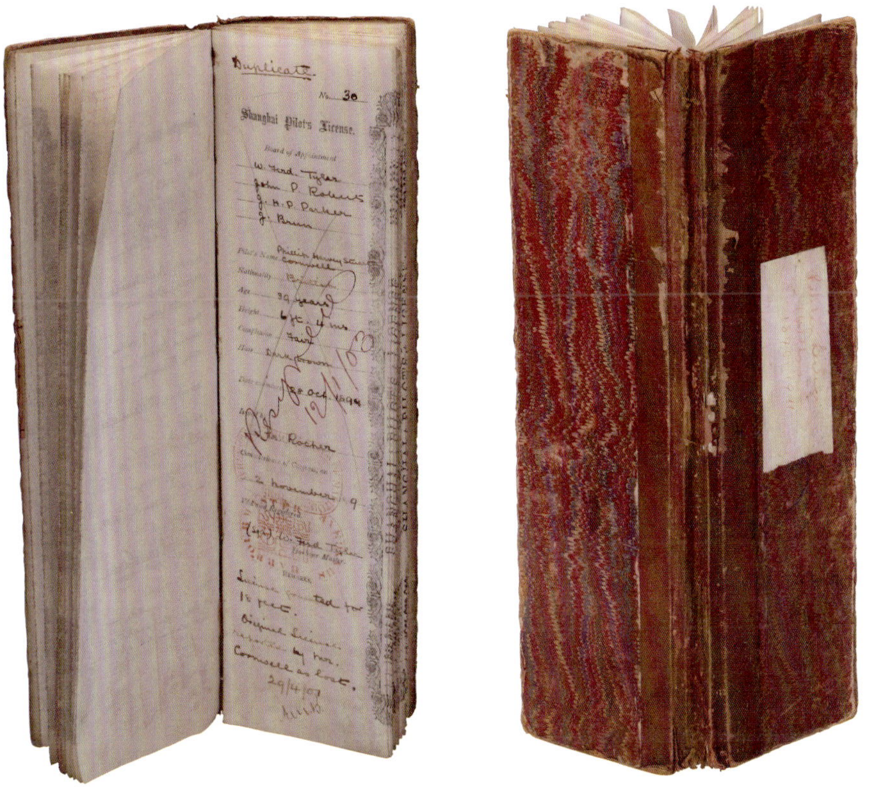

引水员执照存根

Counterfoil of the Pilot License

1896年至1911年

引水，即由熟悉航道并具有驾驶经验的专业人员，引领或驾驶船舶进出港口，或在江、河、内海一定区域内航行。鸦片战争后，中国引水主权丧失，外籍船舶可自雇引水员，外国领事有权向拥有3张船主证明的人员发放引水执照。1868年《引水章程专条》颁布，明确由各口海关理船厅管理引水事宜。此后，各港口引水工作逐步被外籍引水员所把持，中国海防、江防秘密也为外国人所掌握。

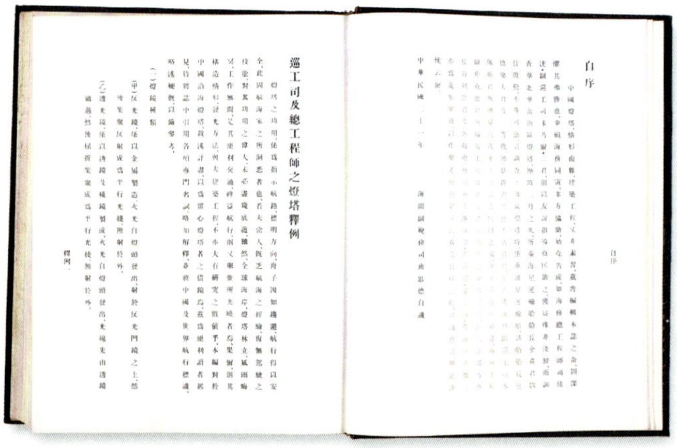

《中国沿海灯塔志》

The Coastwise Lights records of China

1933年

海关副税务司班思德（T.R.Banister）著、署副税务司李廷元译，总税务司署统计科印行，介绍了中国沿海灯塔的起源、发展、构造、形状以及功用，并记载了1866年至1925年兴建的沿海沿江灯塔设备及其照片，调查精确、叙述翔实。

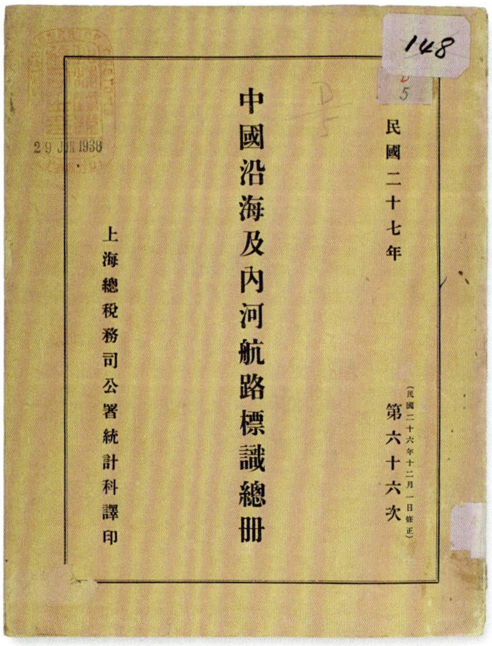

《中国沿海及内河航路标识总册》

A Complete Collection of Signs in China's Coastal and Inland Waterways

1938年

本书内容包括沿海灯站全图、航路标识燃灯规则、雾号说明、各关所属区域及海务界限表，以及长江航路标识说明及水位深度信号等。由于沿海港口开埠后华洋海运船只来往增多，原有简单航道标志已不能保证航行安全，海关成立船钞部，开始改建或新建沿海内河航路标志。截至20世纪30年代初，中国沿海内河灯塔浮标总数已达2000余处，并已开始使用世界新式灯机、雾号。

海务标志铜版

Copper Plate of Marine Sign

民国时期

赫德像基座南面的女神铜像印刷铜版。铜版上的女神手持照明灯具，指引船舶航向，寓意赫德领导的近代海关办理海关港务。赫德铜像于1914年在九江路外滩的江海关大楼前落成，1927年江海关新大楼建成后，铜像亦移至新大楼前，因此铜版上标有“Re-erected 1927”字样。

商标注册
Trademark Registration

根据中英《续议通商行船条约》等不平等条约规定，为维护各国在华商标权益，1904年外务部批准颁行由总税务司署制定的《商标注册试办章程》，规定商部设商标局专门管理商标注册事务，津沪两关设商标挂号分局，专门负责受理商标的挂号、收发、寄递等。总税务司署还制定了实施细则，津海关、江海关开始受理中外厂商商标挂号业务。1923年5月，北洋政府在农商部设立商标局办理商标注册事务，结束了海关经办商标挂号业务的历史。1934年，财政部关务署批准颁行了《海关对于报运之伪造商标或伪造商标之货物或商标与他人注册商标相同者处理办法》，开始查处进出口环节侵犯商标的行为。

According to the unequal treaties, for the purpose of protecting the trademark rights and interests of various countries in China, the *Waiwubu* (the Ministry of Foreign Affairs) approved the *Interim Regulation on Trademark Registration* formulated by the Inspectorate General in 1904, specifying that a registration bureau would be set up under the Ministry of Commerce of the Qing government to be in professional charge of trademark registration, and sub-offices would be set up at Tientsin and Shanghai customs to deal with trademark registration, receiving, sending and delivery. It was replaced by trademark offices under the Ministry of Agriculture and Commerce in May 1923. In 1934, the then Customs Administration of the Ministry of Finance approved and issued regulations and began investigating trademark infringements in import and export.

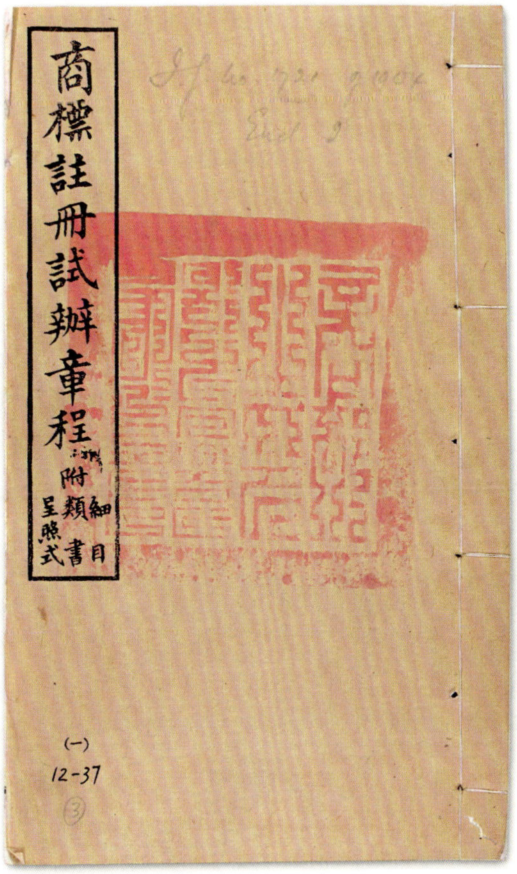

《商标注册试办章程》

Interim Regulation on Trademark Registration

1904年

1904年8月4日，清政府颁布的《商标注册试办章程》，由海关副总税务司裴式楷草拟、总税务司赫德修改、商部修订并经光绪皇帝钦定，是中国历史上的第一部商标注册法规。因英、德、意、比等国的反对，章程中大部分条款被暂缓施行，但第二条在津沪两地海关设立商标挂号分局的规定如期施行，并于同年9月15日正式受理中外厂商的商标备案申请。

海关代办的注册商标

Trademarks Registered by the Chinese Maritime Customs Service

20世纪20年代

20世纪20年代江海关商标挂号分局登记簿中的商标，图案包括人物、花卉、风景等，色彩鲜亮，印制精美。津沪商标挂号分局成立后，负责核实商标注册申请人递交的书面申请，并交至商部商标注册局（因西方列强反对，未能设立）；核实由委托人代办的注册申请，并验凭其委托书或代理凭证；对需注册的商标进行编号，对已注册的商标记录原商标编号，对续用商标则要求提供原商标的印照，以便核查。

頭等玫瑰香皂
BEST TOILET SOAP
J.S. Factory, Shanghai
No. 106

老牌
九鼎香皂
註冊商標
瑞賓自製
J.P. & CO.

中央公園牌香皂
TOILET SOAP
TOILET SOAP
TOILET SOAP
中央公園牌香皂
CENTRAL SOAP WORKS
SHANGHAI CHINA No. 1020
中央公園牌香皂

世界博览会
World Exposition

1867年，受法国邀请，总理衙门通知总税务司署派员参加巴黎国际博览会，赫德派法籍税务司美理登出国参展。1873年起，总理衙门正式授权总税务司署办理筹备、参加国际博览会事宜，并先后组团代表中国参加了1873年维也纳、1876年费城、1878年巴黎、1884年伦敦食品与卫生、1884年新奥尔良（棉花）、1900年巴黎国际博览会，以及1902年河内、1904年圣路易斯、1905年列日世界博览会（1900年巴黎国际博览会后统一改称世界博览会），成为让世界了解中国、让中国走向世界的窗口。但因海关在圣路易斯博览会的参展展品多展示中国落后面貌，引起华侨、留学生及清政府的不满，1905年后清政府将此项事务交商部办理。

In 1867, France held the International Exposition in Paris. China was also invited. The *Zongli Yamen* informed the Inspectorate General to send a mission and Robert Hart dispatched French customs officer Baron de Meritens to the Exposition. Since 1873, the *Zongli Yamen* officially authorized the Inspectorate General to deal with affairs concerning preparations for and participation in world exposition, and missions were successively sent on behalf of China to the 1873 Universal Exhibition in Vienna, the 1876 International Exhibition in Philadelphia, the 1878 Universal Exposition in Paris, the 1884 International Health Exhibition in London, the 1884 Exposition in New Orleans , the 1900 Exposition in Paris, the 1902 Exposition in Hanoi, the 1904 Purchase Exposition in Louisiana and the 1905 Universal and International Exhibition in Liege, becoming a window for the rest of the world to know more about China and for China to go global. Since 1905, this duty of customs was transferred to the Ministry of Commerce.

第一届伦敦世界博览会纪念章

Souvenir Badge of the First International Industrial Exhibition in London

1851年

1851年，伦敦举办了第一届世界博览会（万国工业产品博览会），中国丝绸制品在该届博览会上获奖并名扬天下。该奖章主要颁给参展国代表团高层和获奖者，正面为维多利亚女王、阿尔伯特亲王像，背面为世界博览会主展馆水晶宫。

巴黎国际博览会中国馆照片

China Pavilion at the Pairs World Expo

1878年

1878年海关代表中国参加了巴黎国际博览会，展出的中国馆展品大多由总税务司署从中国各口岸征集，分为木器、瓷器、玉器、金银器、铜锡器等，其中最受欢迎的展品是广州绣屏和象牙折扇。博览会中国馆以“中华公所”命名，建筑和陈设富有民族特色，院中央设有售货小亭，专售瓷器、茶叶、古铜器、雕刻、象牙折扇等中国特色商品。

巴黎博览会中国商品目录

Catalogue of the Chinese Collection of Exhibits at the Paris Exhibition, 1900

1900年

1900年，海关再次代表中国参加了巴黎世界博览会，所征集的展品以象牙、瓷器、织物等工艺品和茶叶、小麦等农作物为主，另带工匠数十人，每天公开演示中国传统手工艺品的制作。中国馆面积约3300平方米，共设5座建筑模拟北京城墙、万里长城、孔庙等地标性建筑。

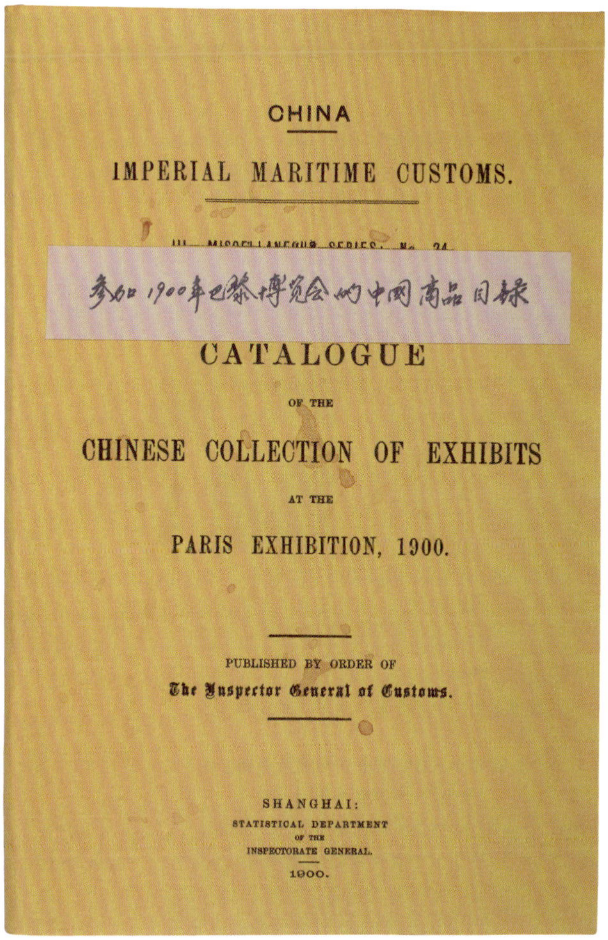

其他兼办
Other Additional Services

第一次鸦片战争后，中国近代海关开始参与政府内外债与赔款及军事、外交事务，并代管京师同文馆。清政府依据条约，指定海关关税作为赔款及外债的担保，各地海关按照总税务司指令偿付所分摊的赔款与外债。民国时期，各地海关还对北洋政府及南京国民政府所发行的内债提供关税担保或以关税拨充内债偿还基金；19世纪60年代，为镇压太平天国起义，总理衙门委派在英国休假的总税务司李泰国代购军舰，但他私自筹建“阿思本舰队”并把控其指挥权，后遭到解散。19世纪70年代，为防范日本侵略中国台湾，总理衙门委托总税务司赫德代购军舰，赫德先后承购炮艇11艘、巡洋舰2艘，为组建“北洋水师”打下基础；为培养外交急需的华人翻译人才，1862年总理衙门根据赫德建议并从海关征收船钞中划拨三成，在北京开办京师同文馆，其外籍教习的聘任及教学的安排等均由总税务司署统一管理。

After the First Opium War, Chinese Maritime Customs began to engage in the foreign debt indemnity of the government, military and diplomatic affairs and the management of *Tungwen Guan*. According to the treaties, the Qing Government designated tariffs as guarantees for indemnity and foreign debts, and various local customs should pay the indemnity according to the amount apportioned to them by the Inspector General. During the period of the Republic of China, local customs would still provide tariff guarantee for the domestic debts issued by the Beiyang Government and Nanjing National Government or appropriated tariffs as the redemption funds of domestic debts. In the 1860s, the *Zongli Yamen* appointed Inspector General Horatio Nelson Lay who was on holiday in Britain to purchase warships in order to suppress the Taiping Rebellion, but he ended up building the “the Sherard Osborn Fleet” without permission and took the command, which was later dissolved. In the 1970s, the *Zongli Yamen* commissioned Inspector General Robert Hart to purchase warships in order to prevent Japan from invading Taiwan of China. He successively purchased 11 gunboats and 2 cruisers, laying the foundation for the establishment of the “Beiyang Fleet”. In order to cultivate Chinese translators for urgent diplomatic needs, the *Zongli Yamen* accepted Robert Hart’s suggestion and appropriated 30 percent from the customs tonnage dues to set up the *Tungwen Guan* in Beijing. The employment of foreign teachers and teaching arrangements of the school were under the unified management of the Inspectorate General.

奕䜣奏拨税银购买外国船炮折

Memorial to the Throne about Purchasing Foreign Ships and Cannons

1862年

总理大臣、恭亲王奕䜣以“贼氛未靖、力求制胜”为由，引述代理总税务司赫德对外洋船炮的描述，奏请动用上海、广东各关的税银，委托赫德购买外洋船炮，交沿海各省雇用本地人学习驾驶，以抗衡“太平天国”。此后，在英国休假的时任总税务司李泰国借代购军舰之机联合英国海军阿思本上校组建了“阿思本舰队”并把控了指挥权，后被遣散。

19世纪70年代，赫德又借防范日本侵略中国台湾之机，说服清政府委托其购买西方先进军舰，并先后从英国阿姆斯特朗公司购买了11艘炮艇、2艘巡洋舰。这些舰船多数被总理衙门分配给李鸿章使用，为组建北洋水师打下了基础。

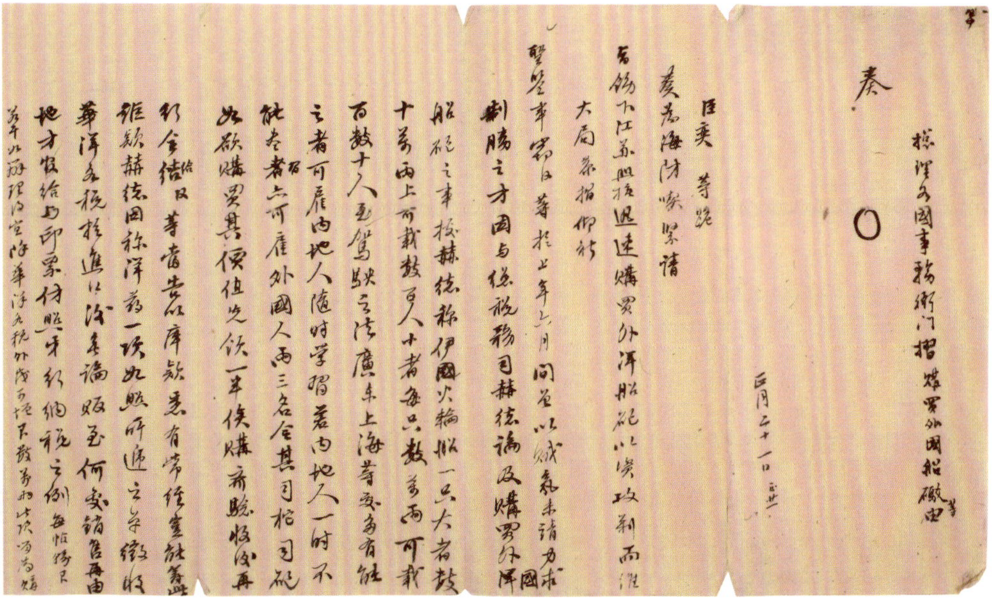

中国订制的蚊炮船

蚊炮船是近代海关为北洋水师代购的军舰，1895年参加了威海卫保卫战，是年2月14日北洋水师投降后被日军俘虏，列入了日本海军编制内。

等待下水的超勇舰

超勇号是世界上第一艘完全摆脱风帆时代窠臼的非装甲巡洋舰，由近代海关代购。1894年9月17日参加了黄海海战，被日舰击沉。

《同文馆题名录》

Triennial Calendar of the Tungwen College

1888年

1862年，为培养中国翻译人才，应对日益增长的外交事务，中国第一座专门培养翻译人员的新式学校——京师同文馆成立，馆址设于北京东堂子胡同49号总理衙门内。同文馆以海关所征船钞的三成用于支付教习薪俸及学生日常生活所需。在1866年之前，京师同文馆的办学目的仅限于培养外语人才。直到总税务司署迁往北京后，总税务司赫德奉总理衙门之命担任京师同文馆监察官，所有同文馆教习均由总税务司协助聘请的外籍人员担任，其余职位则由总理衙门官员担任，并增设各类近代科学课程，京师同文馆成为介绍近代思想进入中国教育制度的先驱。1888年，京师同文馆归入总税务司署编制，1902年京师同文馆改称“译学馆”，重组并入京师大学堂。京师同文馆累计培养了毕业生1000多人，大多成为政府译员、外交官员、海关华员和外文教师等。

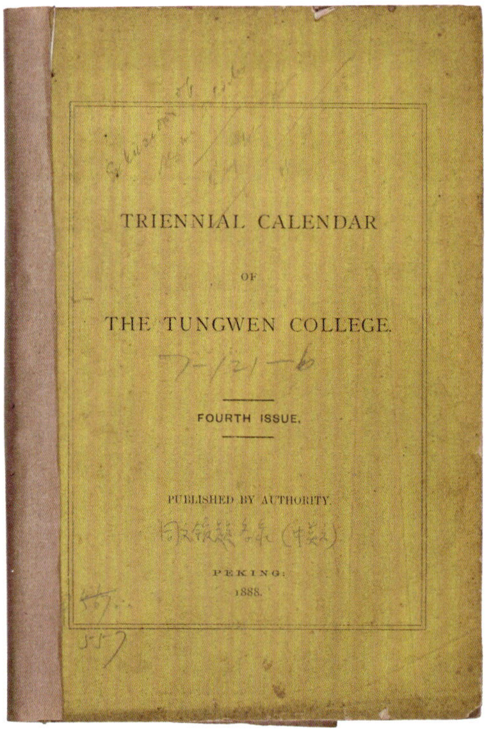

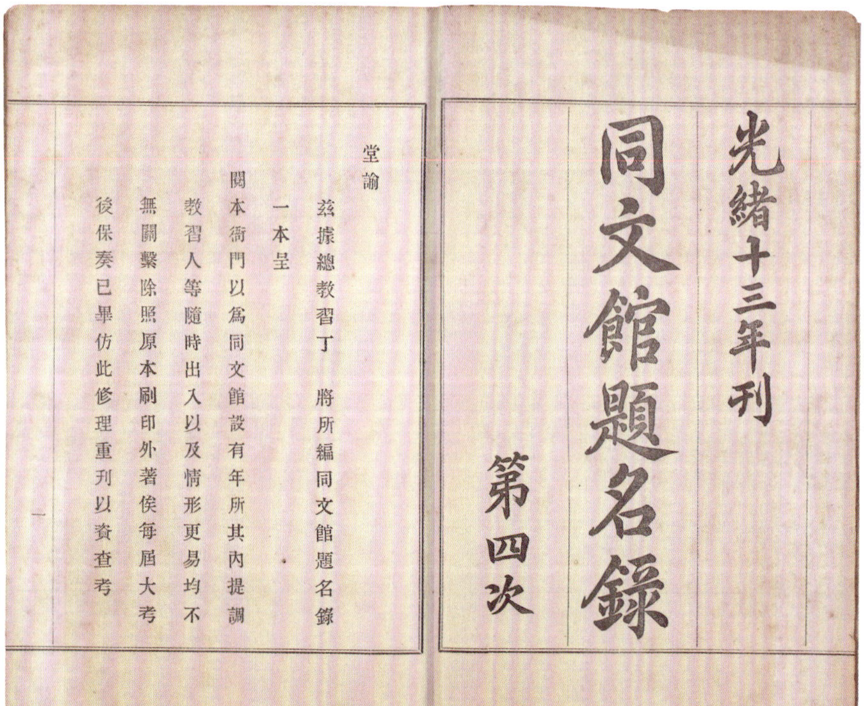

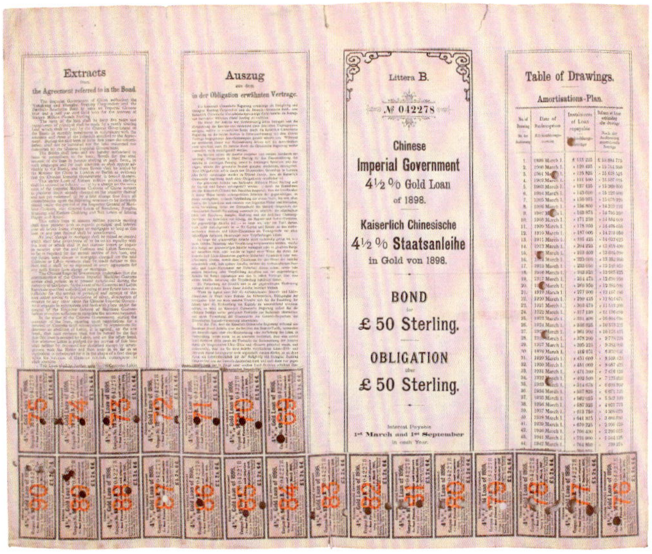

清政府以关税为抵押的借款公债券

Qing Government Bonds Secured on Customs Revenue

1896年

中日甲午战争结束后，根据中日签订的《马关条约》《辽南条约》等不平等条约，中国需在短期内支付日本23050万两库平银。由于战后清政府国库空虚，无力偿付巨额赔款，清政府与俄、法签订借款合同，以4%年息借款1亿两。合同规定，该项借款以中国海关所入税项及存票作为担保。

闽关铜元

“F.K.CUSTOM-HOUSE 10 CASH”

1905年

该铜元属于清光绪元宝，因由闽海关铜币局铸造且署有“闽关”字样得名，是晚清时期唯一由海关铜元局铸造的铜元。其正面中圈内有“光绪元宝”四字、上方署“福建官局造”、左右分署“闽关”；背面中圈内有蟠龙图案、外环以“F.K.CUSTOM-HOUSE”，意为（福建）闽海关。闽海关铜币局正式开办于1905年，开办经费主要来自闽海关，铸造品种单一，目前只发现光绪元宝当十文一种。

全国海关
第一次先进工作者
代表会议纪念

人民海关

People's Customs

The CPC had taken it as an objective to take back customs sovereignty since its founding. In addition to leading the customs staff for progressive activities in the KMT-controlled areas and Japanese-occupied areas, the CPC also built the people's customs successively in the soviet areas, anti-Japanese bases and liberated areas to realize local tariff autonomy, which accumulated experience and cultivated cadres for the founding of new China Customs. After the founding of new China, customs sovereignty was taken back to the people. China Customs has always shared the same outlook and destiny with the country and experienced different periods, including the establishment of new customs, the customs and foreign trade bureau merging and the transfer of administrative functions to lower levels. After the Third Plenary Session of the 11th CPC Central Committee, the centralized and unified vertical management system at customs was recovered, continuously deepening service reform and the principle of "tight control and quick customs clearance" afterwards, which made outstanding contributions to protecting national sovereignty and interests, serving the new pattern of the country's opening-up and promoting socialist modernization.

中国共产党在成立之初，便将收回海关主权作为奋斗目标。除了领导国统区、日占区海关职工进步活动外，还先后在苏区、抗日根据地、解放区等建立人民海关，实现了局部地区的关税自主，为筹建中华人民共和国海关积累了经验、培养了干部。新中国成立后，海关主权回到人民手中。海关与国家同呼吸、与民族共命运，先后经过创建新海关、关局合并、体制下放阶段，十一届三中全会后全国海关恢复集中统一的垂直管理体制，不断深化业务改革，坚持“管得住、通得快”，为维护国家主权和利益、服务国家对外开放和外经贸事业、促进社会主义现代化建设做出了突出贡献。

队伍建设
Team Construction

中华人民共和国成立初期，解放区干部、留任的旧海关人员与青年知识分子共同组成海关队伍的主体；1966至1976年间，海关队伍大幅萎缩；改革开放以后，许多调离海关系统的干部陆续归队，海关队伍重新焕发了生机；2003年，中国海关以实施关衔制为契机，着力打造一支现代化、正规化、准军事化海关队伍；党的十八大以来，中国海关以习近平新时代中国特色社会主义思想为引领，锻造“政治坚定、业务精通、令行禁止、担当奉献”的准军事化纪律部队，努力建设让党中央放心、让人民群众满意的新时代中国特色社会主义新海关。

During the early years after the founding of the People’s Republic of China, cadres in liberated areas, retained staff at old customs and young intellectuals jointly constituted the main part of the customs. After the reform and opening-up, many officials rejoined the customs system to revitalize the customs. In 2003, the customs rank system was adopted to build a modern, normalized and paramilitary customs. Since the 18th CPC National Congress, guided by Xi Jinping Thought on Socialism with Chinese Characteristics for a New Era, China Customs has forged a paramilitary disciplined service that is “firm in political conviction, professionally competent, strictly disciplined, responsible and devoted”, striving to build new socialist customs with Chinese characteristics in the new era which the CPC Central Committee trusts and people are satisfied with.

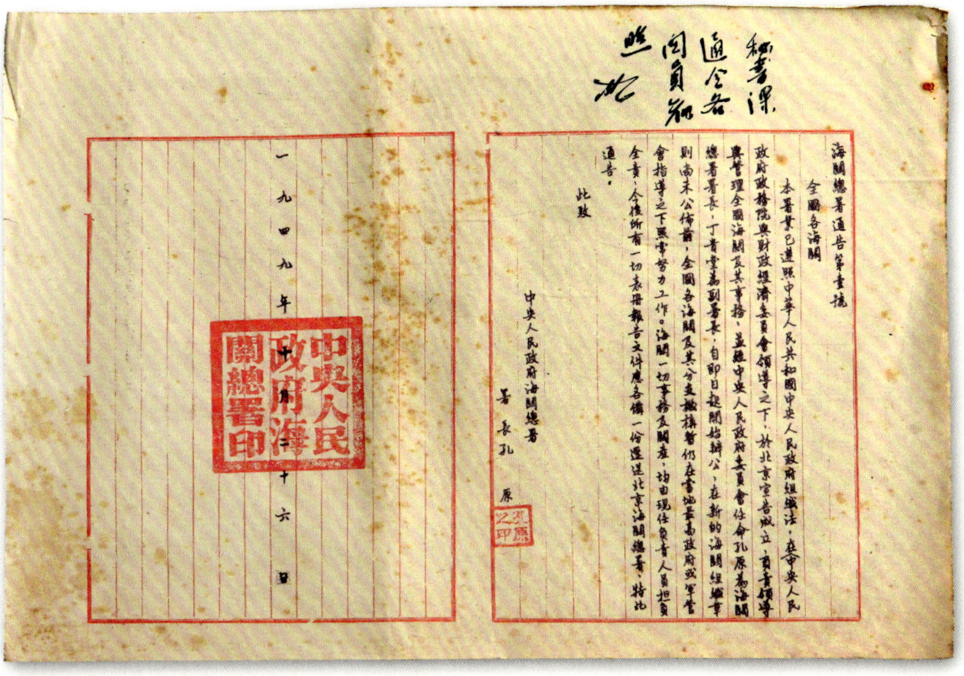

秘書課通令各關員知照

海關總署通告第壹號

全國各海關

本署業已遵照中華人民共和國中央人民政府組織法，在中央人民政府政務院與財政經濟委員會領導之下，於北京宣告成立，負責領導與管理全國海關及其事務，並經中央人民政府委員會任命孔原為海關總署署長，丁貴堂為副署長，自即日起開始辦公，在新的海關組織章則尚未公佈前，全國各海關及其分支機構暫仍在當地最高政府或軍管會指導之下照常努力工作。海關一切事務及關產，均由現任負責人員担負全責，今後所有一切表冊報告文件應各備一份逕送北京海關總署，特此通告。

此致

中央人民政府海關總署

署長孔原

孔原之印

一九四九年十月二十六日

中央人民政府海關總署印

“海关总署通告第壹号”

Notification No.1 of the GACC

1949年

1949年10月26日，中华人民共和国中央人民政府海关总署署长孔原签发的“海关总署通告第壹号”，宣告海关总署正式在北京成立，负责领导与管理全国海关及其事务，标志着中华人民共和国收回海关主权，“把中国大门的钥匙放在自己的袋子里”。

中央人民政府任命通知書
府字第〇叁伍柒號
茲經中央人民政府委員會
第三次會議通過任命孔原為
中央人民政府海關總署署長
特此通知
主席 毛泽东
一九四九年十月十九日
中華人民共和國中央人民政府之印

海关总署首任署长任命书

Appointment Certificate of the First GACC Minster

1949年

1949年10月19日，毛泽东主席签发任命书，任命孔原为中华人民共和国中央人民政府海关总署首任署长。海关总署成立后，依据《关于设立海关原则和调整全国海关机构的指示》精神，领导海关实行集中统一的领导体制，组织制定并由政务院颁布实施《关于关税政策和海关工作的决定》《中央人民政府海关总署试行组织条例》《中华人民共和国暂行海关法》《中华人民共和国海关进出口税则》 等法律法规和30多个海关业务规章制度，为中华人民共和国海关发展打下坚实基础。

全国人民代表大会出席证及公文包

Attendance Certificate of the First National People's Congress and Ding Guitang's Briefcase

20世纪50年代

丁贵堂曾任中国近代海关副总税务司、代理总税务司以及中华人民共和国中央人民政府海关总署副署长、外贸部海关管理局局长。这是他使用过的公文包及1954年9月参加第一届全国人民代表大会的出席证。1961年外贸部海关总署改称海关管理局，丁贵堂担任局长。在担任中华人民共和国海关高级领导职务13年期间，丁贵堂参与组建海关组织机构和制定《中华人民共和国暂行海关法》《中华人民共和国海关进出口税则》等基本法律法规。

注意事项

1. 進入會場時請出示證件
2. 此證可通行各小組會場及各代表住所
3. 如有遺失請卽通知大會秘書處
4. 此證會議閉幕後卽行作廢

姓名 丁貴堂

選舉單位 旅大市

編號 三三四

一九五四年九月六日塡發

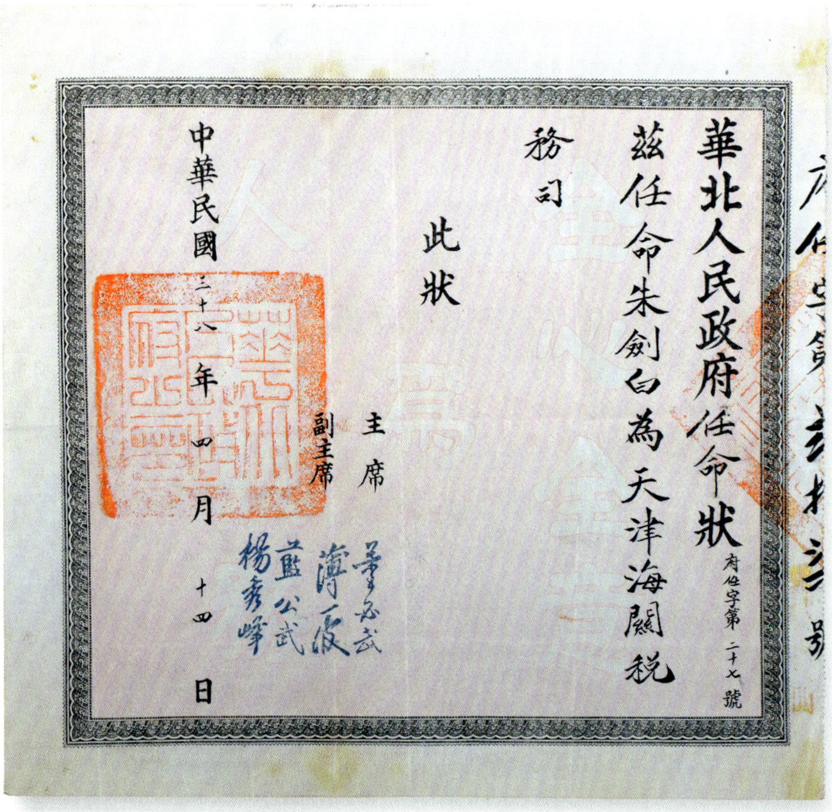
華北人民政府任命狀 府任字第二十七號
茲任命朱劍白為天津海關稅務司
此狀
主席 董必武
副主席 薄一波 藍公武 楊秀峰
中華民國三十八年四月十四日

华北人民政府任命状

Appointment Certificate of North China People's Government

1949年

1948年9月，中华人民共和国中央人民政府的雏形——华北人民政府在石家庄成立，在中国革命政权和民主政治制度史上具有里程碑意义。1949年天津市解放后，华北人民政府任命朱剑白为天津海关税务司。

北京对外贸易学院毕业文凭

Beijing Foreign Trade Institute Diploma

1960年

1960年，曾任外贸部海关管理局局长的朱剑白在北京对外贸易学院（今对外经济贸易大学）学习所取得的毕业文凭。

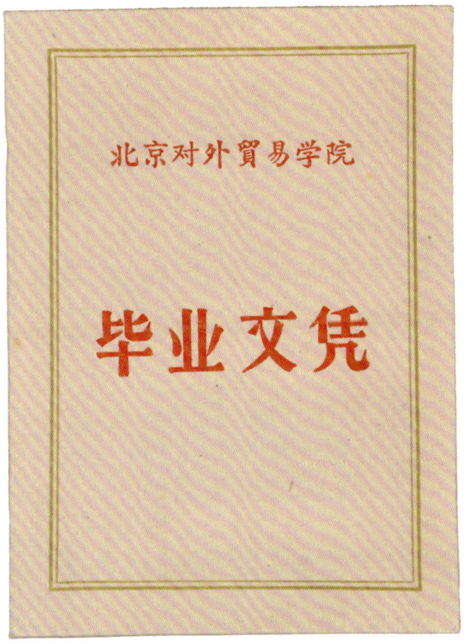

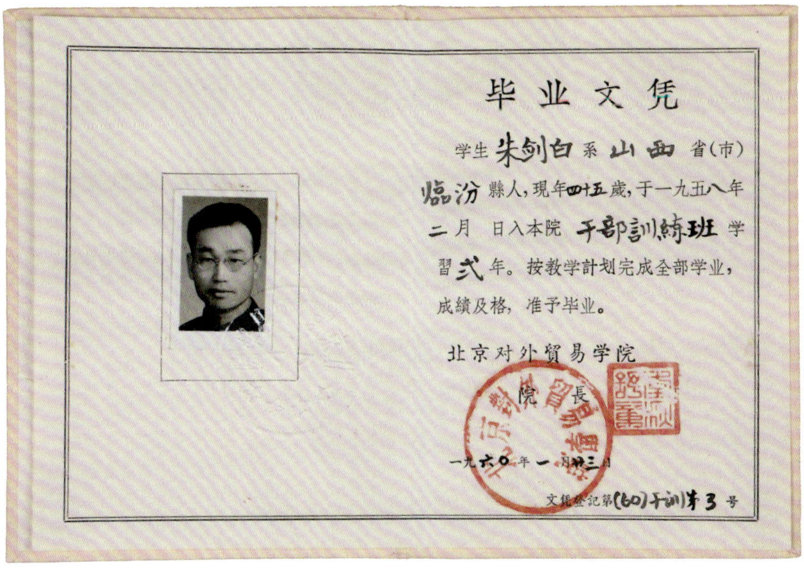

毕业文凭

学生朱剑白系山西省(市)临汾縣人，現年四十五歲，于一九五八年二月　日入本院干部訓練班学習弍年。按教学計划完成全部学业，成績及格，准予毕业。

北京对外貿易学院

院長

一九六〇年一月廿三日

文凭登記第(60)干訓第3号

海关关衔

Customs Rank

2003年

2003年2月28日，第九届全国人民代表大会常务委员会第三十二次会议二审通过《中华人民共和国海关关衔条例》，海关成为中国继人民军队、人民警察后第三支授衔队伍。中国海关关衔分为五等十三级：

一等：海关总监、海关副总监；

二等：一级关务监督、二级关务监督、三级关务监督；

三等：一级关务督察、二级关务督察、三级关务督察；

四等：一级关务督办、二级关务督办、三级关务督办；

五等：一级关务员、二级关务员。

海关制服

Customs Uniform

20世纪50年代至80年代

从1950年起，为了履行职责、表明身份、行使职权，中华人民共和国海关关员统一穿着规定样式的制服并佩戴标志。中华人民共和国海关标志主要有6次变动，与制服的式样变化阶段基本一致，分为1950式、1953式、1966式、1972式、1979式和1985式，制服标志主要包括帽徽、胸章、肩章、领花、臂章、臂套、纽扣等，后期又拓展至带有海关标志的腰带、领带、领带夹等。

1950式关警制服

Uniform for Customs Police Officer in 1950

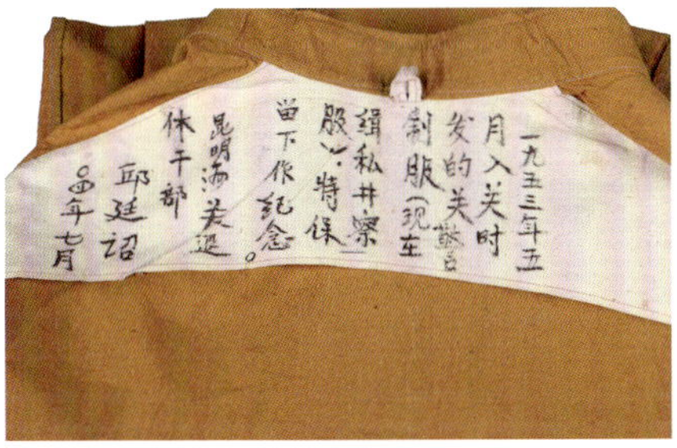

1950式海关证章

Badge for Customs Officer in 1950

1950式关警帽徽

Cap Badge for Customs Police Officer in 1950

1953式海关制服
Uniform for Customs Officer in 1953

1953式海关纽扣
Button for Customs Officer in 1953

1953式海关帽徽
Cap Badge for Customs Officer in 1953

1953式海关臂章
Armband for Customs Officer in 1953

1966式海关制服/袖章

Uniform/Armband for Customs Officer in 1966

1966式海关帽徽

Cap Badge for Customs Officer in 1966

1972式海关制服
Uniform for Customs Officer in 1972

1972式海关臂章
Armband for Customs Officer in 1972

1979式海关女制服
Uniform Shirt for Female Customs Officer in 1979

1979式海关胸章
Badge for Customs Officer in 1979

1979式海关帽徽
Cap Badge for Customs Officer in 1979

1979式海关纽扣
Button for Customs Officer in 1979

1985式海关帽徽
Cap Badge for Customs Officer in 1985

1985式海关领花
Collar Badge for Customs Officer in 1985

1985式海关肩章
Shoulder Board for Customs Officer in 1985

上海海关学校学生肩章
Epaulet for Shanghai Customs School Student

1996至2003年

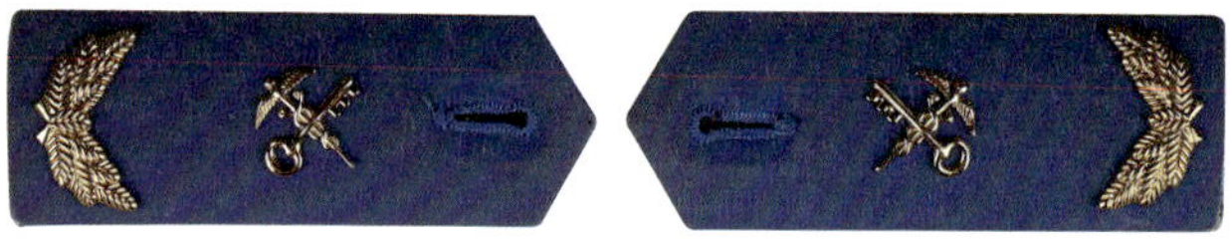

上海海关学校校徽
Insignia of Shanghai Customs School

20世纪末

1953年，海关总署根据海关业务需要并报经中央财经委员会批准，创办上海海关学校，这是中华人民共和国海关第一所具有学历教育资格的中等专科学校。1980年升格为上海海关专科学校；1996年更名为上海海关高等专科学校；2007年3月升格为上海海关学院，为全国唯一一所系统设置海关学科课程和专业的本科院校。

上海海关学校录取通知书

Admission Notice of Shanghai Customs School

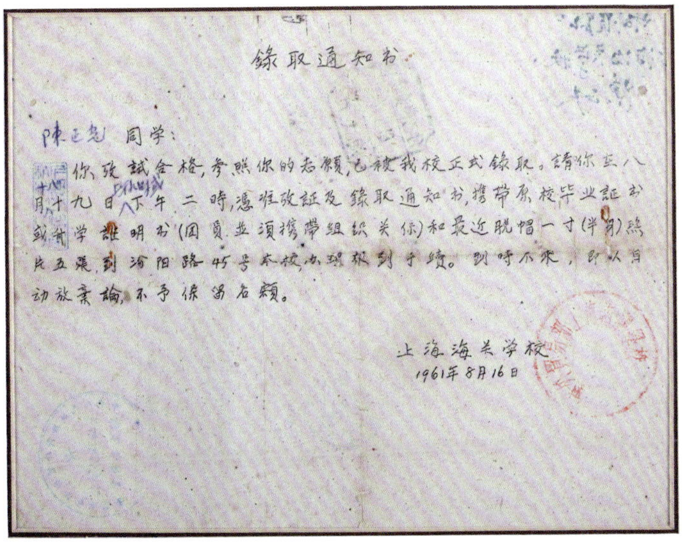

錄取通知书

陳正忠 同学：

你考試合格，参照你的志願，已被我校正式錄取。請你在八月十九日下午二時，憑准考証及錄取通知书，携带原校毕业証书或肄学証明书（团員並須携帶组织关係）和最近脱帽一寸（半身）照片五張，到汾阳路45号本校办理报到手續。到时不来，即以自动放棄論，不予保留名額。

上海海关学校

1961年8月16日

上海海关学校学生证

Student ID of Shanghai Customs School

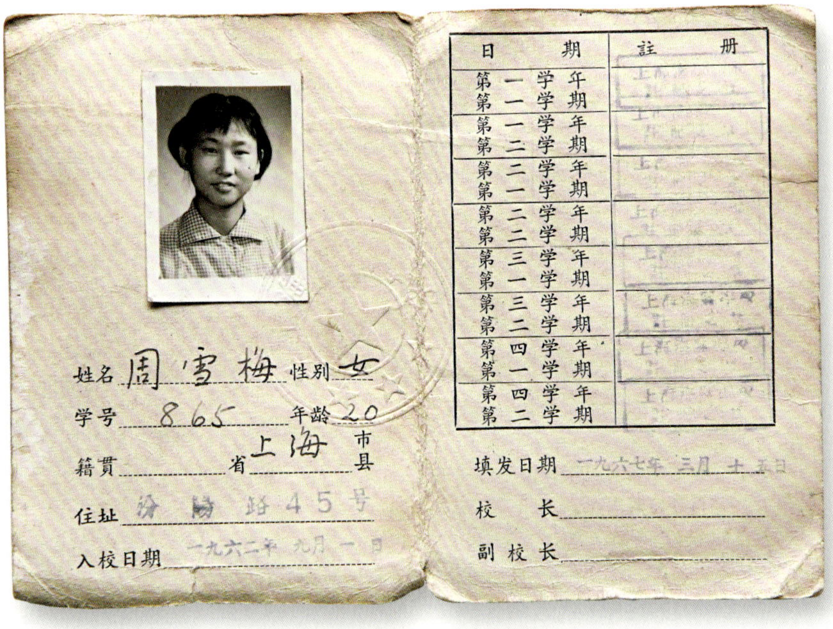

姓名 周雪梅 性别 女

学号 865 年龄 20

籍貫 省 上海 市/县

住址 汾阳路45号

入校日期 一九六二年九月一日

日期	註册
第一学年第一学期	
第一学年第二学期	
第二学年第一学期	
第二学年第二学期	
第三学年第一学期	
第三学年第二学期	
第四学年第一学期	
第四学年第二学期	

填发日期 一九六七年三月十五日

校　长

副校长

争取关权
Struggle for Customs Sovereignty

中国共产党在成立之初，就明确提出了收回海关主权的主张，并领导、支持海关华员开展争取改善华员待遇、抗日救亡运动等进步活动和革命斗争。其中，一些海关华员投身革命、抛家舍业，将自己的安全、生命置之度外，展现了海关人心向光明、爱国爱党的民族精神。中国共产党还领导建立了苏区税关、抗日根据地海关和解放区海关，实现了局部地区的关税自主，为中华人民共和国海关积累了经验、培养了人才。解放战争期间，一大批海关进步华员积极听党话、跟党走，为保护关产、迎接解放做出了贡献。

Since its founding, the CPC had claimed clearly the recovery of customs sovereignty, and led and supported native staff at customs to launch progressive activities and revolutionary struggles to improve their treatment, resist the Japanese aggression and save the nation. Some Chinese employees at customs left their homes and devoted themselves to the revolution, risking their lives for the people. This demonstrated their national spirit of righteousness and patriotism. The CPC also established customs offices in soviet areas, anti-Japanese bases and liberated areas to realize local tariff autonomy, which accumulated experience and cultivated talents for the founding of new China Customs. During the War of Liberation, a large number of progressive customs employees who were loyal to the CPC made contributions to protecting customs' property and preparing for liberation.

海关同人俱乐部印章

Seal of Customs Club

20世纪30年代至40年代

海关同人俱乐部成立于1932年1月，是中华人民共和国成立前上海地区海关下级员工的群众团体，也是旧海关华员群众团体中存在时间最长、人数最多的团体。1946年以后由中共地下党员直接领导开展活动，1949年1月与海关内外班俱乐部合并，成立上海区海关同人进修会。海关同人俱乐部积极开展了各种进步活动，如保障下级员工利益、争取改善工资待遇、开展抗日捐献活动、举办文化教育和福利事业等。抗战胜利后，又开展了反对国民党统治的斗争与迎接解放等活动。

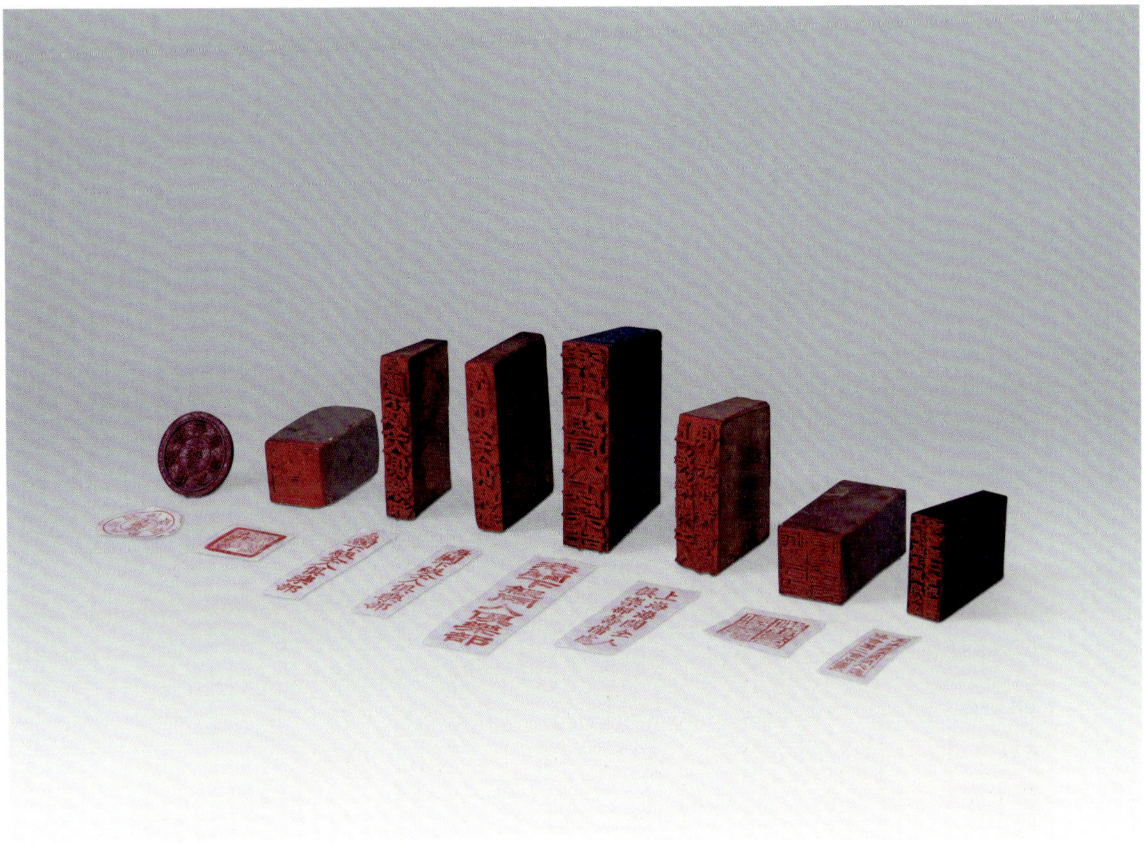

海关乐文社抗日宣传画

Anti-Japanese Posters of Lewen Club

20世纪30年代

1936年9月，中共江海关地下党支部秘密成立，成为党在海关建立的第一个地下组织。乐文社是江海关地下党支部组织成立的海关进步群众团体，为“以文会友，敬业乐文”之意。乐文社组织开展了学习业务、座谈时事、研究文学、编演话剧、教唱歌曲，以及给《关声》撰稿等活动，深受海关职工欢迎。

1937年11月，上海沦陷后，乐文社部分积极分子组织江海关同人组成救亡长征团，离关南下宣传抗日。留沪的积极分子则组成10个“救国十人团”，继续开展小规模的抗日救亡活动。1938年5月，多数共产党员和乐文社骨干被海关当局调离上海，乐文社被迫停止活动。

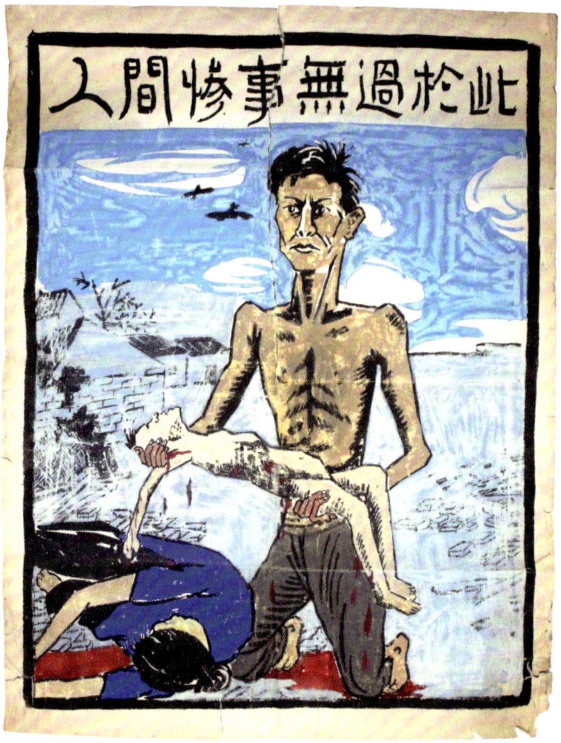

海关乐文社印章

Seal of Lewen Club

20世纪30至40年代

乐文社战时服务团慰劳抗敌战士衣服

Performance Costume of the War-time Service Group of the Lewen Club for Comforting Soldiers Finghting against Enemies

1937年

抗日战争全面爆发后，以乐文社为基础的海关华员战时服务团成立，众多海关华员和家属纷纷参加，积极开展捐献征募、缝制棉衣、慰劳前线将士、慰问伤员和难民、购买救国公债等爱国活动。其中募集捐款金额为上海各团体募捐之首。

海关抗日救亡长征团成员签名留言册

Commemorative Book of Long March Salvation Group of Shanghai Customs Colleagues

20世纪30年代

为了更广泛地宣传、组织抗日救亡，江海关地下党支部组织成立“江海关同人救亡长征团”，用歌咏、话剧、活报剧等形式宣传抗战，江海关、胶海关共11名职工和8名职工亲友报名参加，另外还有随同父母一起的1名不满周岁的婴儿。1937年11月26日，江海关华员举行盛大欢送会。次日，“江海关同人救亡长征团”乘坐法国邮轮离沪南下，赴广州、江门、九龙等地海关积极开展抗日宣传活动。1938年，其中11人赴延安学习并加入中国共产党。

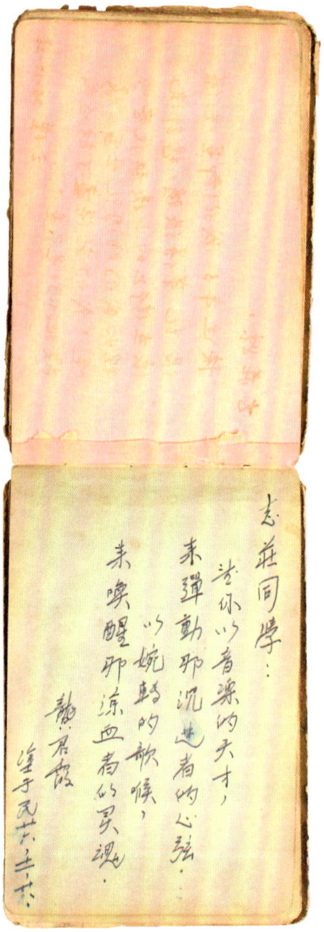

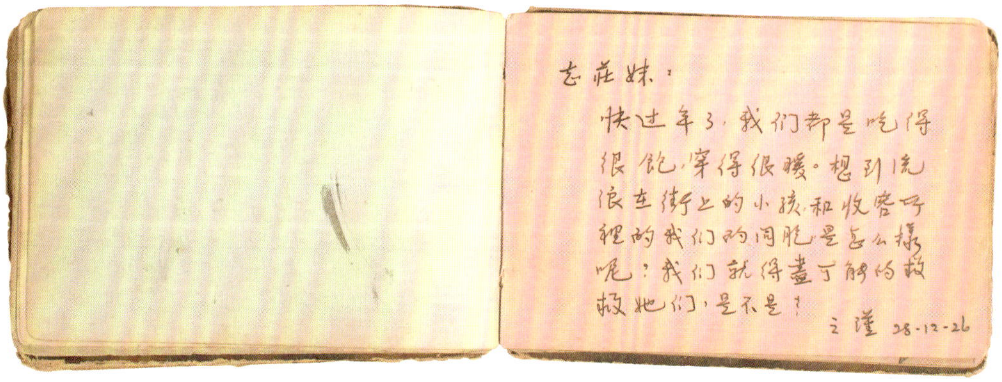

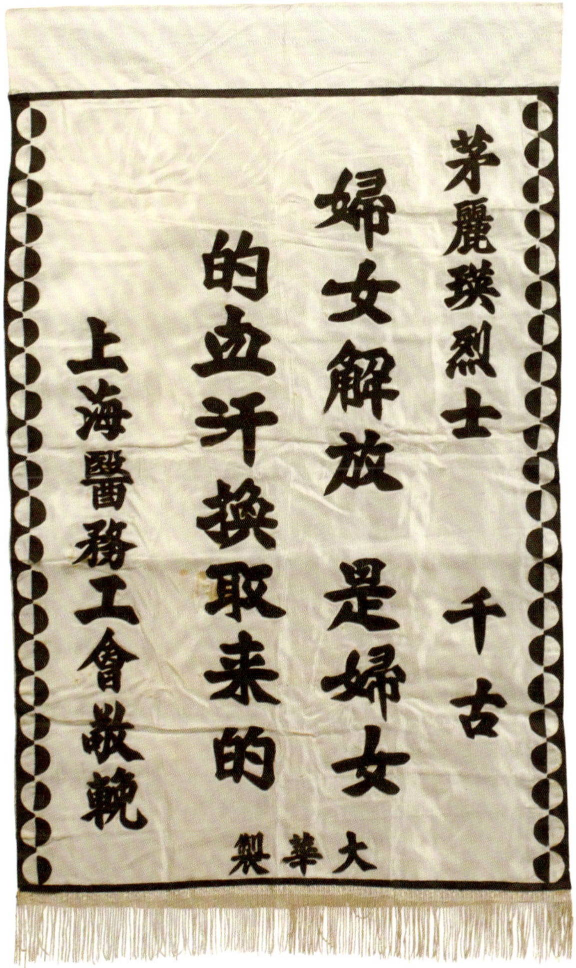

茅丽瑛烈士挽旗

Mourning Flag for Martyr Mao Liying

1939年

1939年12月，茅丽瑛烈士被暗杀牺牲后，上海医务工会赠送的挽旗。茅丽瑛1935年参加上海中国职业妇女会，1936年加入乐文社，1937年随海关抗日救亡长征团南下宣传抗日。1938年回沪后入党，并担任上海中国职业妇女俱乐部主席，积极组织为新四军募捐、义卖等爱国活动。1939年12月12日晚遭汪伪特务枪击，15日不幸逝世，年仅29岁。

消息披露后，上海各界人民团体成立治丧委员会并举行声势浩大的公祭。1949年12月12日，在上海市各界人民举行茅丽瑛烈士殉难十周年悼念大会上，陈毅同志亲笔为她书写了挽词“为人民利益而牺牲是光荣的，人民永远纪念她”。

江海关妇联救济难民义卖物品

Embroidery Articles to Raise Money for Refugee Relief, Sold by the Customs Women's Society

1938年

海关妇女联谊社成立于1938年4月10日，是中国海关成立的第一个群众性妇女组织。1942年后，由于核心力量相继离沪，妇女联谊社的各项工作被迫停止。1949年“三八”妇女节时，海关女职员中的共产党员和积极分子再次组织成立上海区海关妇女联谊社，在中国共产党的领导下开展了救济难民、照顾职工家属、迎接解放等工作。

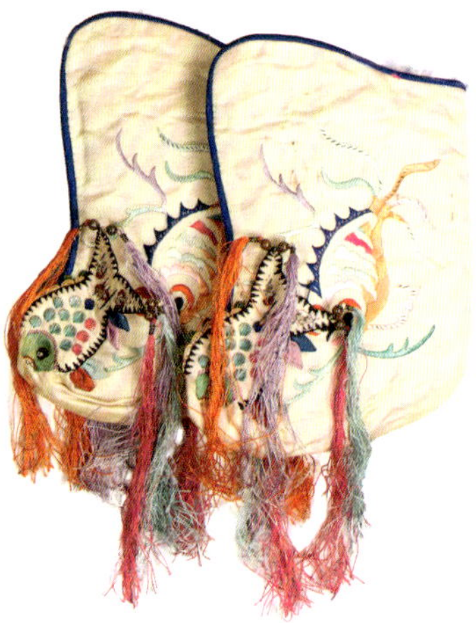

妇女联谊社印章

Seal of Customs Women's Society

20世纪30至40年代

《全国海关华员爱国捐章程》

Constitution of Chinese staff Patriotic Fund

1933年

“九一八”事变后，海关华员开展了捐助抗日军队的爱国活动。据统计，当时全国海关华员每月捐款总数达25000元左右。

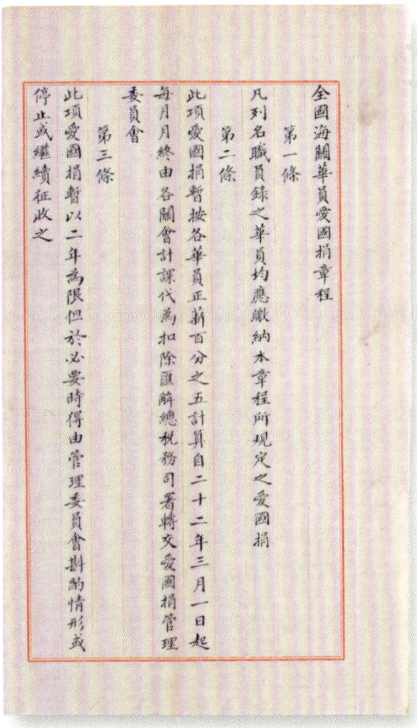

全國海關華員愛國捐章程

第一條

凡列名職員錄之華員均應繳納本章程所規定之愛國捐

第二條

此項愛國捐暫按各華員正薪百分之五計算自二十二年三月一日起每月月終由各關會計課代爲扣除匯解總稅務司署轉交愛國捐管理委員會

第三條

此項愛國捐暫以二年爲限但於必要時得由管理委員會斟酌情形或停止或繼續征收之

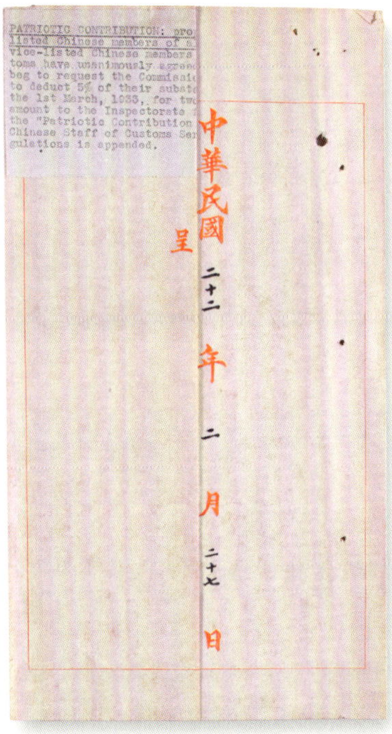

PATRIOTIC CONTRIBUTION: pro
listed Chinese members of
vice-listed Chinese members
toms have unanimously agree
beg to request the Commissi
to deduct 5% of their subst
the 1st March, 1933, for two
amount to the Inspectorate
the "Patriotic Contribution
Chinese Staff of Customs Ser
gulations is appended.

中華民國二十二年二月二十七日 呈

海关俱乐部京剧部春节彩排纪念品

Silk Souvenir for the Spring Festival Rehearsal of Customs Beijing Opera Club

1937年

庆贺厦门关俱乐部京剧部春节彩排成功的纪念品。

《资本论》

Das Kapital

1938年

20世纪40年代江海关地下党员的学习资料。德国思想家马克思创作的政治经济学著作，以剩余价值为中心，对资本主义进行了彻底的批判。郭大力、王亚南翻译，读书生活出版社1938年版，原为江海关地下党员冯华全同志的藏书，20世纪40年代转送给上饶关进步关员潘文凤同志。

同盟胜利公债

Allied Victory Loan

1942年

从1937年9月起，海关华员开始购买救国公债以支持抗战。1942年，国民政府发行“民国三十一年同盟胜利公债”，以英国5000万英镑贷款为担保，年息6%，期限13年，每年付息两次，从1945年起开始还本。海关华员也积极购买此公债。

关东海口管理处旗帜

Banner of Guandong Seaport Management Office

1947年

1945年8月22日，苏军进驻大连，结束了日本对大连长达40年的殖民统治，随之对大连进行了军事管制；11月8日，大连市第一个民主政权——大连市政府成立，旅大地区成为由苏军军事管制、中国共产党领导的特殊解放区。1946年10月，旅大金行政联合办事处设立，成为当地最高的行政机关；1948年4月，关东公署设立，统辖大连市、旅顺市、金县和大连县；1949年4月，改为旅大行政公署。1946至1947年，大连海口管理处、关东海口管理处相继成立，履行海关和海务港务职能。

“海关”胸章

Badge for Customs Staff

1947年

1945年8月，抗日战争胜利后，山东解放区政府接管烟台、威海等地的敌伪海关机构，取消了税务司制度，组建了新的人民海关，烟台海关也因此成为中共领导下最早建立的人民海关。此后又相继建立了一系列海关机构、海关分支站所等。1949年山东全境解放，各解放区海关部分撤销或合并。山东解放区海关为粉碎敌人的经济封锁、发展解放区经济、支援人民解放战争做出了重大贡献。同时，为接管旧海关建立新海关积累了经验，培养和输送了大批海关干部，为中华人民共和国海关建设提供了重要支持。

关栈临时出入证

Temporary Pass of Customs Warehouse

1947年

山东解放区海关关员进出关栈时所佩戴的工作凭证。

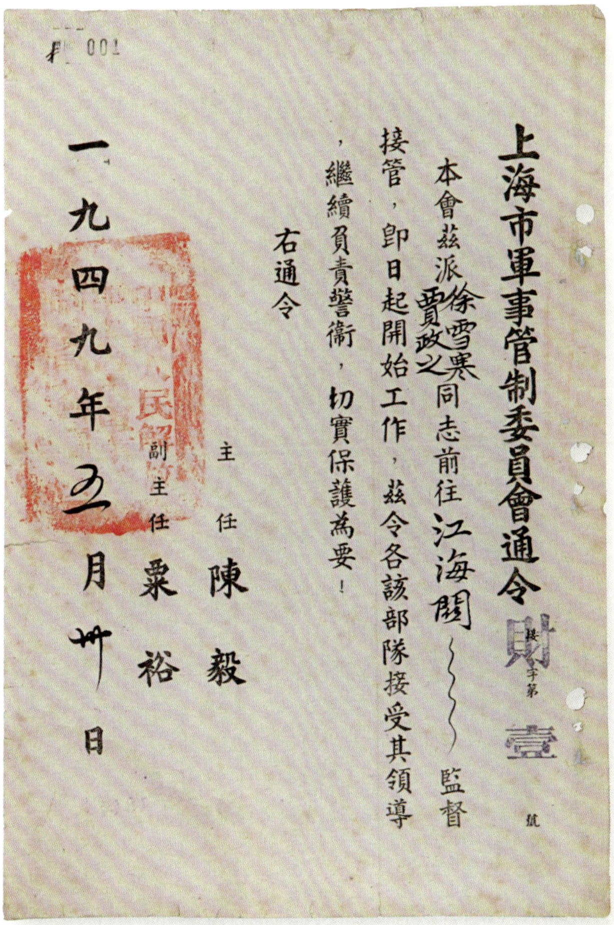
上海市軍事管制委員會通令　財接字第壹號

本會茲派徐雪寒賈振之同志前往江海關監督接管，即日起開始工作，茲令各該部隊接受其領導，繼續負責警衛，切實保護為要！

右通令

主任　陳毅

副主任　粟裕

一九四九年五月卅日

上海军事管制委员会通令

Shanghai Municipal Military Control Committee Circular

1949年

1949年5月27日，上海解放。5月30日，军管会主任陈毅、副主任粟裕签署委任令，委派徐雪寒、贾振之为接管海关总税务司署和江海关的接收专员，负责接管事宜。贾振之后来成为中华人民共和国上海海关第一任关长。

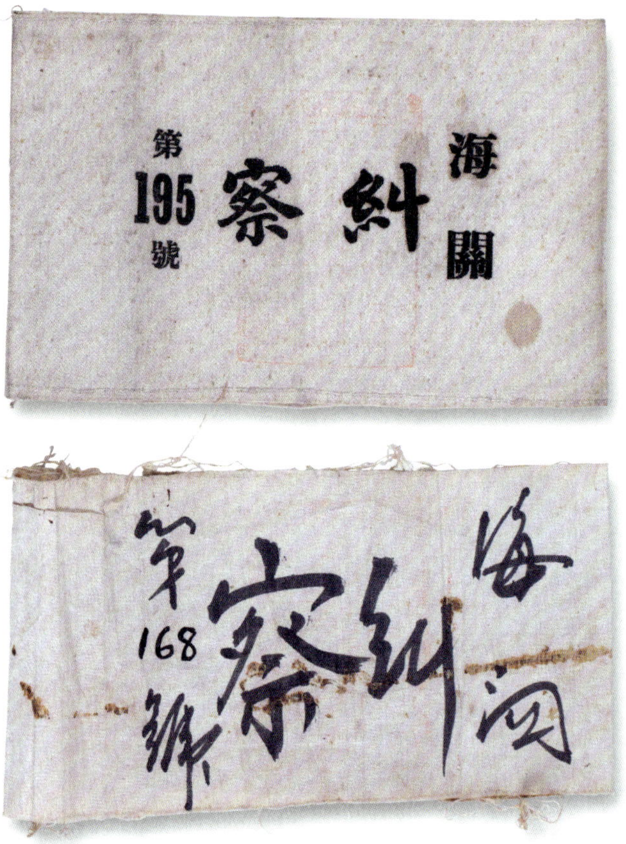

“海关纠察”袖章

Armbands of “Customs Picket”

1949年

1949年3月底上海解放前夕，中共上海市委指示江海关党总支成立海关纠察队，在负责保护关产、档案与保障职工安全的同时，根据上级党组织的部署，也负责中心区的治安保卫工作。海关纠察队由60多个分队、500余人构成，统一佩戴臂章，并利用执勤便利将位于浦东的江海关军火仓库武器发放给浦西的海关纠察队员，使得海关纠察队成为上海地下党掌握中最强的一支武装队伍，为解放上海贡献了重要力量。

上海区海关特种委员会工作人员出入证

Pass of Shanghai Customs Special Committee Staff

1949年

1949年上海解放前夕，中国共产党将国民党在上海区海关（含总税务司署、江海关、海务科、税务专门学校）成立的应变委员会改组为特种委员会，通过中共地下党员和旧海关中倾向进步的中高级职员获得实际领导权，做好保护关产、迎接解放工作。

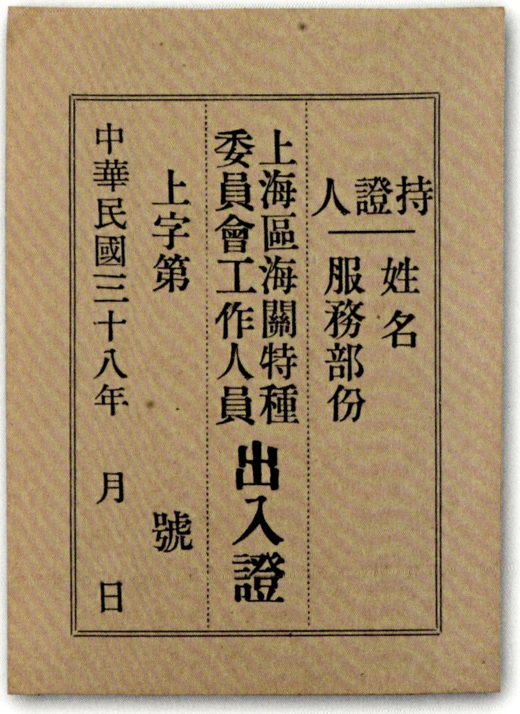

海关通行证

Customs Pass

1949年

上海解放前夕，江海关制发的用于出入外滩海关大楼的通行证，以甄别身份、防止敌人混进大楼破坏。

刊登“深圳海关高悬红旗”消息的报纸

Article about Red Flag Displaying on Customs Building in Shenzhen

1949年

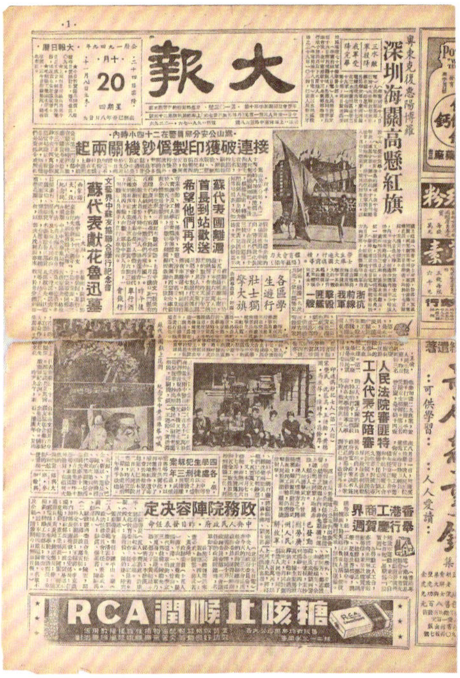

1949年10月20日的《大报》刊载名为“深圳海关高悬红旗”的消息，介绍了解放军于10月15日至18日解放广东惠州、深圳等地，并接管深圳海关的情况。

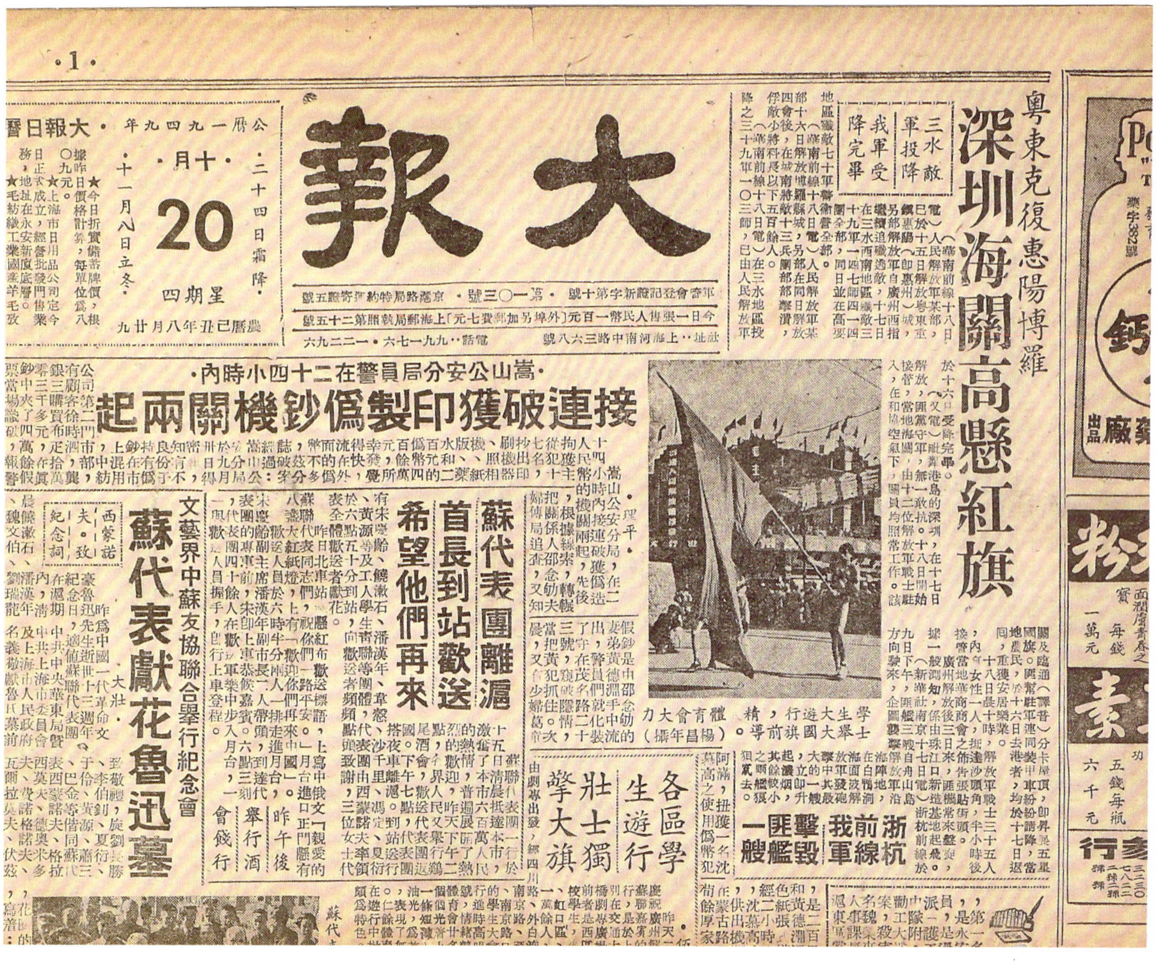

大報

公曆一九四九年 十月 20 星期四

農曆己丑年八月廿九

二十四日霜降 十一月八日立冬

粵東克復惠陽博羅

深圳海關高懸紅旗

三水敵軍投降 我軍受降完畢

嵩山公安分局警員在二十四小時內

接連破獲印製僞鈔機關兩起

蘇代表團離滬 首長到站歡送 希望他們再來

文藝界中蘇友協聯合舉行紀念會

蘇代表獻花魯迅墓

各區學生遊行 壯士獨擎大旗

浙前線我軍擊毀匪艦

九龙关全体职工致海关总署宣布断绝与国民政府关系的电文

Telegraph of Kowloon Customs on Cutting Ties with the Government of KMT

1949年

九龙关职工致函海关总署的电文，宣布与国民政府脱离关系，接受中华人民共和国中央人民政府海关总署领导。中华人民共和国成立前夕，九龙关（今深圳海关）地下党员为了策划起义成立护产小组，以打麻将的形式进行秘密聚会，并借机劝说九龙关英籍税务司经蔚斐答应起义、保全关产。1949年10月19日，九龙关宣布起义，保护了大批关产。

1950年，经过海关总署和九龙海关精心策划、严密组织，滞留香港的27艘缉私艇摆脱各种干扰于夜间悄悄驶回广州，划归公安部队和人民解放军，为组建人民海军、解放沿海岛屿发挥了重要作用。

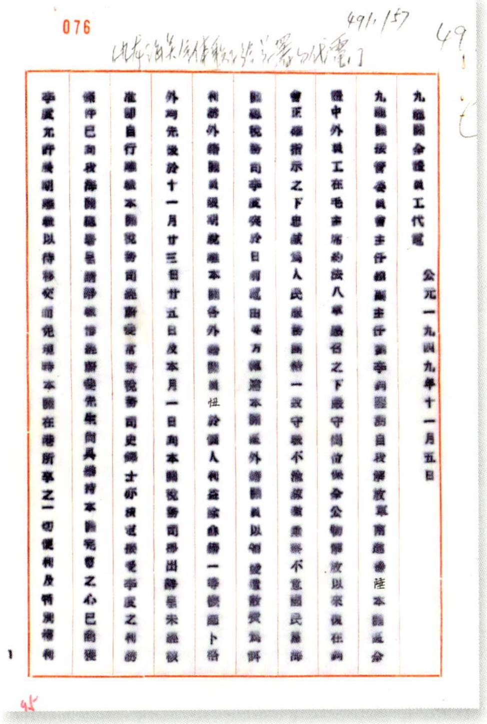

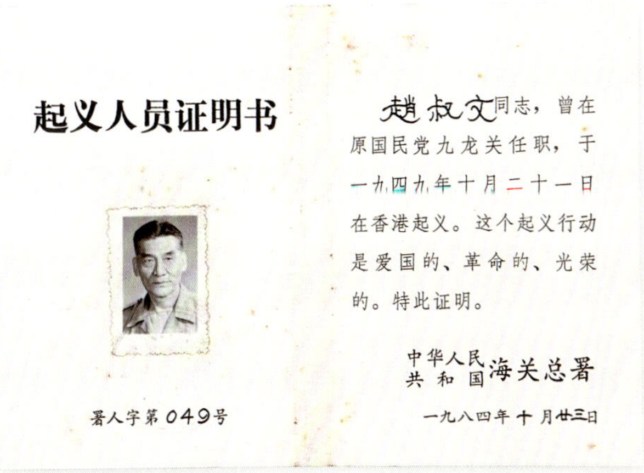

起义人员证明书

趙叔文同志，曾在原国民党九龙关任职，于一九四九年十月二十一日在香港起义。这个起义行动是爱国的、革命的、光荣的。特此证明。

中华人民共和国海关总署

一九八四年十月廿三日

署人字第049号

九龙关起义证明书及纪念盘

The Certificate and Commemorative Copper Dish of the Kowloon Customs Uprising

1984年

在九龙关起义35周年之际，海关总署在深圳举办仪式，向九龙关人员颁发证书。

边关精神
Border Safeguarding Spirit

我国陆地边境线总长2万多公里，与14个国家接壤，共设有边境口岸88个，包括呼和浩特、满洲里、大连、长春、哈尔滨、南宁、昆明、拉萨、兰州、乌鲁木齐等海关所属的口岸。这些海关自然条件恶劣，但关警员克服各种艰难困苦，用自己的青春忠于祖国，用自己的热血为国把关，谱写着和平年代可歌可泣的“边关精神”。

China has a vast territory with more than 20,000 km of Land boundary and 14 bordering countries. Along the border are 88 border ports, including Customs Houses subordinate to Hohhot, Manzhouli, Dalian, Changchun, Harbin, Nanning, Kunming, Lhasa, Lanzhou and Urumqi Customs. Despite the harsh natural conditions, customs officers overcame all hardships and devoted themselves to the country to safeguard its border with their heroic acts in the peaceful age.

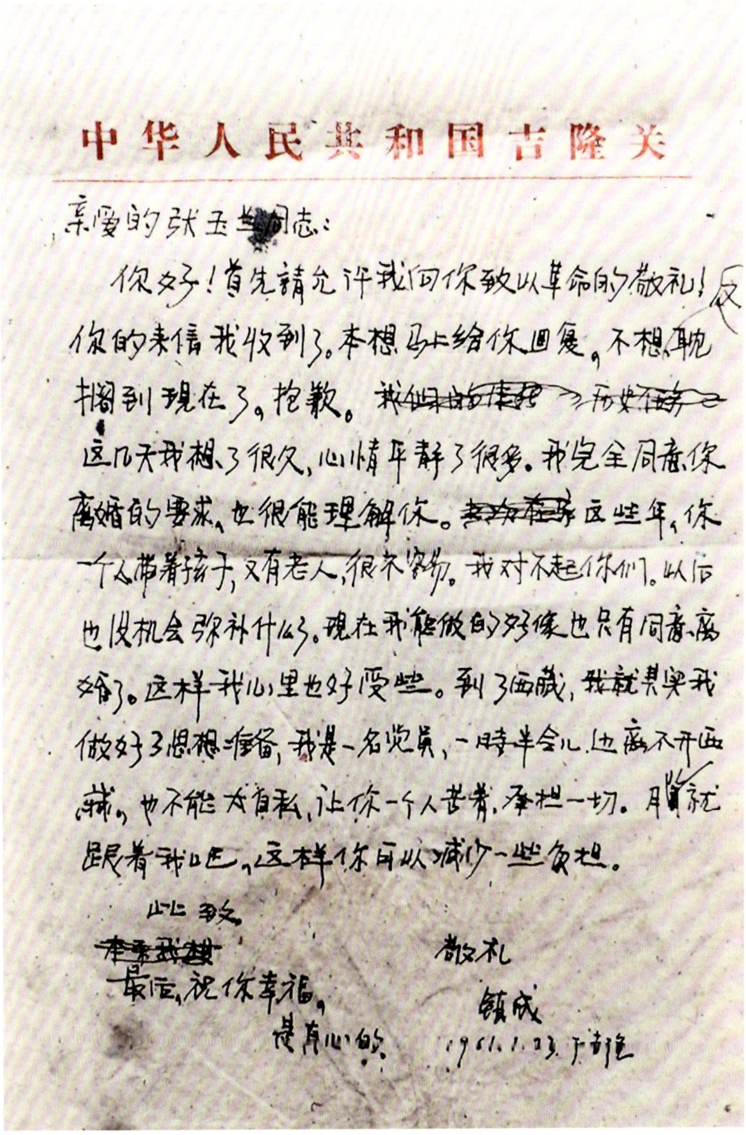

中华人民共和国吉隆关

亲爱的张玉兰同志：

你好！首先请允许我向你致以革命的敬礼！

你的来信我收到了。本想马上给你回复，不想耽搁到现在了。抱歉。~~[illegible]~~

这几天我想了很久，心情平静了很多。我完全同意你离婚的要求，也很能理解你。~~[illegible]~~这些年，你一个人带着孩子，又有老人，很不容易。我对不起你们。以后也没机会弥补什么了。现在我能做的好像也只有同意离婚了。这样我心里也好受些。到了西藏，~~我就~~其实我做好了思想准备，我是一名党员，一时半会儿也离不开西藏，也不能太自私，让你一个人去承担一切。所以就跟着我吧，这样你可以减少一些负担。

此致

~~[illegible]~~

敬礼

最后，祝你幸福。

是真心的。

镇成

1961.1.23. 于吉隆

王镇成写给爱人的一封信

A letter from Wang Zhencheng to his beloved

1961年

王镇成同志1959年从广东汕头海关抽调至西藏工作，1960年1月5日赴吉隆筹备建关。在西藏工作期间，王镇成与妻儿两地分居，无法及时照顾家庭。为了不拖累爱人，王镇成答应了独自承担家庭重任、不堪分离之苦的妻子的离婚请求，并写了一封回信给妻子。然而，信还没寄出，王镇成同志就在1961年1月28日从日喀则出差返回吉隆的途中因车祸殉职，年仅29岁。原件现存拉萨海关。

“艰苦奋斗模范海关”荣誉证书

Certificate of Exemplary Hard-working Customs

2005年

红其拉甫海关隶属乌鲁木齐海关，地处被称为“生命禁区”的帕米尔高原，从海拔5600米的明铁盖到海拔5200米的红其拉甫达坂，到海拔4700米的水布浪沟，再到海拔4200米的皮拉力，然后到海拔3200米的塔什库尔干县城，直到重回海拔4900米的国门一线开展安全准入检查，多年来担负着红其拉甫和卡拉苏口岸的进出境监管任务，形成了“特别能吃苦、特别能忍耐、特别能战斗、特别能奉献”的精神。2005年6月3日，国务院授予该关“艰苦奋斗模范海关”荣誉称号。

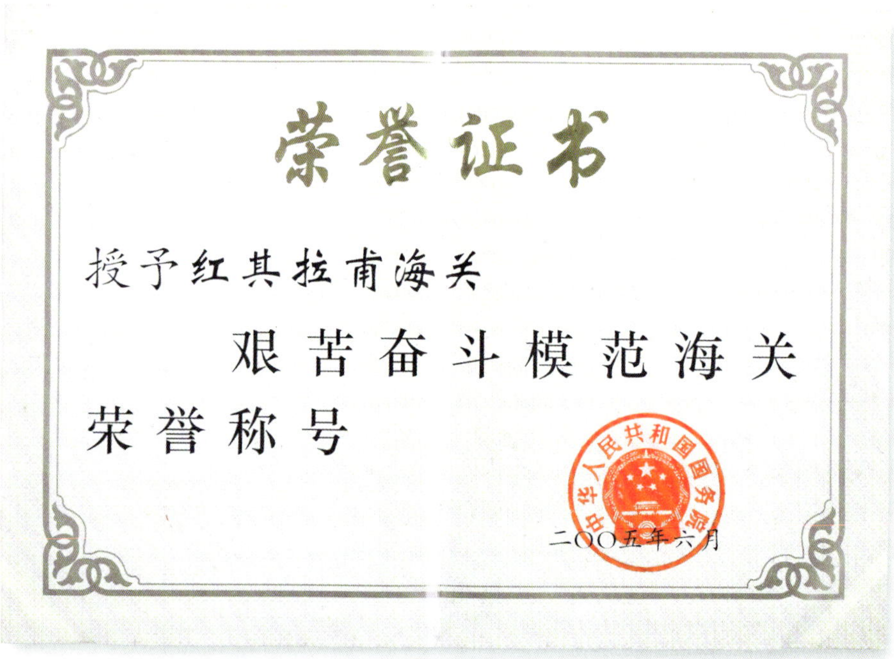

荣誉证书

授予红其拉甫海关

艰苦奋斗模范海关

荣誉称号

中华人民共和国国务院

二〇〇五年六月

边关关员破冰取水

水布浪沟支关旧影

拉水车

Water Cart

20世纪80年代

红其拉甫海关关员使用过的拉水车。红其拉甫海关自然环境十分恶劣，建关初期没有自来水，海关关员在冬天只能冒着零下40℃的严寒，拉着水车去凿冰取水。

边关关员戈壁取水

路牌

Guideboard

20世纪80年代

红其拉甫海关使用过的路牌。

氧气瓶

Oxygen Bottle

20 世纪80年代

红其拉甫海关关员使用过的氧气瓶。红其拉甫海关是中国与巴基斯坦唯一的陆路进出境通道。该关位于祖国西部帕米尔高原的冰峰雪岭之中，平均海拔3200米，平均气温在零下2℃，空气中含氧量只有平原地区的52%。

高压锅

Pressure Cooker

20 世纪80年代

红其拉甫海关关员使用过的高压锅。由于地处高原、气压偏低，水在80℃左右就已经沸腾，关员们必须使用高压锅才能喝上开水。

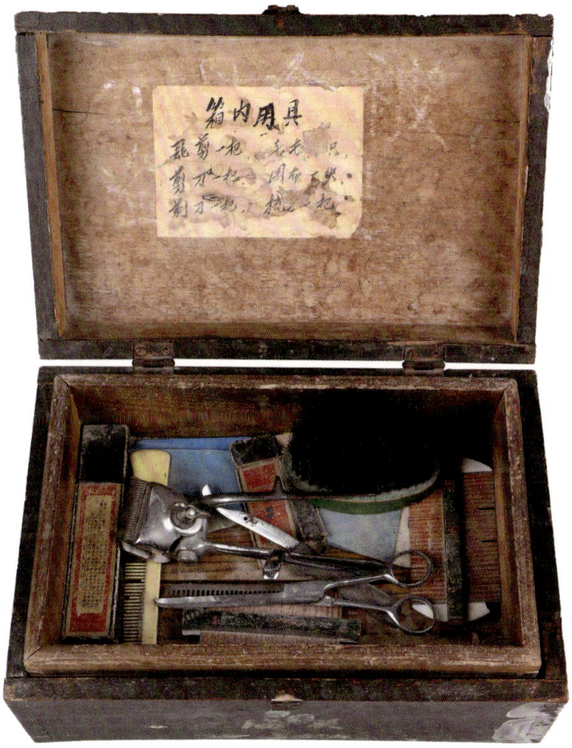

理发工具

Barber Tools

20世纪70至80年代

由于边关生活条件艰苦、外出不便，南宁凭祥分关关员自备理发工具修剪头发。

海关荣誉
Customs Honor

海关是一支具有强烈职业荣誉感、自豪感的队伍。解放战争时期颁发的奖章记录了海关关员对革命事业的忠诚与奉献。中华人民共和国成立以后，随着队伍建设的现代化、正规化、准军事化，一代代海关关警员坚守岗位、履行职责，吃得起苦头、受得住清贫、耐得住寂寞、经得起考验，在平凡岗位上干出了不平凡的业绩。

Customs officers are a team with a strong sense of professional honor and sense of pride. Medals awarded during the War of Liberation recorded the loyalty and dedication of the customs staff to the revolutionary cause. After the founding of the People's Republic of China, with the modernization, normalization and paramilitarization of the team construction, generations of customs officers kept to their posts to fulfill their duties. They have withstood the test of hardships and loneliness and have made extraordinary accomplishments at ordinary posts.

立功章、奖章证和奖品

Medals and Prize

1947年

山东解放区胶东区用于奖励在解放区海关各项工作中做出贡献的模范人员的勋章及奖品。

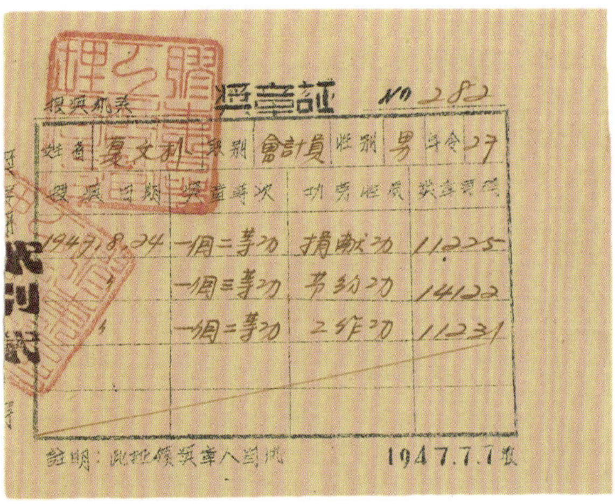

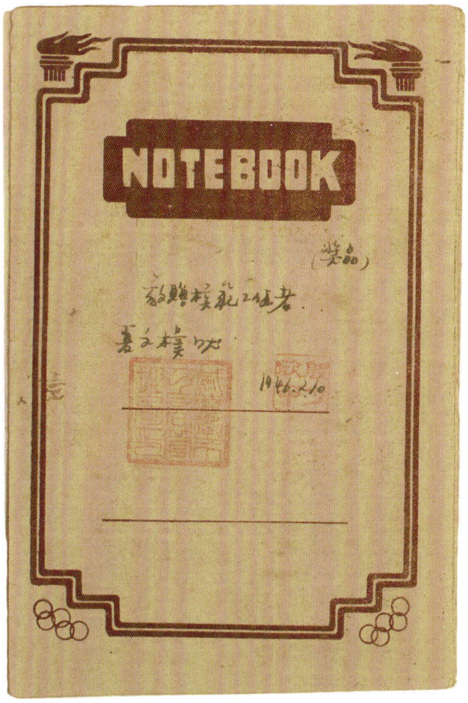

汉口关员渡海作战光荣章

Certificate of Hankow Customs Staff

1950年

1950年，汉口关（今武汉海关）15名从事海务工作的关员自愿报名参加解放海南岛战争，受到海关总署和汉口关的表彰。

抗美援朝捐款收据

Receipt of Donation for “the War to Resist US Aggression and Aid Korea”

1951年

1951年6月25日，时任外贸部海关总署财务处处长陈铁保同志将设计关徽所获奖金壹佰零伍万伍仟元（旧币）捐给海关总署抗美援朝支会的收据。此外，他还从个人工资中拿出壹佰万元（旧币）通过中国银行支援抗美援朝。“抗美援朝”战争爆发后，全国海关开展捐款购买“中国海关号”飞机支援前线的运动。广大关员积极响应，捐款总额足够购买三架飞机。

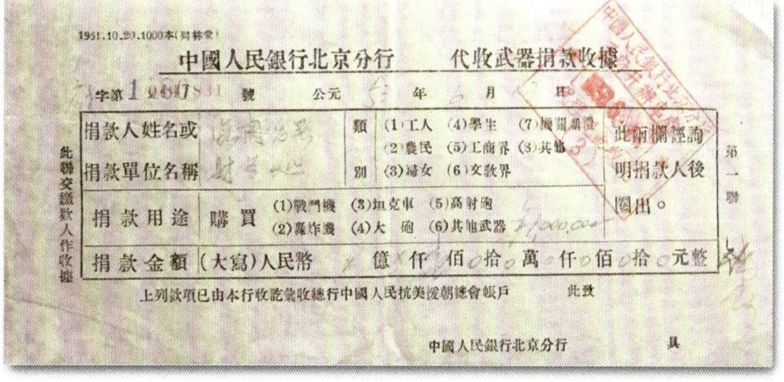

1951.10.20.1000本

中國人民銀行北京分行　代收武器捐款收據

字第　號　公元　年　月　日

捐款人姓名或捐款單位名稱		類別	(1)工人 (4)學生 (7)機關團體 (2)農民 (5)工商界 (8)其他 (3)婦女 (6)文教界	此兩欄證諭明捐款人後圈出。
捐款用途	購買	(1)戰鬥機 (2)轟炸機 (3)坦克車 (4)大砲 (5)高射砲 (6)其他武器		
捐款金額	(大寫)人民幣　億　仟　佰　拾　萬　仟　佰　拾　元整			

此聯交繳款人作收據　第一聯

上列款項已由本行收訖彙收總行中國人民抗美援朝總會帳戶　此致

中國人民銀行北京分行　具

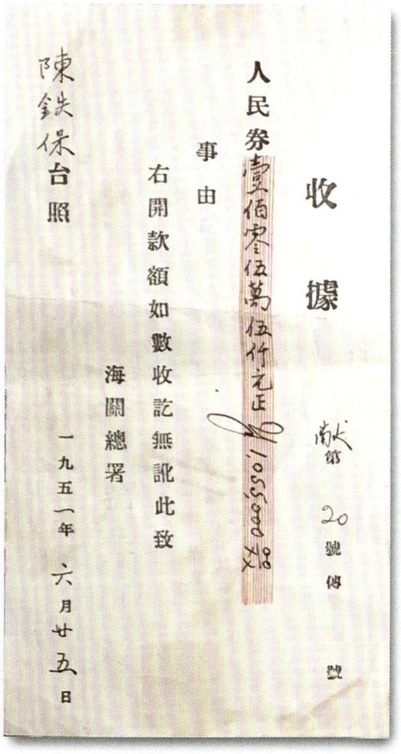

收據

人民券壹佰零伍萬伍仟元正 ¥1,055,000.00

事由

右開款額如數收訖無訛此致

陳鉄保台照

海關總署

一九五一年六月廿五日

第20號

全国海关第一次先进工作者代表会议纪念章

Souvenir Badge for the First National Outstanding Customs Staff Representative

1956年

1956年12月18日，全国海关第一次先进工作者代表会议在北京召开，中共中央主席毛泽东、副主席刘少奇、朱德等接见了全体代表。

全国海关第二次先进工作者代表会议纪念章

Souvenir Badge for the Second National Outstanding Customs Staff Representative

1960年

1960年5月20日至28日，全国海关第二次先进集体和先进工作者代表会议在北京召开，周恩来、朱德、邓小平等党和国家领导人接见了会议代表。

海关工作纪念章

Gold, Silver and Bronze Customs Medals

1987年

从1987年起，海关总署对长期在海关任职的关员颁发荣誉纪念章，工作满30、20、10年者分别获得金、银、铜质纪念章，以进一步激发海关关员的职业荣誉感和自豪感。

中国海关荣誉纪念章

China Customs Honorary Medal

2009年

2009年，在海关总署庆祝中华人民共和国成立60周年大会上，向从事海关工作30年以上的人员颁发了荣誉纪念章。

国家科学技术进步奖

Medal and Certificates of the National Award for Science and Technology Progress

1992年、1997年、2001年

海关报关自动化系统工程、海关EDI通关系统、全国报关单联网核查系统工程先后于1992年、1997年、2001年获“国家科学技术进步奖”一等奖、三等奖、二等奖。

国家科学技术进步奖，是国务院设立的国家科学技术奖五大奖项（国家最高科学技术奖、国家自然科学奖、国家技术发明奖、国家科学技术进步奖、国际科学技术合作奖）之一。主要授予在技术研究、技术开发、技术创新、推广应用先进科学技术成果、促进高新技术产业化，以及完成重大科学技术工程、计划等过程中做出创造性贡献的中国公民和组织。

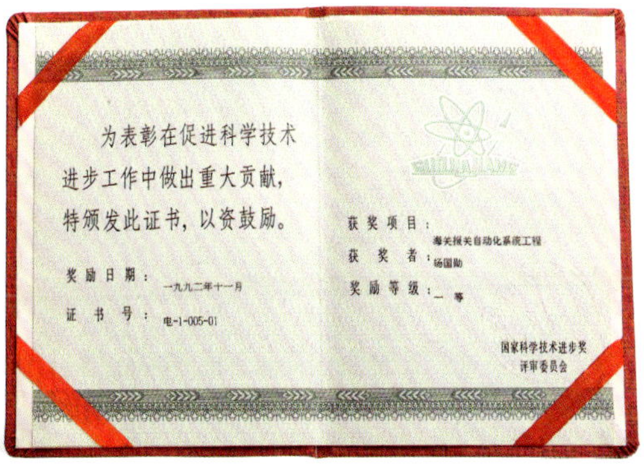

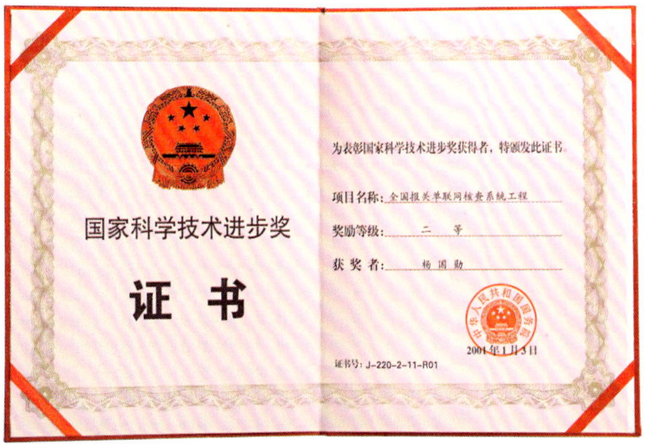

海关监管

Customs Supervision and Control

Supervision and control is one of the basic functions of the customs. From the Western Zhou Dynasty to the time before the founding of the People's Republic of China, all import and export goods, means of transport and entry-exit personnel were supervised and controlled by supervisory authorities with customs powers. After the founding of the People's Republic of China, the customs started to exercise effective supervision and control over inbound and outbound means of transport, goods and articles in accordance with law. Since the reform and opening-up, the customs has adhered to the balance of tight control and quick customs clearance. It vigorously promotes paperless clearance, nationwide integrated clearance, and "the oversight model of random inspection and public release", implements "integration of multiple inspections" and unified declaration of customs and inspection integration, optimizes the business environment of ports, and improves customs clearance efficiency, to accelerate the development of China's export-oriented economy.

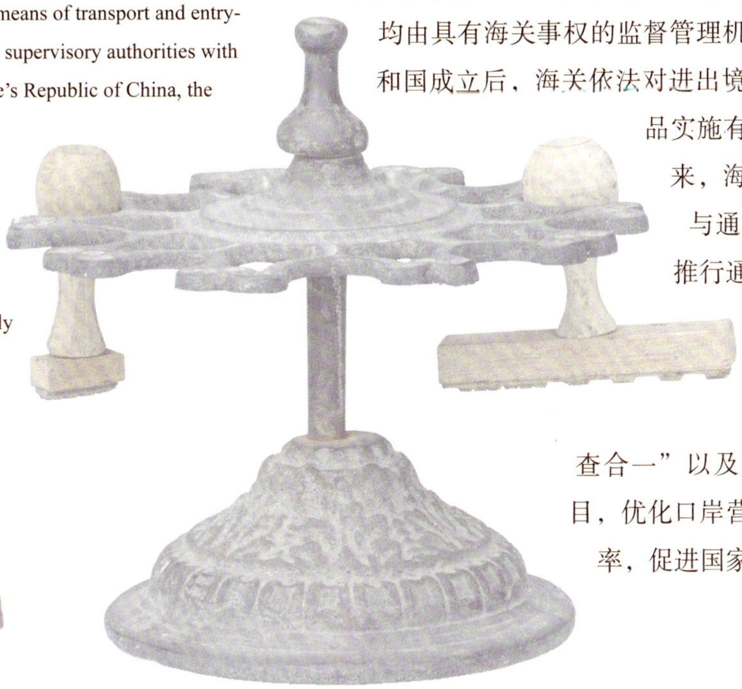

监管是海关的基本职能之一。自西周至中华人民共和国成立前，凡进出口货物、运输工具及进出关境的人员均由具有海关事权的监督管理机构监管。中华人民共和国成立后，海关依法对进出境运输工具、货物和物品实施有效监管。改革开放以来，海关坚持把握好管得住与通得快的平衡点，大力推行通关无纸化作业、全国通关一体化、“双随机、一公开”监管改革，并实施“多查合一”以及关检融合整合申报项目，优化口岸营商环境，提高通关效率，促进国家外向型经济发展。

鄂君启节

Jie(Passports) for Qi, the King of State E

战国中期

战国中期楚怀王颁发给鄂地封君“启”经商的水陆通行证及免税凭证，分为舟节和车节两种，记载了楚怀王颁发该节的过程以及鄂君“启”经商的水路、陆路交通运输线路，商品种类，限额和纳税情况。原件现存国家博物馆、安徽博物院。

厦门关监督庄伟刚签署的护照

Passport signed by Zhuang Weigang, Supervisor of Amoy Maritime Customs

1933年

厦门关监督颁发给思明县永康钱庄运输银元的许可证。

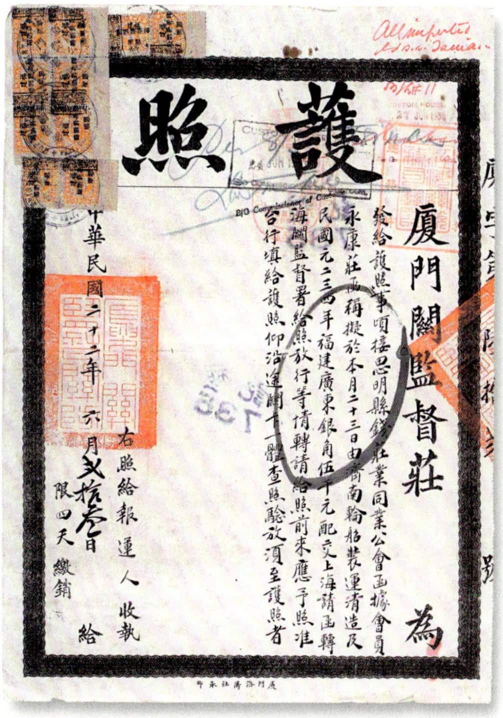

護照

厦門關監督莊　為

發給護照事頃據思明縣錢莊業同業公會函據會員永康莊函稱擬於本月二十三日由濟南輪船裝運清造及民國元二三年福建廣東銀角伍千元配交上海請函轉海關監督署給照放行等情轉請給照前來應予照准合行填給護照仰沿途關卡一體查照驗放須至護照者

右照給報運人　收執

中華民國二十二年六月　日給

限四天繳銷

护照与核准书

License and Certificate

民国时期

民国时期，海关对军事物资运输实行护照（许可证）管理制度，军事当局或商人装运的军事物资，一律凭财政部等部门发放的运输护照验核放行。

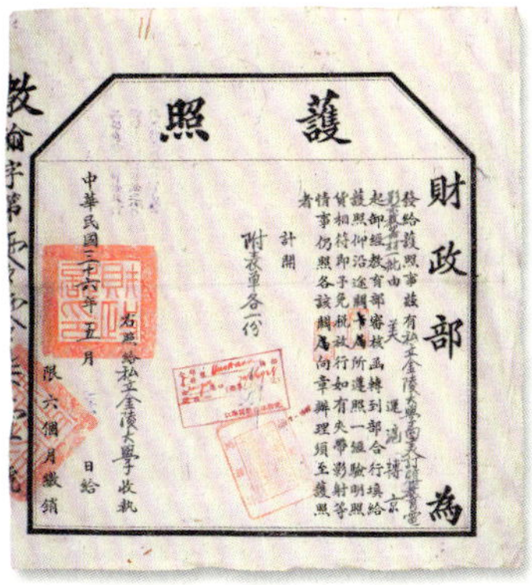

財政部　為

護照

1947年财政部运输护照

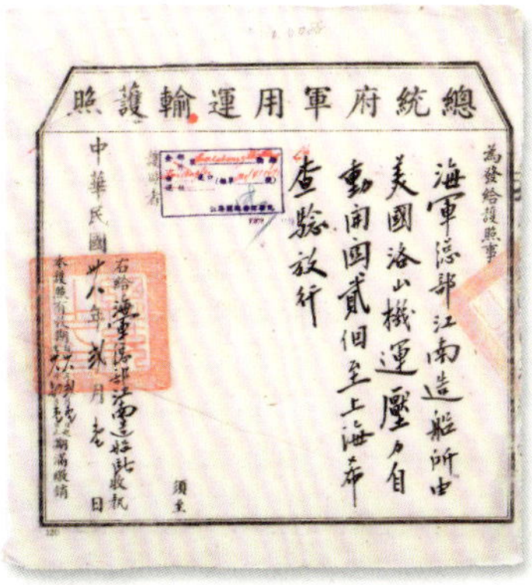

總統府軍用運輸護照

1949年总统府军用运输护照

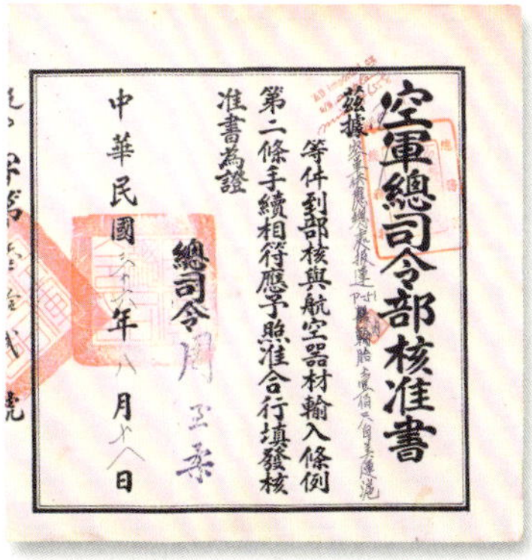

空軍總司令部核准書

1947年空军总司令部核准书

海关报关单证

Declaration Documents

20世纪30至40年代

包括普通卸货准单、1939年领事签证货单、海关出口及转口税缴纳证、1949年转口税收据、货样收据、旅客证明等。

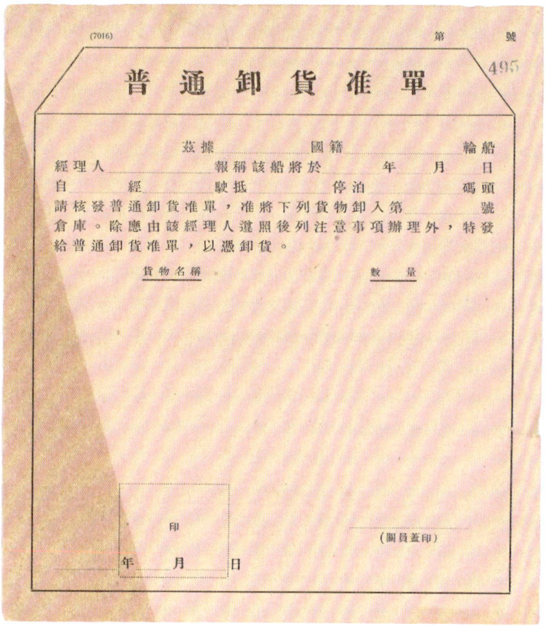
(7016)　　第　　號 495

普通卸貨准單

茲據　　國籍　　輪船
經理人　　報稱該船將於　　年　　月　　日
自　　經　　駛抵　　停泊　　碼頭
請核發普通卸貨准單，准將下列貨物卸入第　　號
倉庫。除應由該經理人遵照後列注意事項辦理外，特發
給普通卸貨准單，以憑卸貨。

貨物名稱　　數量

印
年　　月　　日

(關員蓋印)

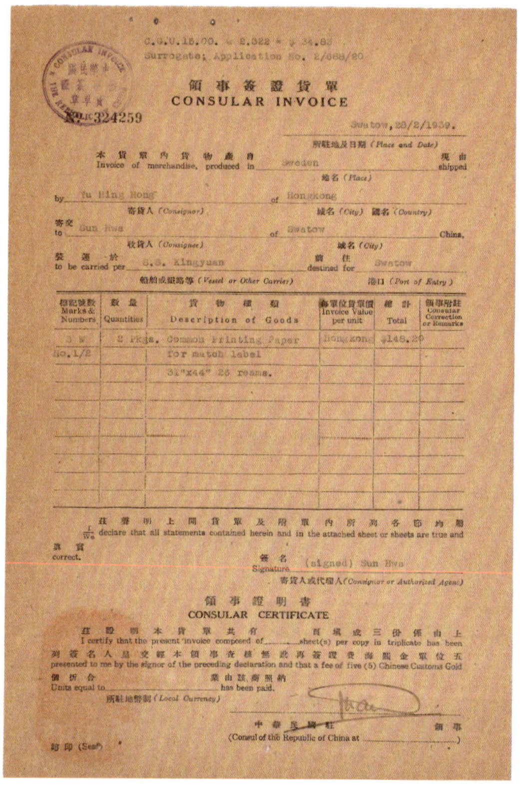
C.G.U.15.00. @ 2.322 = $ 34.83
Surrogate; Application No. 2/668/20

領事簽證貨單
CONSULAR INVOICE

No. 324259

Swatow, 28/2/1939.
所駐地及日期 (Place and Date)

本貨單內貨物產自　　現由
Invoice of merchandise, produced in Sweden shipped
地名 (Place)

by Yu Bing Hong of Hongkong
寄貨人 (Consignor)　　城名 (City) 國名 (Country)

寄交
to Sun Hwa of Swatow China.
收貨人 (Consignee)　　城名 (City)

裝運於　　前往
to be carried per S.S. Kingyuan destined for Swatow
船舶或鐵路等 (Vessel or Other Carrier)　　港口 (Port of Entry)

標記號數 Marks & Numbers	數量 Quantities	貨物種類 Description of Goods	每單位貨單價 Invoice Value per unit	總計 Total	領事附註 Consular Correction or Remarks
S W	2 Pkgs.	Common Printing Paper	Hongkong	$148.20	
No.1/2		for match label			
		31"x44" 26 reams.			

茲聲明上開貨單及附單內所列各節均屬真實
I/We declare that all statements contained herein and in the attached sheet or sheets are true and correct.

簽名
Signature (signed) Sun Hwa
寄貨人或代理人 (Consignor or Authorized Agent)

領事證明書
CONSULAR CERTIFICATE

茲證明本貨單共有　　頁填成三份係由上列簽名人呈交經本領事查核無訛再簽證費海關金單位五個折合　　業由該商照納
I certify that the present invoice composed of ____ sheet(s) per copy in triplicate has been presented to me by the signor of the preceding declaration and that a fee of five (5) Chinese Customs Gold Units equal to ____ has been paid.
所駐地幣制 (Local Currency)

中華民國駐　　領事
(Consul of the Republic of China at ____)

鈐印 (Seal)

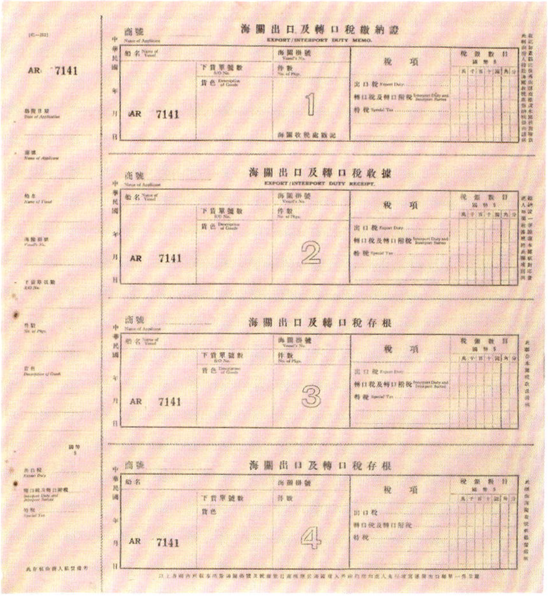
AR 7141

海關出口及轉口稅繳納證
EXPORT/INTERPORT DUTY MEMO.

商號 Name of Applicant
船名 Name of Vessel　海關掛號 Vessel's No.
下貨單號數 S/O No.　件數 No. of Pkgs.
貨色 Description of Goods
稅項：出口稅 Export Duty；轉口稅及轉口附稅 Interport Duty and Interport Surtax；特稅 Special Tax
稅銀數目
AR 7141　1
海關收稅處戳記

海關出口及轉口稅收據
EXPORT/INTERPORT DUTY RECEIPT.

商號 Name of Applicant
船名 Name of Vessel　海關掛號 Vessel's No.
下貨單號數 S/O No.　件數 No. of Pkgs.
貨色 Description of Goods
稅項：出口稅 Export Duty；轉口稅及轉口附稅 Interport Duty and Interport Surtax；特稅 Special Tax
AR 7141　2

海關出口及轉口稅存根

AR 7141　3

海關出口及轉口稅存根

AR 7141　4

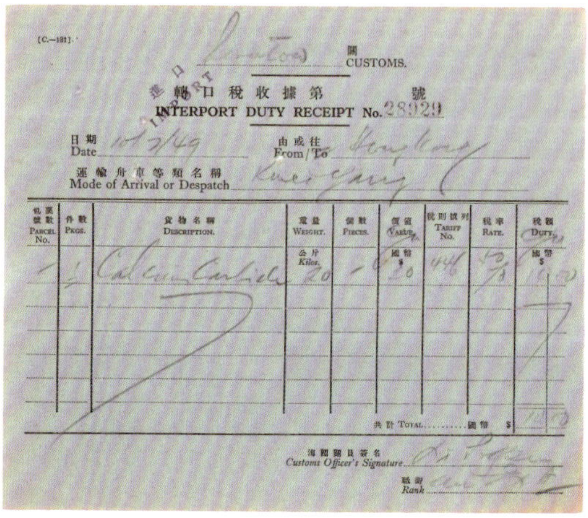
[C.—181]

關
CUSTOMS.

轉口稅收據第　　號
INTERPORT DUTY RECEIPT No. 28929

日期 Date　　由或往 From/To
運輸舟車等類名稱 Mode of Arrival or Despatch

包裹號數 Parcel No.	件數 Pkgs.	貨物名稱 Description.	重量 Weight.	個數 Pieces.	價值 Value.	稅則號列 Tariff No.	稅率 Rate.	稅額 Duty.
			公斤 Kilos.		國幣 $			國幣 $

共計 Total……國幣 $

海關關員簽名
Customs Officer's Signature

職銜
Rank

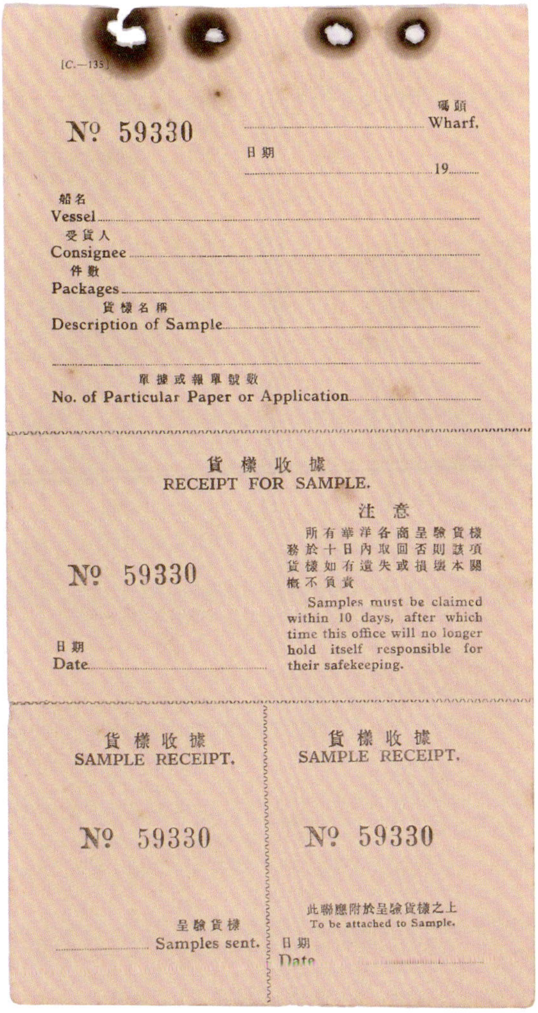

[C.—135]

碼頭
.... Wharf.

№ 59330

日期
.... 19.........

船名
Vessel.........

受貨人
Consignee.........

件數
Packages.........

貨樣名稱
Description of Sample.........

單據或報單號數
No. of Particular Paper or Application.........

貨樣收據
RECEIPT FOR SAMPLE.

注意

所有華洋各商呈驗貨樣務於十日內取回否則該項貨樣如有遺失或損壞本關概不負責

Samples must be claimed within 10 days, after which time this office will no longer hold itself responsible for their safekeeping.

№ 59330

日期
Date.........

貨樣收據
SAMPLE RECEIPT.

№ 59330

呈驗貨樣
.... Samples sent.

貨樣收據
SAMPLE RECEIPT.

№ 59330

此聯應附於呈驗貨樣之上
To be attached to Sample.

日期
Date.........

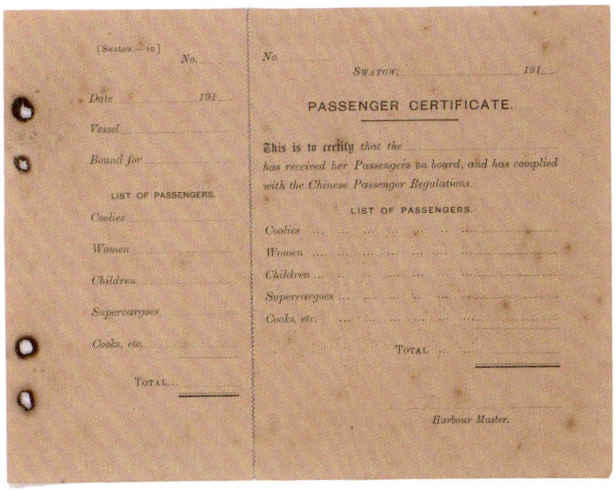

[Swatow.—10]

No.

Date .... 191...

Vessel.........

Bound for.........

LIST OF PASSENGERS.

Coolies.........

Women.........

Children.........

Supercargoes.........

Cooks, etc.........

TOTAL.........

No.

SWATOW, ... 191...

PASSENGER CERTIFICATE.

This is to certify that the .... has received her Passengers on board, and has complied with the Chinese Passenger Regulations.

LIST OF PASSENGERS.

Coolies ....

Women ....

Children ....

Supercargoes ....

Cooks, etc. ....

TOTAL ....

Harbour Master.

布样

Fabric Swatch Catalogue

1930年至1931年

20世纪30年代海关监管的纺织品样例。

《报关须知》

Customs Clearance Procedure

1947年

此书收录办理海关报关的各项须知章程、事项、手续等，是指引报关人员工作的工具书。

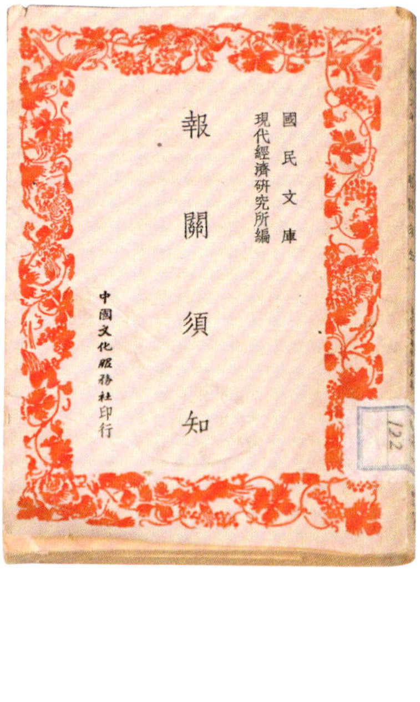

國民文庫
現代經濟研究所編
報關須知
中國文化服務社印行

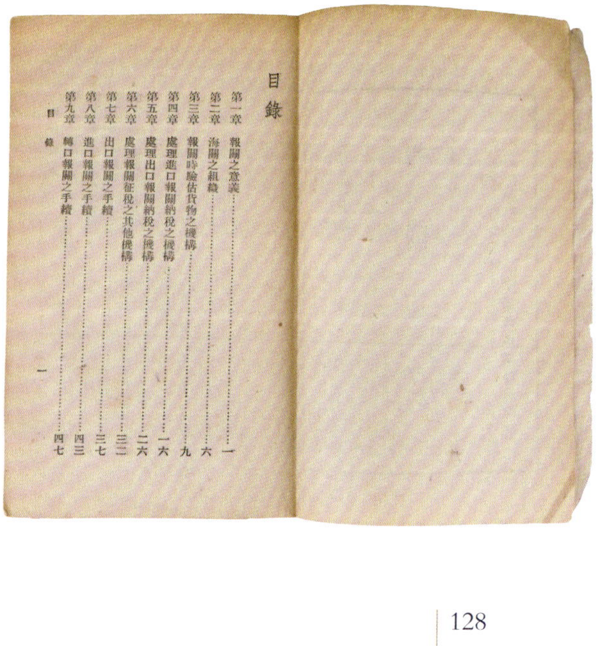

目錄

第一章 報關之意義……一
第二章 海關之組織……六
第三章 報關時驗估貨物之機構……九
第四章 處理進口報關納稅之機構……一六
第五章 處理出口報關納稅之機構……二六
第六章 處理報關征稅之其他機構……三二
第七章 出口報關之手續……三七
第八章 進口報關之手續……四三
第九章 轉口報關之手續……四七

目錄 一

洋货进口报单

Import Declaration Form of Foreign Goods

1947年

1946年2月14日，总税务司署为适应抗战胜利后的需要，通令各关使用新式进口报单。

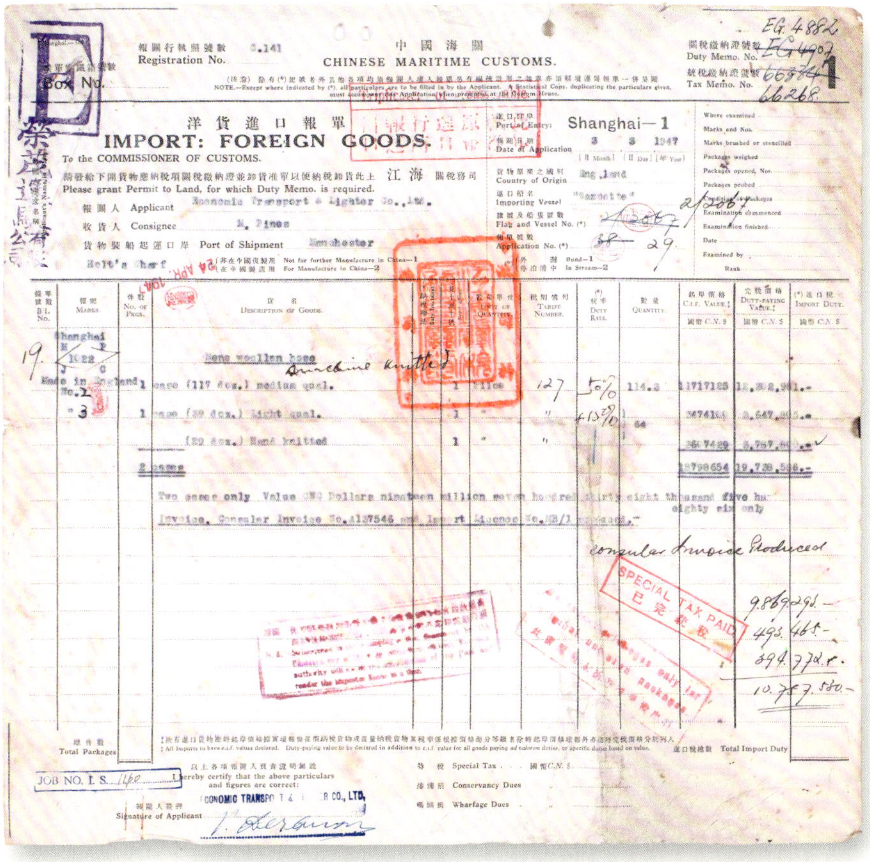

中國海關
CHINESE MARITIME CUSTOMS.

Box No.

報關行執照號數 Registration No.

關稅繳納證號數 Duty Memo. No. EG 4882 ~~EG 4907~~
統稅繳納證號數 Tax Memo. No. 66268

NOTE.—Except where indicated by (*), all particulars are to be filled in by the Applicant. A Statistical Copy, duplicating the particulars given, must accompany this Application when presented at the Custom House.

洋貨進口報單
IMPORT: FOREIGN GOODS.

To the COMMISSIONER OF CUSTOMS.

請發給下開貨物應納稅項關稅繳納證並卸貨准單以便納稅卸貨此上 江海 關稅務司
Please grant Permit to Land, for which Duty Memo. is required.

報關人 Applicant
收貨人 Consignee
貨物裝船起運口岸 Port of Shipment

非在中國復製用 Not for further Manufacture in China—1
在中國製造用 For Manufacture in China—2

進口口岸 Port of Entry: Shanghai—1
報關日期 Date of Application 3 3 1947 (月 Month) (日 Day) (年 Year)
貨物原來之國別 Country of Origin England
進口船名 Importing Vessel
旗號及船隻號數 Flag and Vessel No. (*)
報單號數 Application No. (*) ~~38~~ 29

外灘 Bund—1
停泊浦中 In Stream—2

Where examined
Marks and Nos.
Marks brushed or stencilled
Packages weighed
Packages opened, Nos.
Packages probed
Condition of Packages
Examination commenced
Examination finished
Date
Examined by
Rank

24 APR. 1947

提單號數 B/L. No.	標記 Marks	件數 No. of Pkgs.	貨名 Description of Goods	數量單位 Unit of Quantity	稅則號列 Tariff Number	(*) 稅率 Duty Rate	數量 Quantity	起岸價格 C.I.F. Value‡ 國幣 C.N.$	完稅價格 Duty-paying Value‡ 國幣 C.N.$	(*) 進口稅 Import Duty 國幣 C.N.$
19.	Shanghai M P 1022 J C Made in England No. 2		Mens woollen hose (machine knitted)							
		1	case (117 doz.) medium qual.		127	50%	114.3	11717125		
	3	1	case (39 doz.) Light qual.		"	15 2/10				
			(29 doz.) Hand knitted		"					
		2 cases							19,738,586.-	

Two cases only Value CNC Dollars nineteen million seven hundred thirty eight thousand five hundred eighty six only

Consular Invoice Produced

SPECIAL TAX PAID 已完稅

9.869.293.-
493.465.-
394.772.5.
10.757.580.-

‡ All Imports to have c.i.f. values declared. Duty-paying value to be declared in addition to c.i.f. value for all goods paying ad valorem duties, or specific duties based on value.

總件數 Total Packages

進口稅總數 Total Import Duty

JOB NO. I. S. 1160

以上各項報關人負責證明無訛
I hereby certify that the above particulars and figures are correct:

報關人簽押 Signature of Applicant

特稅 Special Tax 國幣C.N.$
濬浦捐 Conservancy Dues
碼頭捐 Wharfage Dues

海关业务单证

Customs Documents

20世纪50年代

中华人民共和国海关成立初期使用的业务单证。

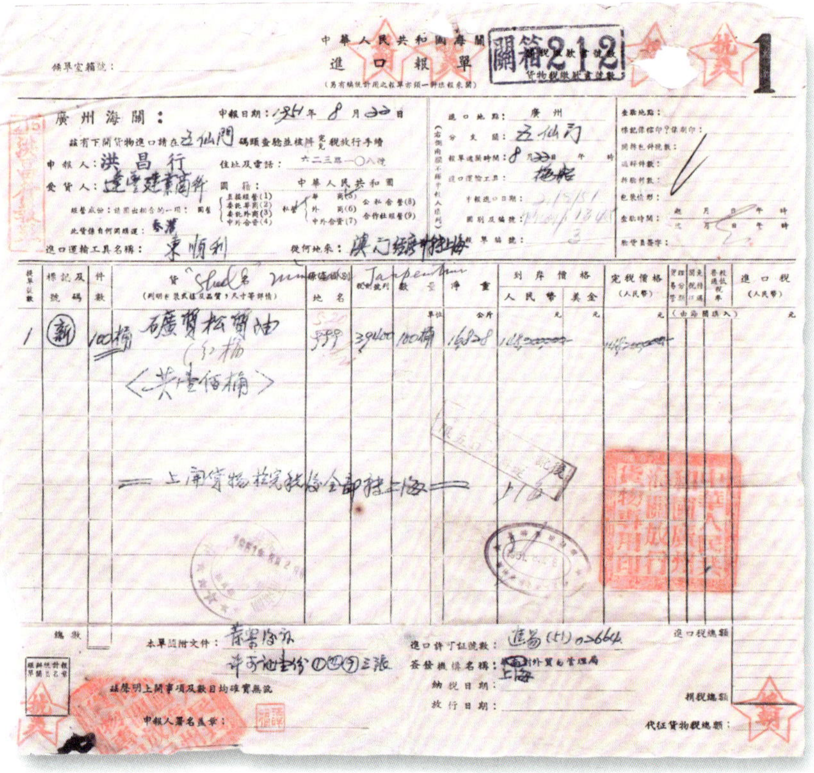

1951年8月广州海关进口货物报关单

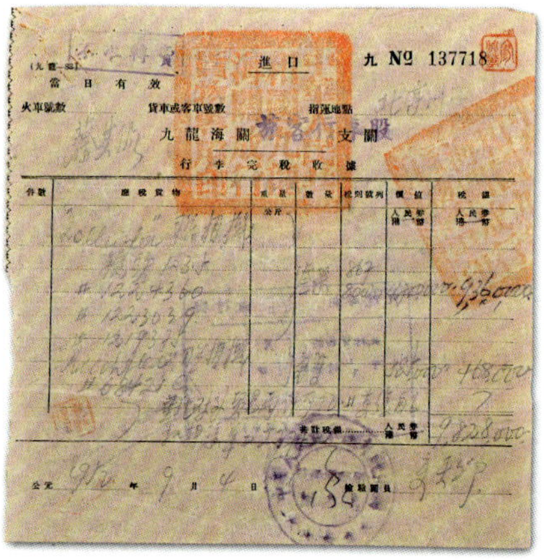

1952年九龙海关行李完税收据

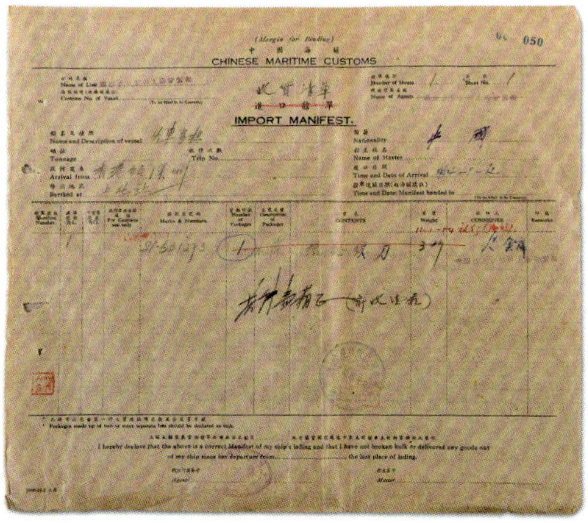

1954年转口输入货物收货清单

中国外贸进出口总额首次突破1万亿美元的报关单

Declaration Form Marking the Breakthrough of One Trillion US Dollars of Gross Value of China's Foreign Trade

2004年

改革开放以后，中国外贸持续快速发展。2004年中国货物进出口总额首次突破1万亿美元大关，提前6年实现规划目标。中国在世界贸易排名也由2003年的第4位升至第3位，成为名副其实的贸易大国。这是突破1万亿美元的标志性报关单。

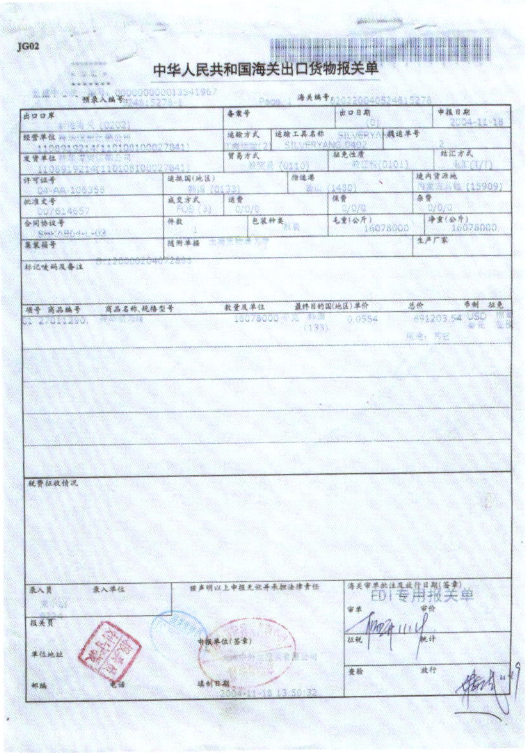
中华人民共和国海关出口货物报关单

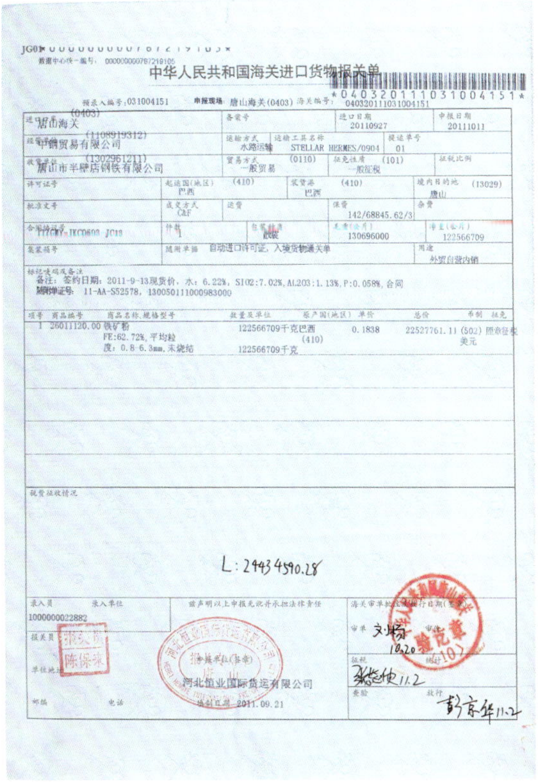
中华人民共和国海关进口货物报关单

中国外贸进出口额突破3万亿美元的报关单

Declaration Form Marking the Breakthrough of Three Trillion US Dollars of Gross Value of China's Foreign Trade

2010年

2010年，中国货物进出口贸易总额达2.97万亿美元，跃居世界第一，2011年10月11日，唐山市半壁店钢铁有限公司向唐山海关申报从巴西进口的铁矿粉1.2万吨，为中国货物进出口总值突破3万亿美元的标志性报关单。

关检融合后第一张报关单

The First Customs Declaration form after China's Inspection and Quarantine Functions Integrated into Customs

2018年

2018年，党中央决策部署将出入境检验检疫管理职责和队伍划入海关总署，4月20日，新转隶人员统一以海关名义对外开展工作，全国306个对外开放口岸统一使用“中国海关”标识；8月1日，报关单、报检单合二为一，海关监管、检验检疫两大口岸通关作业环节历史性融为一体。机构改革后，通关流程和环节大幅精简优化，原报关、报检共229个申报项目合并精简至105个，达到“1+1>2”的效果。

中华人民共和国海关出口货物报关单

预录入编号：[illegible]　海关编号：[illegible]　页码/页数：1/1

境内发货人　出境关别　出口日期 20180801　申报日期 20180801　备案号
境外收货人　运输方式　运输工具名称及航次号　提运单号
生产销售单位　监管方式 (0110)　征免性质 (101)　许可证号
合同协议号　贸易国（地区）(HKG) 香港　运抵国（地区）(HKG) 香港　指运港 俄罗斯　离境口岸
包装种类 (99)　件数　毛重（千克）　净重（千克）3321.93　成交方式 (3) FOB　运费　保费　杂费
随附单证及编号
标记唛码及备注

项号	商品编号	商品名称及规格型号	数量及单位	单价/总价/币制	原产国（地区）	最终目的国（地区）	境内货源地	征免
1 (0)	[illegible]	UPS电源 1|0|功率:6KW、3KW等|HUAWEI牌|型号:UPS2000-G-6KRTL、UPS2000-G-3KRTL等	3台 3台	1243.6333 3730.90 美元	中国 (CHN)	俄罗斯联邦 (RUS)		照章征税 (1)
2 (0)	[illegible]	以太网交换机 1|0|用途:数据通信设备用|通讯方式-有线|[illegible]|网络种类:以太网|HUAWEI牌|型号:CE6810-48S4Q-LI、CE686	16台 16台	1106.[illegible] 17703.16 美元	中国 (CHN)	俄罗斯联邦 (RUS)		照章征税 (1)
3 (0)	[illegible]	光纤交换机 1|0|用途:光纤数据传输设备用|通讯方式:有线|品牌:HUAWEI|型号:OceanStor SNS2624|是否加密:非加密	2台 2台	[illegible] 11023 美元	中国	俄罗斯联邦		照章征税 (1)
4 (0)	[illegible]	路由器 1|0|用途:数据通信设备|通讯方式:有线|适用网络种类:有线网络|HUAWEI牌|型号:AR550-SFE-D-H、AR1220EV、AR122	11台 11台	[illegible] 8974.06 美元	中国 (CHN)	俄罗斯联邦 (RUS)		照章征税 (1)
5 (0)	[illegible]	磁盘阵列 1|0|品牌:HUAWEI|型号:OceanStor 5800 V5|[illegible]	1台 1台	106185.90 106185.90 美元	中国 (CHN)	俄罗斯联邦 (RUS)		照章征税 (1)
6 (0)	[illegible]	服务器(不带显示器) 1|0|机型:[illegible]|CPU:2*2.6GHz、2*2400MHz等内存:2*32GB、6*8GB等硬盘:无、8*300GB等|HUAWEI牌|型号:[illegible]	36台 36台	9998.8291 359957.86 美元	中国 (CHN)	俄罗斯联邦		照章征税 (1)

特殊关系确认：否　价格影响确认：否　支付特许权使用费确认：否　自报自缴：否
报关人员　报关人员证号　电话　兹申明对以上内容承担如实申报、依法纳税之法律责任　海关批注及签章
申报单位 [illegible]　申报单位（签章）

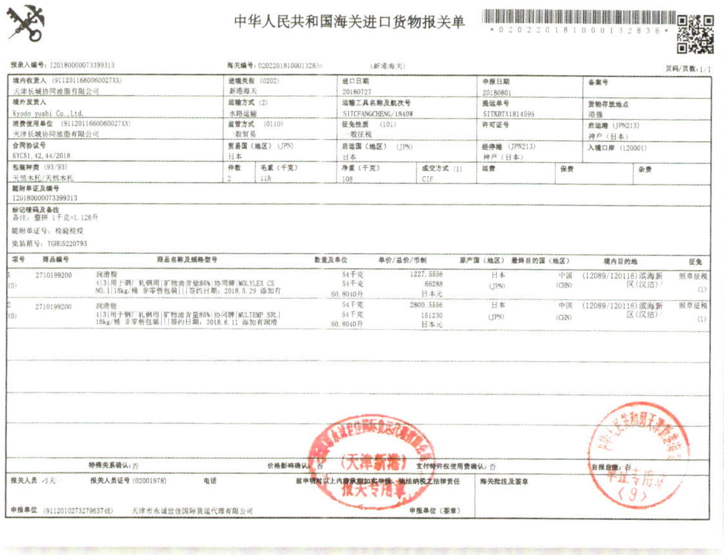

中华人民共和国海关进口货物报关单

020220181000132836

预录入编号：I20180000073399313　海关编号：020220181000132836　（新港海关）　页码/页数：1/1

境内收货人 (9112011660060027XX) 天津长城协同油脂有限公司　进境关别 (0202) 新港海关　进口日期 20180727　申报日期 20180801　备案号
境外发货人 Kyodo yushi Co.,Ltd.　运输方式 (2) 水路运输　运输工具名称及航次号 SITCFANGCHENG/1840W　提运单号 SITKBTX1814595　货物存放地点 港福
消费使用单位 (9112011660060027XX) 天津长城协同油脂有限公司　监管方式 (0110) 一般贸易　征免性质 (101) 一般征税　许可证号　启运港 (JPN213) 神户（日本）
合同协议号 KYC51,42,44/2018　贸易国（地区）(JPN) 日本　启运国（地区）(JPN) 日本　经停港 (JPN213) 神户（日本）　入境口岸 (120001)
包装种类 (93/93) 天然木托/天然木托　件数 2　毛重（千克）118　净重（千克）108　成交方式 (1) CIF　运费　保费　杂费
随附单证及编号 I20180000073399313
标记唛码及备注
备注：整拼 1千克=1.126升
随附单证号：检验检疫
集装箱号：TGHU5220793

项号	商品编号	商品名称及规格型号	数量及单位	单价/总价/币制	原产国（地区）	最终目的国（地区）	境内目的地	征免
1 (0)	2710199200	润滑脂 4|3|用于钢厂轧钢用|矿物油含量85%|协同牌|MOLYLEX CS NO.1|18kg/桶 非零售包装||签约日期：2018.5.29 添加有	54千克 54千克 60.8040升	1227.5556 66288 日本元	日本 (JPN)	中国 (CHN)	(12089/120116)滨海新区(汉沽)/	照章征税 (1)
2 (0)	2710199200	润滑脂 4|3|用于钢厂轧钢用|矿物油含量85%|协同牌|MULTEMP SRL|18kg/桶 非零售包装||签约日期：2018.6.11 添加有润滑	54千克 54千克 60.8040升	2800.5556 151230 日本元	日本 (JPN)	中国 (CHN)	(12089/120116)滨海新区(汉沽)/	照章征税 (1)

特殊关系确认：否　价格影响确认：否　支付特许权使用费确认：否　自报自缴：否
报关人员 刁天一　报关人员证号 (02001978)　电话　兹申明对以上内容承担如实申报、依法纳税之法律责任　海关批注及签章
申报单位 (91120102732796374E) 天津市永诚世佳国际货运代理有限公司　申报单位（签章）

监管工具

Tools of Supervision and Control

旋转式印章架

Customs Seal Rack

清晚期

厦门关用于办理报关手续的旋转印章架，可同时挂10枚印章，提高工作效率。

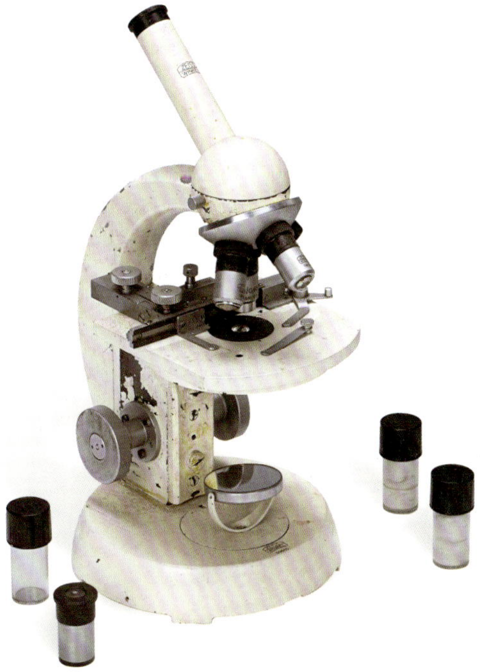

显微镜

Microscope

民国时期

闽海关用于监管货物并征税的化验仪器。

钎子
Drill Rod
晚清时期

海关查验谷物类货物所用监管工具。

大杆秤
Steelyard
晚清时期

潮海关关员查验货物时使用的称重衡器。

比重计、温度计
Hydrometer / Thermometer
民国时期

粤海关用于液体类（含油类）商品测量、化验的比重计、温度计。

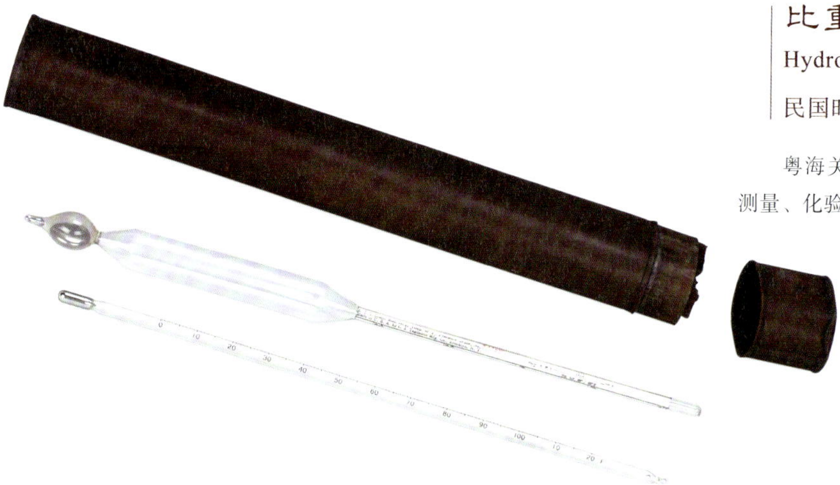

施封锁、铅封

Customs Seal

20世纪40年代

海关用于封存货物物品的锁具。铅封破坏后不能再次使用，施封锁标有特定编号和海关关名。

查验工具

Examination Tools

20世纪60年代至90年代

中华人民共和国海关监管中使用的施封钳、钻具、锁针。

金属探测器

Metal Detector

20世纪80年代

20世纪80年代海关旅检现场使用的金属探测器，可探测隐藏在人体身上的各类金属物体，包括首饰、电器元器件等。

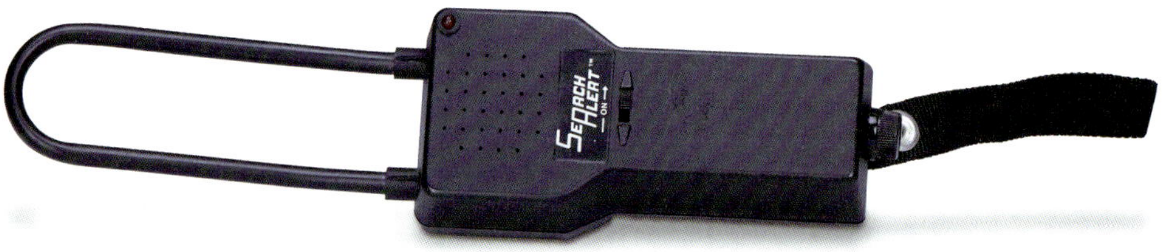

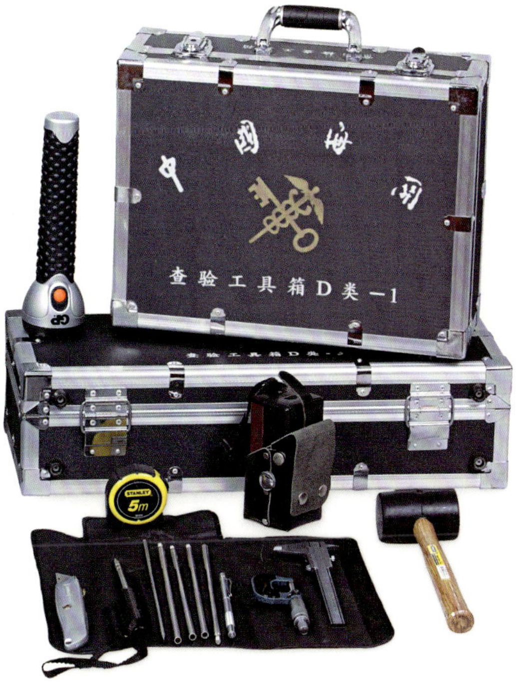

查验工具箱

Tool Kit for Customs Inspection

21世纪初期

各地海关使用的组合式查验工具箱。

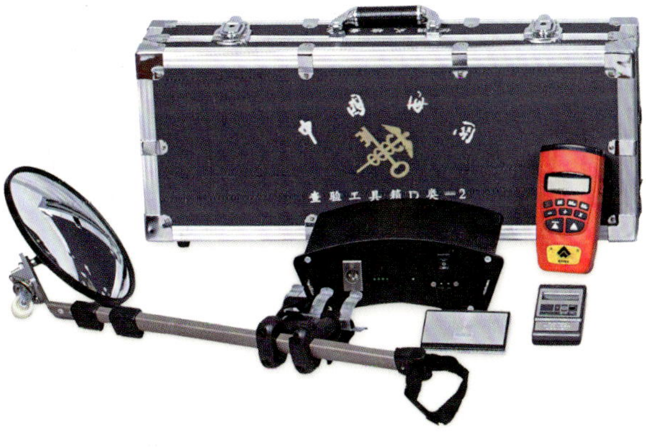

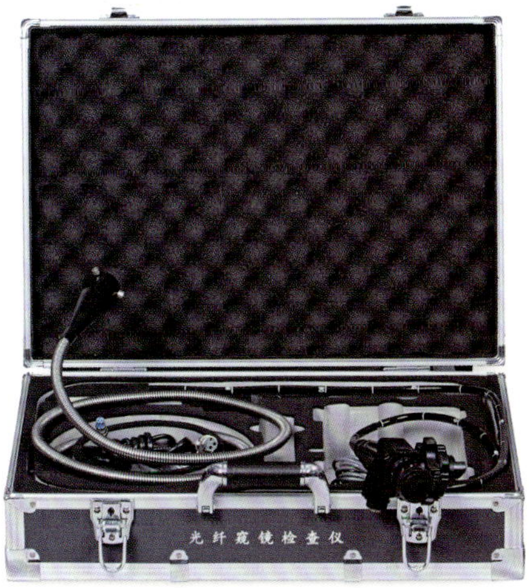

“H915” 系统机芯

The Core Part of H915 Mobile Container Inspection System

1994年

1994年，世界上最早投入商业运用的移动式集装箱检查系统分别在深圳皇岗海关、文锦渡海关部署。这是其主机机芯，可以在不打开车厢货柜的情况下，通过X光射线将内容物图像显现出来，以确定其中是否藏匿走私物品，曾经被誉为海关查验现场的“火眼金睛”。1998年以来，清华同方公司联合中国海关研发的H986集装箱/货柜车大型检查系统先后在全国海关运用并推广至世界有关国家海关。

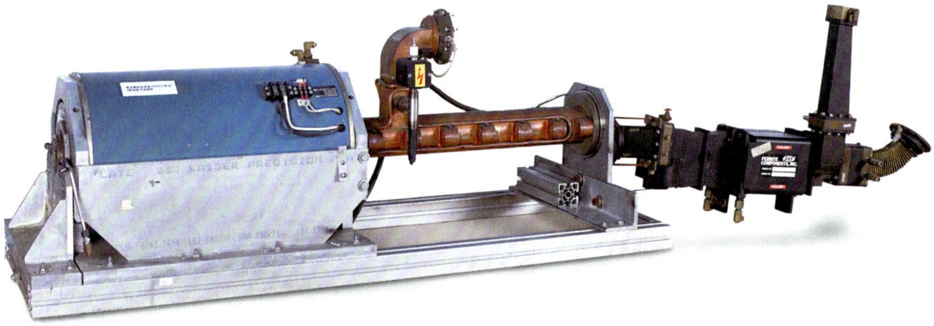

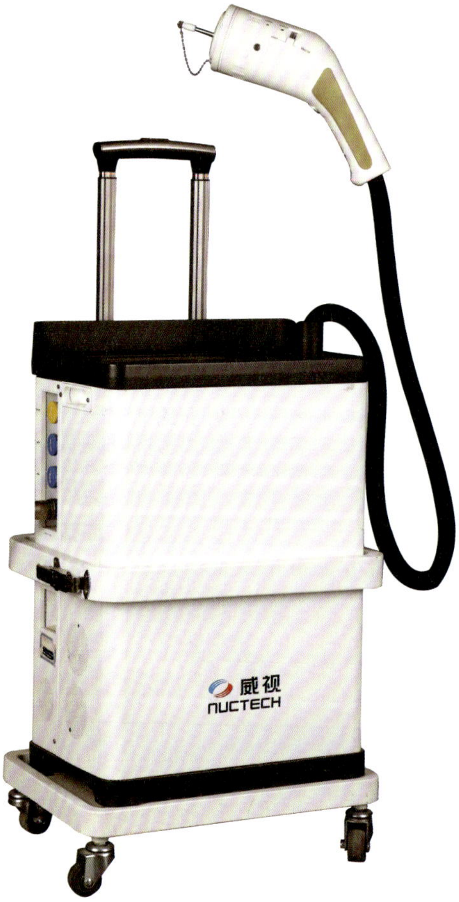

电子鼻

Electronic Nose System

2019年

北京海关联合清华同方股份有限公司主持的北京市科学技术委员会项目“动植食产品快速通关查验设备——‘电子鼻’研制与应用”孵化出的新型产品。该仪器采用气相色谱—离子迁移谱（MCC-IMS）联用技术，可快速检测海关重点关注的动植物及其制品、食品、毒品、爆炸物、集装箱熏蒸剂、化学战剂及有毒有害气体，亦可应用于化工园区气体泄漏、消防勘验等场合。

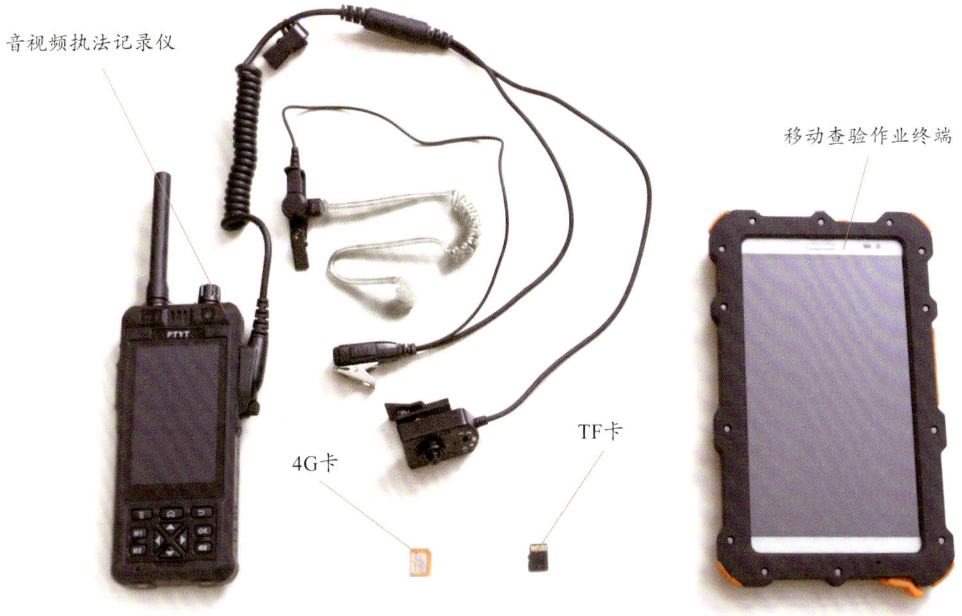

海关单兵移动应用设备

Equipment for Single Person Operation

当代

海关正在推广使用的新式现场作业工具，外观类似平板电脑。每台终端都链接着海关总署研发的移动查验作业系统，通过拍照取证等方式，使得查验证据现场固化，强化了查验执法过程的监督，从而防控风险。通过系统辅助，利用集体智慧解决疑难问题，为查验人员提供实时信息支持，提高查验效率。

手持激光设备

Hand-held Laser Equipment

2019年

用于海关现场对未知化学物质快速定性的检测设备。该设备采用分子指纹光谱分析技术，结合自建的可靠数据库以及精准的识别算法，可在不接触样品的情况下快速识别可疑毒品、毒品前体、易制毒化学品、工业原料等在内的不明化学物质，还可以用于对象牙饰品等濒危动植物制品、芬太尼及其衍生物等禁止进出境物品的快速鉴定。

青花缠枝莲纹碗

Blue-and-white Porcelain Bowl with Interlaced Floral Design

明代初期

从海底打捞出水的古代外销瓷器，是我国对外贸易和海上丝绸之路的历史证物。

三彩划花小罐

Tri-colored Jar

辽代

外销陶瓷器皿，是我国对外贸易发展历程的见证物。

绍英隆顾绣丝发庄黑红漆描金花卉纹方盒

Red and Black Painted Square Box with Gold Outline and Flower Pattern

清代

外销漆盒，盒面上绘有梅兰竹菊四君子图，产自广州。

柳亭人物故事图檀木首饰盒

Sandalwood Jewelry Box with the Picture of Willow, Pavilion and Characters

清代

檀香木制成，盒子四面浮雕柳树亭台人物图，盒面中间为需要定制专属徽号和商铺名称的客户预留空白。

黑漆描金制茶图茶叶盒

Black-painted Tea Caddy with Outline in Gold and Tea Making Picture

清代

外销茶具，产自中国广东，木胎，髹黑漆。盒面装饰采用了描金工艺，是当时最受欧洲欢迎的工艺之一，绘制了清代晚期制茶、贩茶的场景。盒内放有一个锡制茶叶盒，锡盒盖上有錾刻纹饰和象牙提纽。随着茶叶的输入以及饮茶风气盛行，英国等欧洲国家的茶具需求也在与日俱增。由于早期欧洲茶叶非常珍贵，所以茶叶盒配有锁孔，一般钥匙只掌握在主人的手里，防止茶叶被仆人偷喝。而漆器可以有效地防止茶叶受潮发霉，里面锡罐的设置也增强了密封性。19世纪中叶开始，英国人在印度、斯里兰卡等殖民地大量开辟茶园，茶叶数量激增，价格下滑，加锁的茶叶盒就渐渐不再流行。

青花缠枝花卉纹盘

Blue-and-white Porcelain Dish with Design of Entangled Floral Branches

清代

外销陶瓷器皿，是我国对外贸易发展历程的证物。青花瓷是一种白底蓝花的釉下彩瓷器，此青花盘口沿饰回纹一周，盘内及外壁绘有缠枝莲花、宝相花等吉祥图案。

双面广绣绶带鸟纹玳瑁骨折扇

Hawksbill Fold Fan with Bird Pattern in Double-sided Canton Embroidery

清代

有别于以竹木为扇骨的传统折扇，盛行于18、19世纪的外销折扇多用象牙、玳瑁、砗磲、檀香木等珍贵材质为骨。此玳瑁骨折扇扇面绶带鸟采用双面广绣技法，既有浓郁的广东地方工艺特色，又符合西洋定制者审美喜好，属东西方文化交融的产物。

黑漆描金人物故事纹双面折扇

Black-painted Double-faced Fold Fan with Gold Outline and Character Story Picture

清代

黑漆描金，是以黑漆为底色，用金粉或银粉描绘的一种装饰手法。19世纪早期，最早的黑漆描金外销扇开始出现。此折扇20档黑漆描金扇骨以丝带连缀，正反面使用青、赤两种金粉描绘了道光中晚期流行的“满大人”庭院人物故事题材纹饰，顶部以禽鸟装饰相间隔，两边扇骨利用朱漆描绘龙纹。

咸豐元年
咸豐元年

税收征管

Taxation

征税是海关的基本职能之一。西周设置“讥而不征”的关津，春秋战国时期关津开始征收通过税或进出境税，始有“关市之征”。唐至明代，市舶（使）司负责征收舶脚；明代中后期，漳州月港督饷馆征收水饷（船舶吨税）和陆饷（进出口货物税）；清代前中期，闽、粤、江、浙四海关颁布税则并征税；近代海关关税自主权和税款收支保管权丧失。中华人民共和国成立后，收回海关主权，实行独立自主的关税政策，海关依法征收关税、船舶吨税，并代征进口环节增值税、消费税等。海关税收是中央财政收入的重要来源，是国家宏观调控的工具，成为保护和促进国内产业健康发展的重要屏障。

Taxation is one of the basic functions of the customs. In the Western Zhou Dynasty, passes were set up for “examining travelers but levying no duties from them”, and during the Spring and Autumn Period as well as the Warring States Period, transit duties or entry and exit taxes were levied at passes, which was the start of “taxation at the customs passes”. From the Tang Dynasty to the Ming Dynasty, *Shiboshi* or *Shibosi* were responsible for levying anchorage tax. In the middle and late Ming Dynasty, Yuegang Tariff Supervising Bureau in Zhangzhou levied marine rates (ship tonnage dues) and land rates (import and export cargo tax). In the Early and Middle Qing Dynasty, the customs of Fuzhou, Guangzhou, Shanghai, Ningbo promulgated tariff regulations and levied customs duties. In modern times, the customs autonomy, the tariff autonomy and the right to customs revenue custody were lost. After the founding of the People’s Republic of China, we recovered the customs sovereignty and implemented an independent tariff policy. The customs levy customs duties and tonnage dues in accordance with the law, and is authorized to levy import value-added taxes and consumption taxes. Customs revenue is an important source of central government fiscal revenue and a tool of national macro-control, which has become an important barrier for protecting and promoting the sound development of domestic industries.

税银货币
Customs' Ingot and Currencies

云南牌坊银锭
Silver Ingot in Memorial Gate Shape from Yunnan

清代

铸有“陈元昌号汇号纹银”字样。牌坊锭是云南最具代表性的一种银锭，因形状酷似牌坊而得名，光绪早期出现于云南地区，是中国历代银锭里字戳铭使用最多、最精美的一类银锭。清代晚期，牌坊银锭成为云南边境贸易的主要流通货币，甚至随着滇缅行商外流至东南亚各国。陈元昌在清代是云南较有名的半官半私“汇号制银处”，但大部分时间皆发行地方法定商号汇票，验造发行的银锭数量很少。

粤海关十两银锭
Ten-tael Silver Ingot of Canton Customs

1851年

粤海关咸丰元年（1851年）铸，是中国海关行政管理权沦丧前最后一批税收银锭之一。自明代隆庆年间实施督饷制度后，中外商人皆使用银锭缴纳关税。海关征税后将碎银熔解之后重铸成十两一锭、中间微束腰、两头鼓起的砝码形银锭，银锭上刻有海关名字、纪年等内容，便于统一上缴国库。由于晚清时期战争赔款导致白银大量外流，现存的粤海关银锭屈指可数。

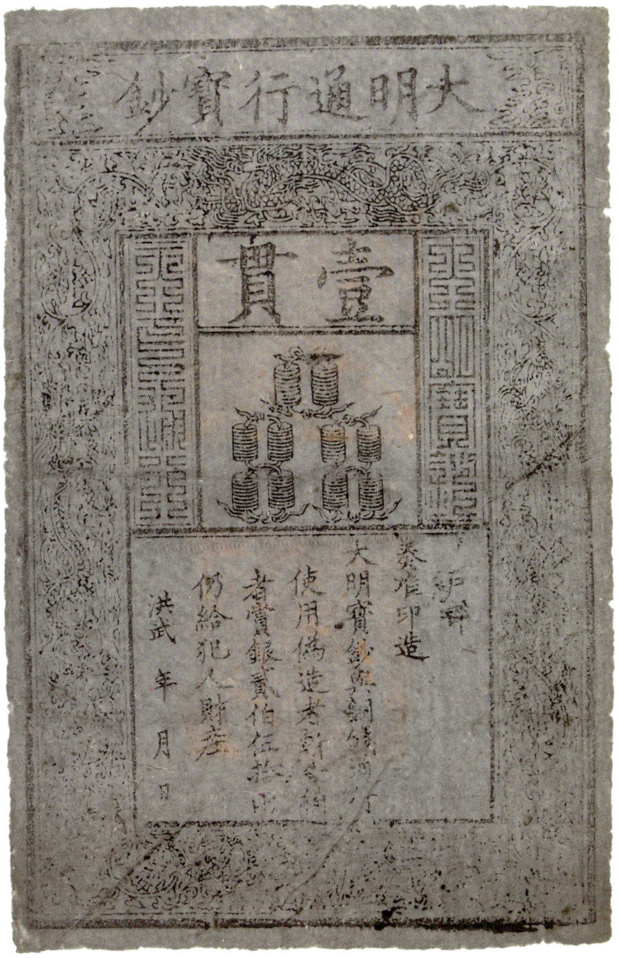

大明宝钞

Banknote from the Ming Dynasty

14世纪晚期

明太祖朱元璋登基后于洪武七年（1374年）发行的纸币。大明宝钞发行后与铜钱通行，在全国范围内流通。但因发行与支出数量激增，宝钞持续大幅贬值，每况愈下。政府为“疏通钞法”，于宣德四年（1429年）在南京与北京之间的运河沿岸设立7个钞关，隶属于户部，过往船只均以大明宝钞缴纳商货税款，钞关自此诞生。尽管正德年间大明宝钞被废止不用，但因其得名的“钞关”却一直延续至清代，成为征收货税机构的代名词。

户部官票

Note of the Ministry of Revenue

1856年

发行于清咸丰三年（1853年），以银两为单位，既可用于缴纳税款，也可加盖“粮台”字样作为军饷之用，咸丰十一年（1861年）停止发行，同治元年（1862年）全部停用。

户部官票发行时只可以在市场上换成银钱，但没有规定能在官银钱号中兑现，因此官票在实际流通中变成了不能兑现的纸币，导致官票非但不能兑换银两，甚至连制钱都很难换到，拿到官票的人只能低价出手。地方上一些官吏和外国商人就用低价买进官票，用以充当赋税来获取高额利润。

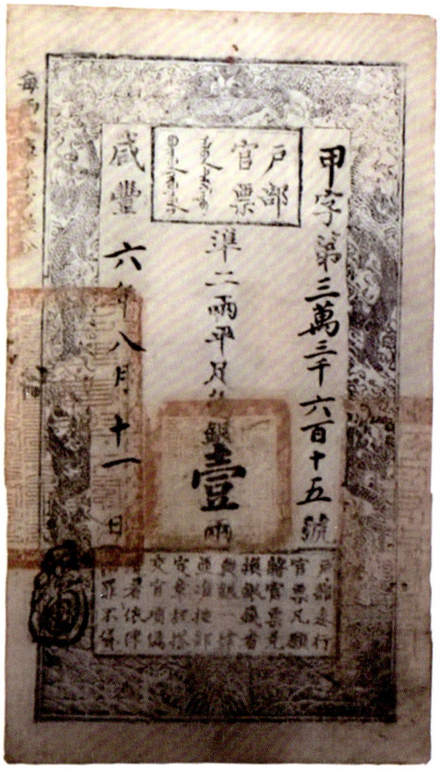

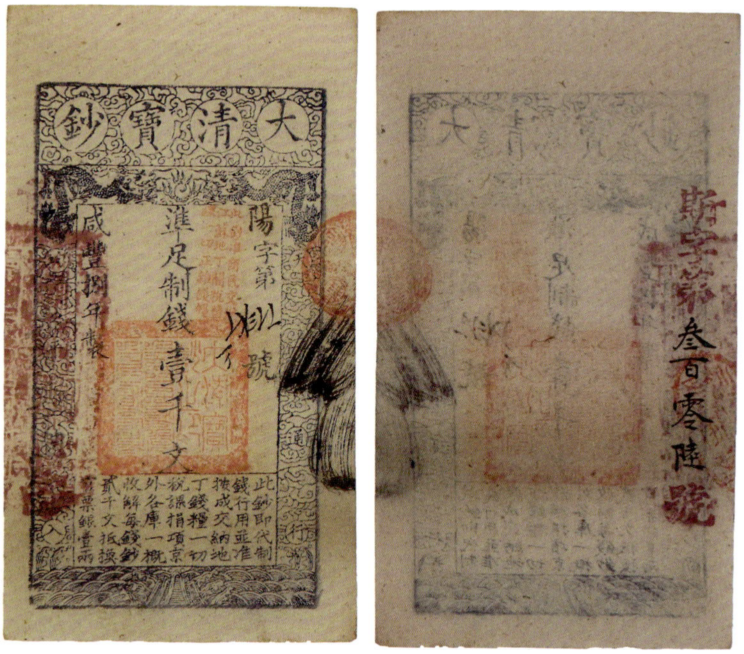

大清宝钞

Banknote from the Qing Dynasty

19世纪50年代至60年代

发行于清咸丰三年（1853年），以制钱为单位，可用于缴纳各类税款，咸丰十一年（1861年）停止发行，同治元年（1862年）全部停用。

西班牙本洋

Spanish Silver Dollar

19世纪晚期

银币正面图案是西班牙国王头像，背面图案是垂双柱的西班牙皇室徽记。1521年，墨西哥沦为西班牙的殖民地，西班牙统治者利用当地丰富的银矿铸造银币，明代后期开始流入广东、福建一带，清康熙年间开放海禁后又大量流入上海。1823年前后，墨西哥摆脱西班牙殖民统治，不再大量铸造供应双柱本洋，而代之以自铸的鹰洋。本洋逐渐退出市场。

“中外通宝关平银壹两”银元

“One Haikwan Tael” Silver Dollar

清晚期

“关平银”为近代海关征税时使用的货币单位，是鸦片战争后为统一通商各口与国外贸易往来而建立的一种纳税货币单位，并非实银。为统一标准，遂以对外贸易习惯使用的“司马平”（“平”即砝码），又称“广平”，取其一两作为关平两的标准单位。一关平两的虚设重量为583.3英厘，或37.7495克（后演变为37.913克）的足色纹银（含93.5374%纯银）。海关在征收关税时，依据当地实际采用的虚银两与纹银的折算标准进行兑换。

关金券

The Customs Gold Unit

1930年

1929年世界银价大落，影响海关关税收入。1930年，国民政府决定海关进口税征金，设置“海关金单位”，与黄金保持1：0.601866克固定比价，合0.40美元。1931年5月，中央银行正式发行“海关金单位兑换券”，简称“关金券”，作为缴纳关税之用。1942年，国民政府宣布法币和关金可以相互兑换，关金券就此失去原来的发行意义而成为大面额流通货币，1948年国民政府实施币制改革，发行金圆券，关金券作废。关金券正面均采用孙中山头像，下部印关金面额，背面则是江海关大楼的图案，只在花边设计和面额的背景纹样等细节方面有所差异。

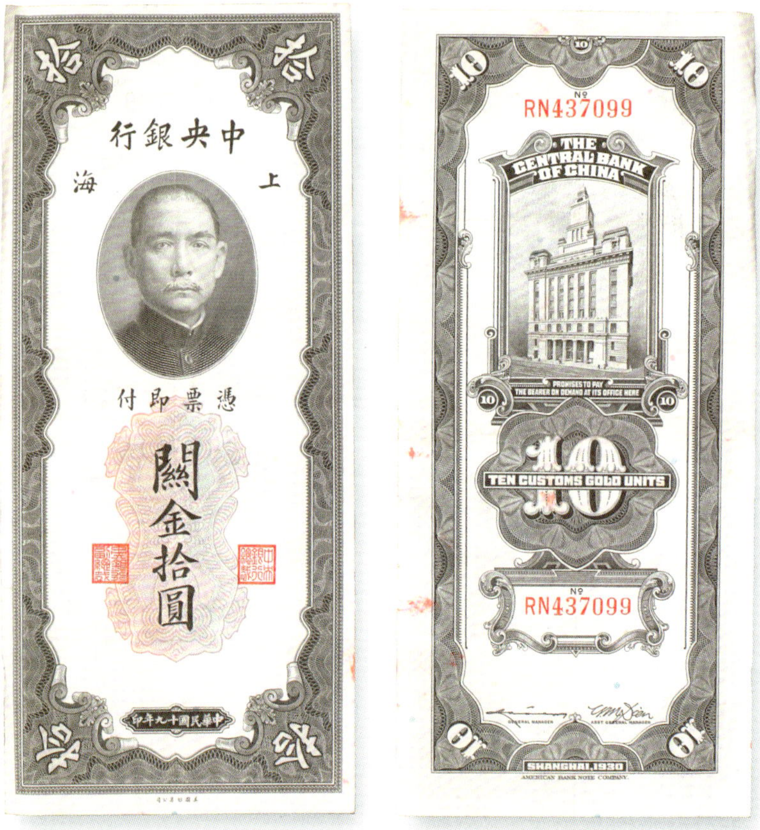

金圆券

Gold Yuan Certificate

1949年

国民政府为挽救解放战争后期的财政崩溃而发行的货币。1948年8月，国民政府实行币值改革，用金圆券代替法币，强制将黄金、白银和外币兑换为金圆券。后期因为滥发造成恶性通货膨胀、物价飞涨，致使大量城市中产阶级破产，也成为国民党统治迅速土崩瓦解的原因之一。1949年4、5月，南京、上海解放，人民政府宣布停止金圆券流通。

中央信托局支票

China Central Trust Cheque

20世纪30年代至40年代

1935年，为应对抗日战争紧急需要，中央信托局成立，定位为中央银行附设机构，总局设于上海。此支票可作缴纳关税用途。

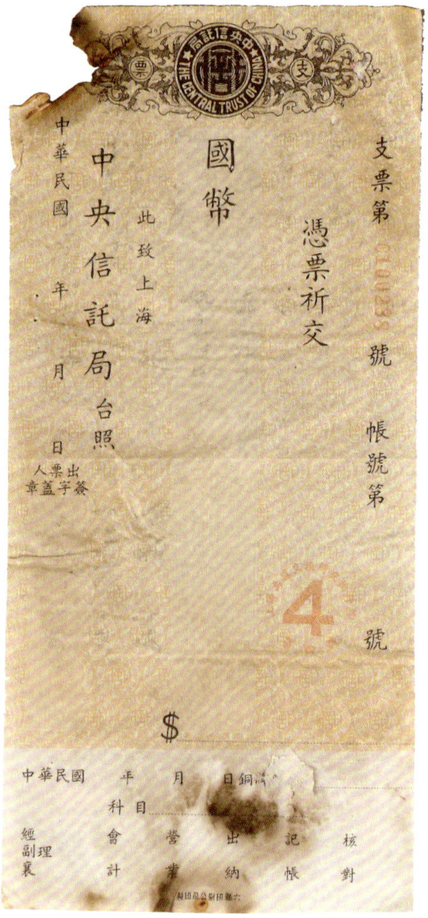

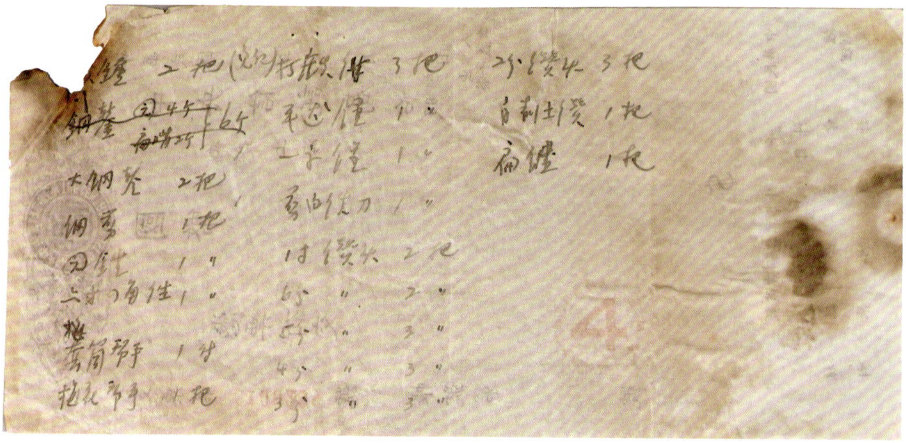

川陕省苏维埃铜币

Copper Coin Issued by Sichuan and Shaanxi Provincial Soviet Government

20世纪30年代

1933年，中共川陕省第一次党员代表大会和川陕省第一次工农兵代表大会相继召开，组建了中共川陕省委，成立了川陕省苏维埃政府，被毛泽东称为“中华苏维埃共和国的第二疆域”。为统一币制、稳定金融秩序，苏区政府在四川省通江县城郊西寺设造币厂，用古老的熔铸法铸造带有镰刀斧头图案的铜币。

皖西北特区苏维埃银行一元币

One Yuan Note Issued by the Soviet Bank in the Northwest Anhui Soviet Area

20世纪30年代

皖西北特区苏维埃银行建立之初发行。1931年5月，皖西北特区苏维埃政府成立，特区是鄂豫皖苏区的一部分，其在成立之初就建立了皖西北特区苏维埃银行，经营业务包括发行革命货币、代理金库、办理财政存款、拨付红军和军政机构经费等。1932年该纸币停止发行，统一改用鄂豫皖省苏维埃银行纸币。

海关税收清折

Lists of Customs Duty Collection

1905年

海关监督上报的各关税收清折，原件现存中国第一历史档案馆。晚清时期，海关监督负责关税的保管与支放，并办理所属常关税及海关洋税的奏销，每三个月将税款的出、入、调、存情况上报户部（后为度支部）并请求核准。

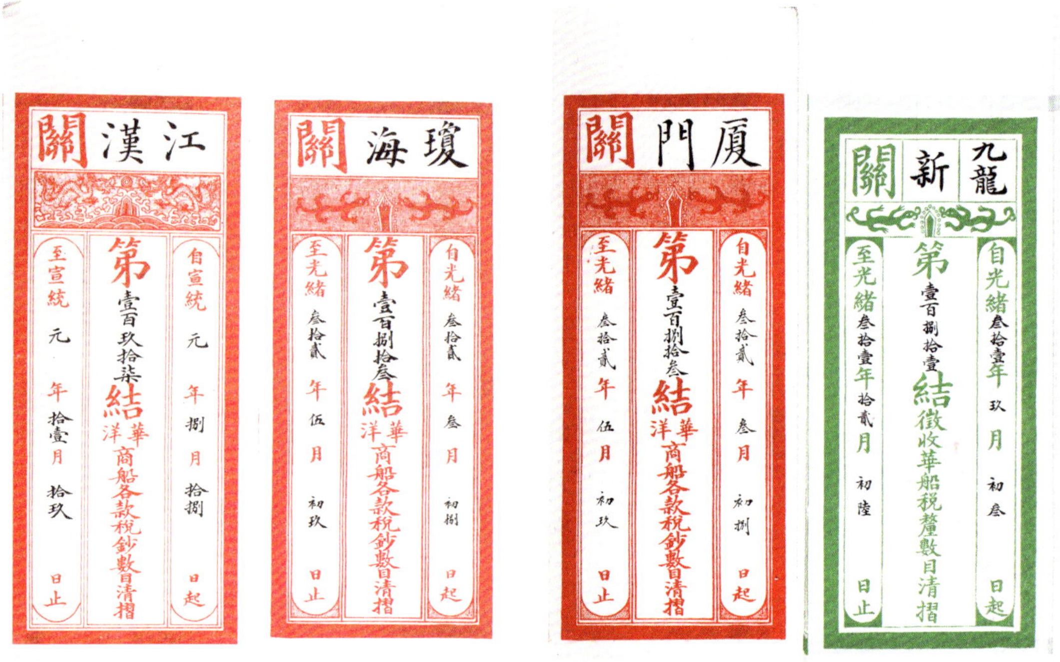
江漢關
自宣統元年捌月拾捌日起
第壹百玖拾柒結
洋華商船各款稅鈔數目清摺
至宣統元年拾壹月拾玖日止

瓊海關
自光緒叁拾貳年叁月初捌日起
第壹百捌拾叁結
洋華商船各款稅鈔數目清摺
至光緒叁拾貳年伍月初玖日止

厦門關
自光緒叁拾貳年叁月初捌日起
第壹百捌拾叁結
洋華商船各款稅鈔數目清摺
至光緒叁拾貳年伍月初玖日止

九龍新關
自光緒叁拾壹年玖月初叁日起
第壹百捌拾壹結
徵收華船稅釐數目清摺
至光緒叁拾壹年拾貳月初陸日止

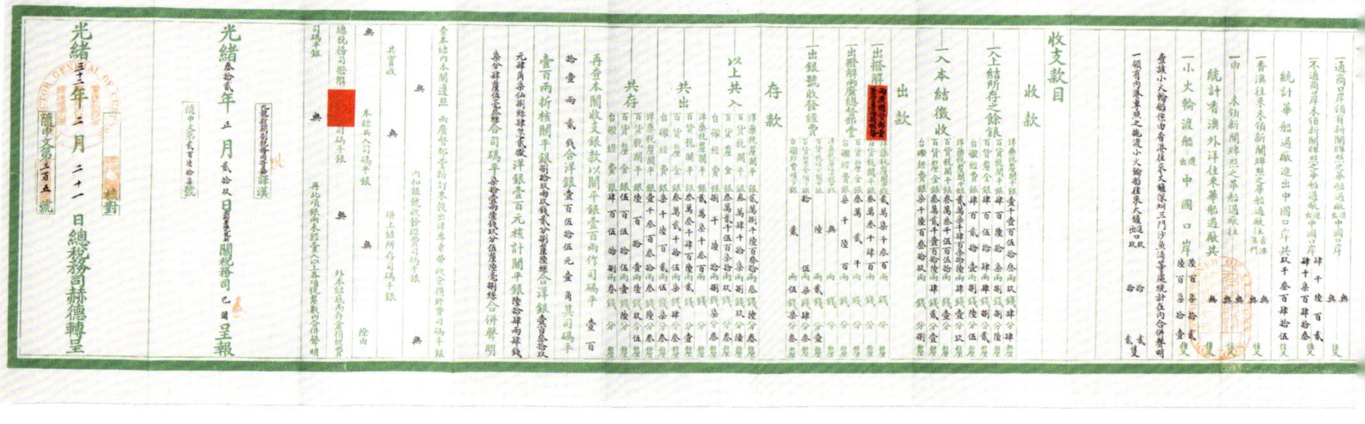

吴淞分关征税税银清单

Duty List of Woosung Sub-office

20世纪20年代

吴淞分关原为海关监督属下的常关机构，1901年11月按《辛丑条约》划归外籍税务司掌控的江海关管辖。

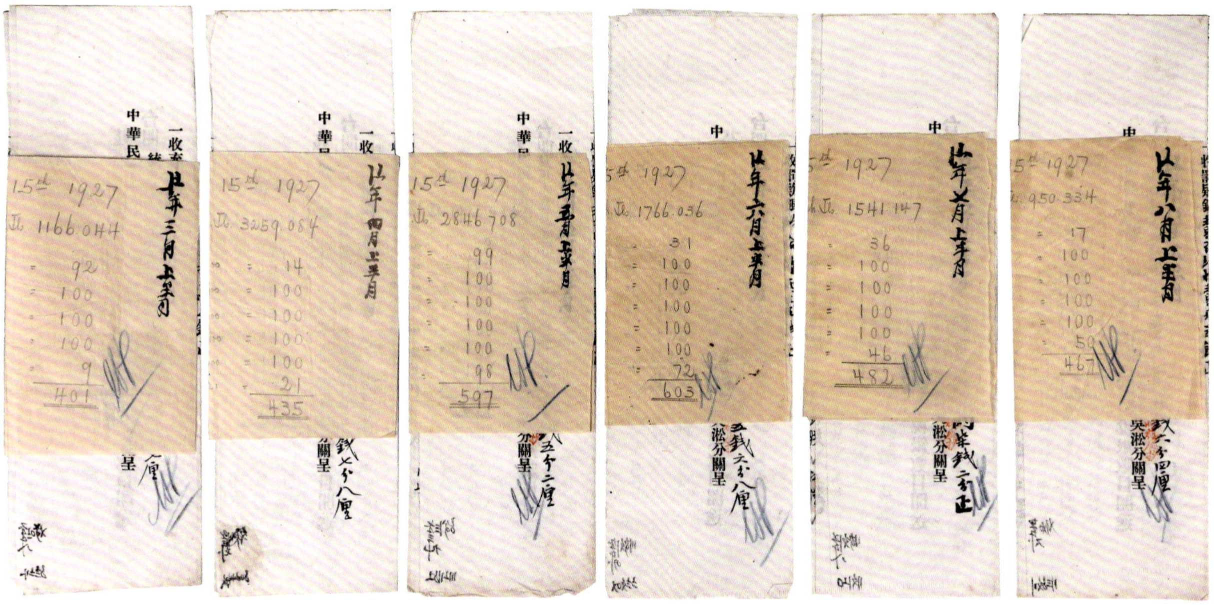

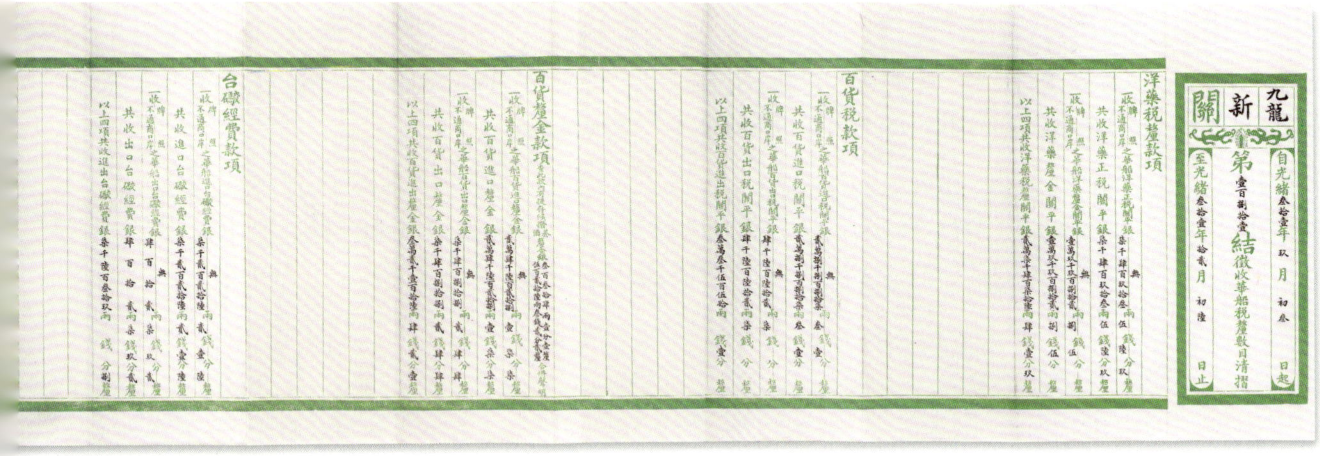

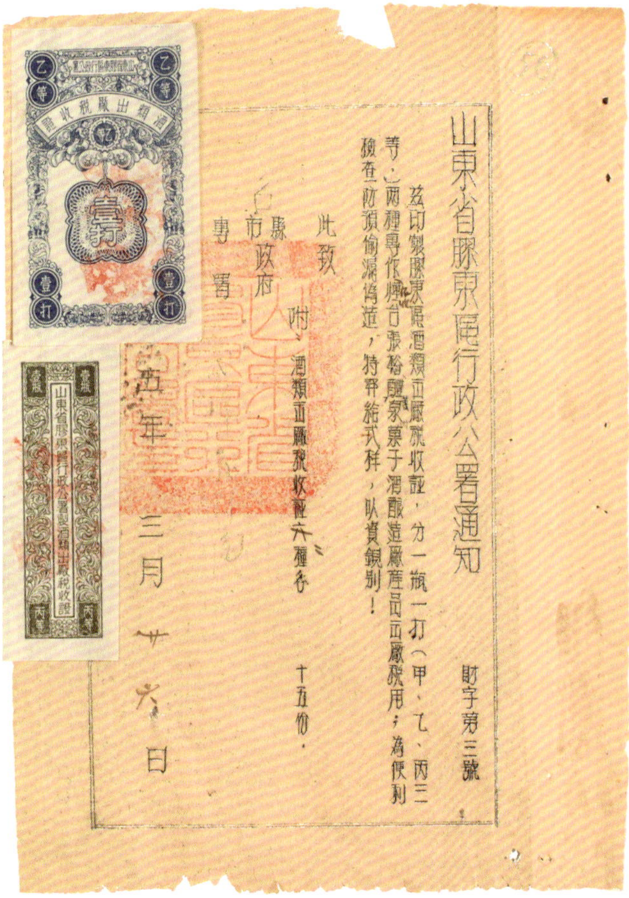

山东解放区酒类出厂税收证

Revenue Stamp of Liquor Product in Shandong Liberated Area

20世纪40年代

山东解放区内实施酒类专酿，1946年3月26日，胶东区行政公署下达《关于酒类税收证明的通知》，并附有酒类专用税收证，解放区海关关员凭此证查验放行。

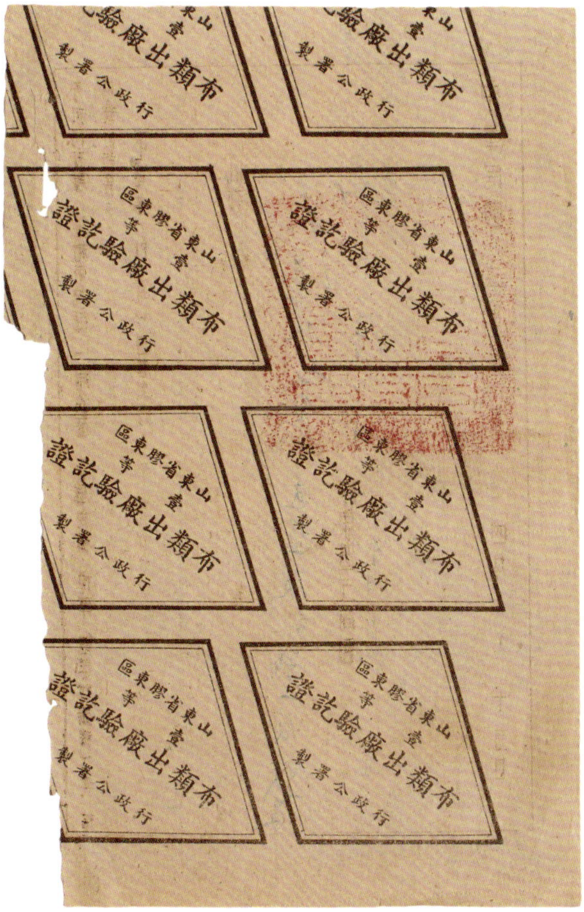

布类出厂验讫证

Delivery Inspection Certificate for Cloth

1943年

山东解放区胶东区行政公署制发的一等布类出厂验讫证。

山东解放区印花税票

Revenue Stamps Issued by Shandong Liberated Area

1947年

山东胶东解放区发行。有5、6、9、50、100元等面值，背面印有文字。税票即完税凭证，主要包括两类：一种是税收完税证，包括通用完税证、定额完税证和印花税票；另一种是税收缴款书。印花税票是印花税的完税证明，其外形与邮票相似，有精美的设计图案、凿打齿孔等，并有一定的面值。印花税在中共革命根据地和解放区的发展较为曲折，最开始被认为是苛捐杂税，受到排斥和取缔；之后又从实际出发开征印花税。自1938年开始，各根据地和解放区开征印花税，各区自行设计印制税票。

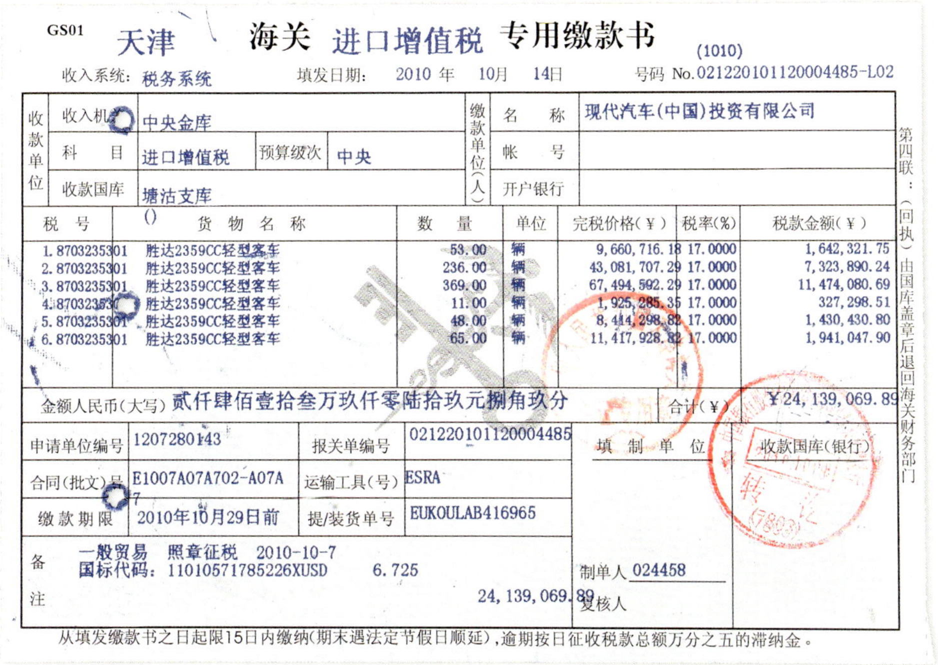

GS01 天津 海关 进口增值税 专用缴款书 (1010)

收入系统：税务系统 填发日期：2010 年 10月 14日 号码 No.021220101120004485-L02

收款单位	收入机关	中央金库		缴款单位(人)	名 称	现代汽车(中国)投资有限公司
	科 目	进口增值税	预算级次 中央		帐 号	
	收款国库	塘沽支库			开户银行	

税 号	() 货 物 名 称	数 量	单位	完税价格(￥)	税率(%)	税款金额(￥)
1. 8703235301	胜达2359CC轻型客车	53.00	辆	9,660,716.18	17.0000	1,642,321.75
2. 8703235301	胜达2359CC轻型客车	236.00	辆	43,081,707.29	17.0000	7,323,890.24
3. 8703235301	胜达2359CC轻型客车	369.00	辆	67,494,592.29	17.0000	11,474,080.69
4. 870323[illegible]	胜达2359CC轻型客车	11.00	辆	1,925,285.35	17.0000	327,298.51
5. 8703235301	胜达2359CC轻型客车	48.00	辆	8,414,298.82	17.0000	1,430,430.80
6. 8703235301	胜达2359CC轻型客车	65.00	辆	11,417,928.82	17.0000	1,941,047.90

金额人民币(大写) 贰仟肆佰壹拾叁万玖仟零陆拾玖元捌角玖分 合计(￥) ￥24,139,069.89

申请单位编号	1207280143	报关单编号	021220101120004485	填 制 单 位	收款国库(银行)
合同(批文)号	E1007A07A702-A07A7	运输工具(号)	ESRA		
缴款期限	2010年10月29日前	提/装货单号	EUKOULAB416965		

备注 一般贸易 照章征税 2010-10-7
国标代码：11010571785226XUSD 6.725
24,139,069.89

制单人 024458
复核人

第四联：（回执）由国库盖章后退回海关财务部门

从填发缴款书之日起限15日内缴纳(期末遇法定节假日顺延)，逾期按日征收税款总额万分之五的滞纳金。

海关税收突破万亿元专用缴款书

Special Payment Letter of Import Duty

2010年

2010年10月14日，中国海关征收关税、进口环节税、船舶吨税等总额突破1万亿人民币大关；2018年全国海关税收入库19727亿元，为增强中央财力做出了突出贡献。

查缉走私

Anti-smuggling

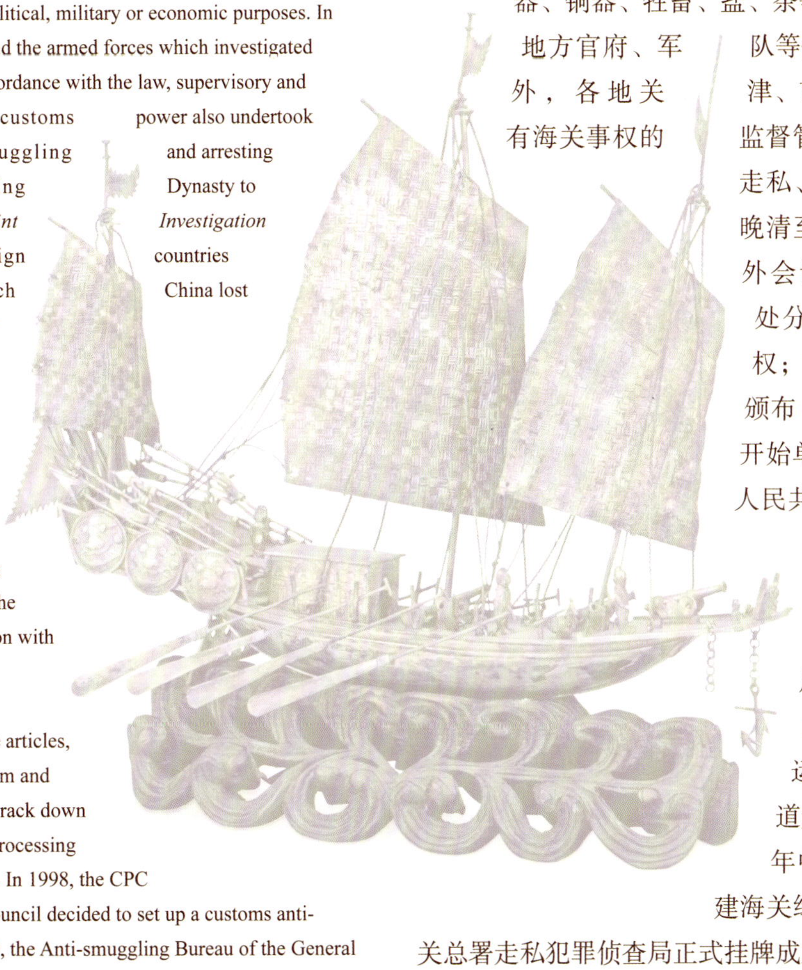

Anti-smuggling is one of the basic functions of the customs. Since the Western Zhou Dynasty, governments of dynasties had issued bans to manage and control the gold, silver, iron, copper ware, weapons, livestock, salt, tea and other important materials for political, military or economic purposes. In addition to the local governments and the armed forces which investigated and seized prohibited articles in accordance with the law, supervisory and administrative authorities with customs power also undertook the tasks of ensuring anti-smuggling and arresting smugglers. From the Late Qing Dynasty to the Beiyang Government, the *Joint Investigation Rules* between China and foreign countries was implemented, through which China lost its jurisdiction over punishment for violations and the final decision of cases. In June 1934, Nanjing National Government promulgated the *Customs Preventive Law*, through which customs started to independently handle smuggling cases. After the founding of the People's Republic of China, the customs strengthened the cooperation with frontier forces, Ministry of Public Security and other departments, to investigate smuggling of destructive articles, daily necessities, etc. After the reform and opening-up, the customs started to crack down smuggling in freight channels and processing trade channels and marine channels. In 1998, the CPC Central Committee and the State Council decided to set up a customs anti-smuggling police force, and in 1999, the Anti-smuggling Bureau of the General Administration of Customs was founded. The customs integrate administrative law enforcement and criminal law enforcement, and intensify pressure on smuggling, which have made important contributions to the maintenance of the state's foreign economic and trade order and the promotion of all-round economic and social development.

查缉走私是海关的基本职能之一。自西周起，历朝历代出于政治、军事、经济等目的，多次颁布禁令对金银、铁器、铜器、牲畜、盐、茶等重要物资实行管制。除地方官府、军队等依律对违禁物品进行查缉外，各地关津、市舶司、沿海四海关等具有海关事权的监督管理机构，亦承担着查缉走私、处罚走私人员的任务。晚清至北洋政府时期，实行中外会讯办法，我国丧失违章处分管辖权和案件最终裁决权；1934年6月南京国民政府颁布《海关缉私条例》，海关开始单独处理走私案件。中华人民共和国成立后，海关加强与边防部队、公安等部门合作，重点查处政治破坏性物品和日常生活用品等走私行为；改革开放后，海关严厉打击货运渠道走私、加工贸易渠道走私、海上走私等；1998年中共中央、国务院决定组建海关缉私警察队伍，1999年海关总署走私犯罪侦查局正式挂牌成立，海关综合行使行政执法、刑事执法两种手段，保持反走私高压态势，为维护国家对外经济贸易秩序、促进经济社会全面发展做出重要贡献。

“缉捕巡船”模型

Artwork of Anti-smuggling Ship

晚清时期

清代以广式帆船为原型制作的银质“缉捕巡船”模型。清代前期，各海关均设有巡哨船队，负责“稽查偷漏，而不征税”，功能类似近代的缉私艇。此模型取材于清朝广东水师查缉走私、维持港口水道和海上丝绸之路外销贸易秩序的船只。船身以锤揲、錾刻等技法精制而成，通体银质附原木座，船尾有“缉捕巡船”4字。甲板上设有火炮，两侧护板上置戟、矛，悬挂兽面纹藤编盾牌。

望远镜
Telescope
晚清时期

近代海关缉私时使用的望远镜。

海关关警训练所第二期结业纪念手册

Commemorative Handbook of the Second Customs Guard Training Camp

1948年

包括关警队分布地域图、人员通讯录以及长官、教官、职员留言页。近代海关成立初期，因查私任务繁重，各关大多根据当地实际情况建立了武装缉私队伍，有些称为巡缉队或关勇队，有些叫作关警队或港警队，业务量特别大的关区还建立了两个以上的武装缉私队。

关警进关后，均须参加关警训练班，接受英式训练，包括列队、射击、山地缉私技巧等，考验合格后方可上岗。海关总税务司署在上海成立了全国性的关警培训基地，配备专职教官进行训练，有时还选派关警前往香港警察学校接受强化训练。九龙关、江海关等关区也设立了各自的关警培训基地。

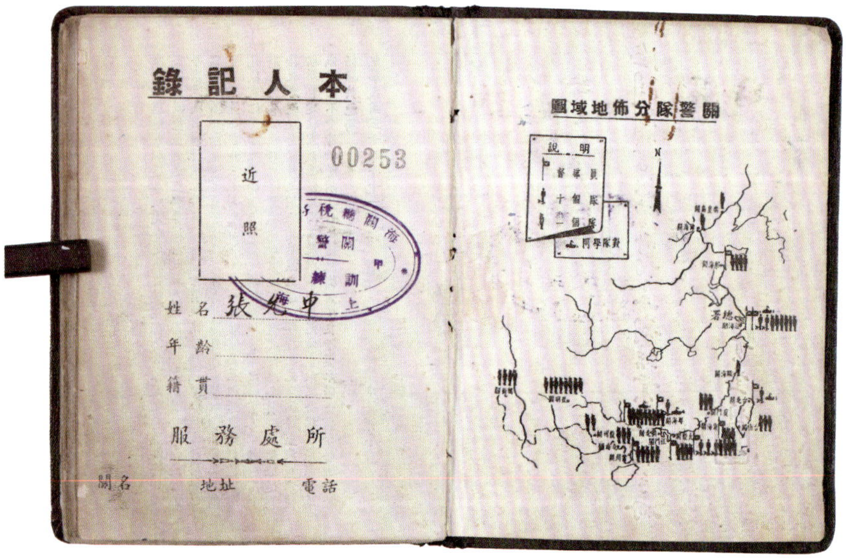

禁烟督察处上海市办事处私土毒品收据

Receipt for the Seized Opium, Issued by Shanghai office of Opium Suppression Bureau

1936年

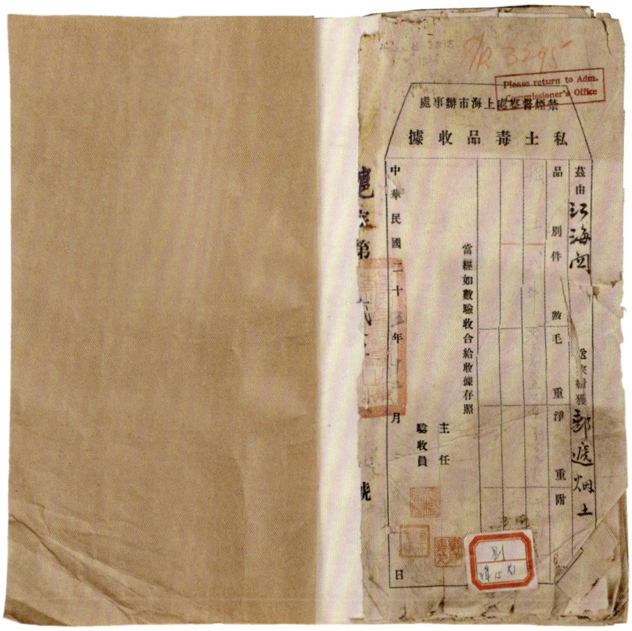
禁烟督察处上海市办事处
私土毒品收据
Please return to Adm. Commissioner's Office

江海关缉获毒品上交禁烟督察处的收据。1934年5月，国民政府军事委员会设立禁烟督察处，接办禁烟督察事宜，并掌控烟草税。同年6月，国民政府颁布《海关缉私条例》，规定海关统一对私货进行依法处理的职权，但对缉获毒品、军火等特殊物品的处理另有规定。同年9月，关务署转发财政部训令，对海关缉获的鸦片及大麻等毒品，指定交由禁烟督察处统一处理。

“永安号”巡艇报警钟

Ship Bell on the “WING ON” Anti-smuggling Boat

1948年

九龙关“永安号”缉私艇上的铜钟。1934年，海关缉私舰队正式建立，有大小缉私舰37 艘、缉私艇数十艘。1937年，抗战全面爆发，沿海地区相继沦陷，各关均停止海上缉私工作。抗战胜利后，海关购买美军退役舰艇60多艘，重建华中、华南和华北缉私舰队，其中华南缉私舰队基地设在九龙关。

走私西药密报信封

Envelop of a Confidential Letter Reporting a Smuggling Case

1949年

线人发给江海关税务司的缉私密报。各通商口岸新关设立后，为收集当地走私情报和线索，各关除了派出关员穿着平民服装明察暗访外，还鼓励商人、民众等密报有关私运、私销及私藏走私物品的情形，并承诺海关将对提供线报的人员保守秘密，并给予奖励。对派出的化装侦探，各关规定在内部文函中不得提及其身份和其他信息，严格保护暗访人员信息和安全。

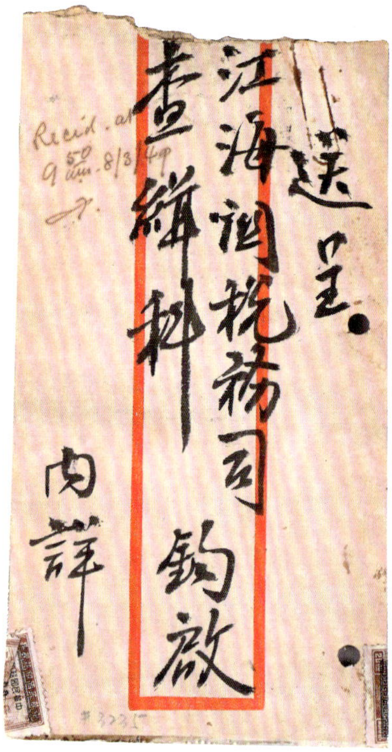

《在反走私战线上》电影胶片

Filmstrip of *On the Anti-Smuggling Front*

1979年

1979年，外贸部海关管理局将全国海关反走私斗争展览摄制成《在反走私战线上》影片在全国各地放映，加大反走私宣传力度。

“海关902”艇

Revenue Cutter 902

20世纪晚期

“902艇”长58.5米、宽7.8米，总排水量400吨，最大航速29.5节。1989年在拱北海关服役，2009年退役。服役20年间，“902艇”共航行28万海里，查获海上走私案件总案值3.5亿元，为打击海上走私立下了赫赫战功；并且在服役过程中先后45次安全接送党和国家领导人，为中央领导同志视察特区工作、指导改革开放事业做出了贡献。1992年1月23日，邓小平同志乘坐它从深圳前往珠海，在1小时45分钟的航程中，发表了著名的“南方谈话”的一部分，为中国的改革开放指明了方向。

1992年邓小平同志乘坐“海关902”艇发表“南方谈话”时的座椅。

打私成果
Anti-smuggling Achievements

海关查获藏私物品
Smuggled Items

20世纪50年代

20世纪50年代，海关查获的藏有手表的椰子壳、竹篮、脸盆等，是当时日用品走私的证据。

剑齿虎头骨化石

Smilodon Skull Fossil

中至上新世

中国海关缉私成果。剑齿虎是史前时期最大的猫科动物，或因气候和物种间竞争而灭绝。

孔子鸟化石

Confuciusornis Fossil

早白垩世

中国海关缉私成果。孔子鸟是白垩纪古鸟属，目前已知最早拥有无齿角质喙部的鸟类。

满洲龟及北票鲟化石

Manchurochelys Fossil / Peipiao Sturgeon Fossil

早白垩世

中国海关缉私成果。满洲龟生活在晚侏罗纪至早白垩纪时期，多分布于辽宁省北票地区。北票鲟属软骨硬鳞鱼类，内骨骼为软骨质，外骨骼（鳞片）退化，化石多发现于辽宁北票地区白垩纪地层中。

潜龙化石

Hyphalosaurus Fossil

早白垩世

中国海关缉私成果。潜龙一般生活在淡水湖泊中，成年体长约1米，头颅和躯体较小，脖子和尾巴较长。潜龙化石常见于白垩纪晚期至始新世。

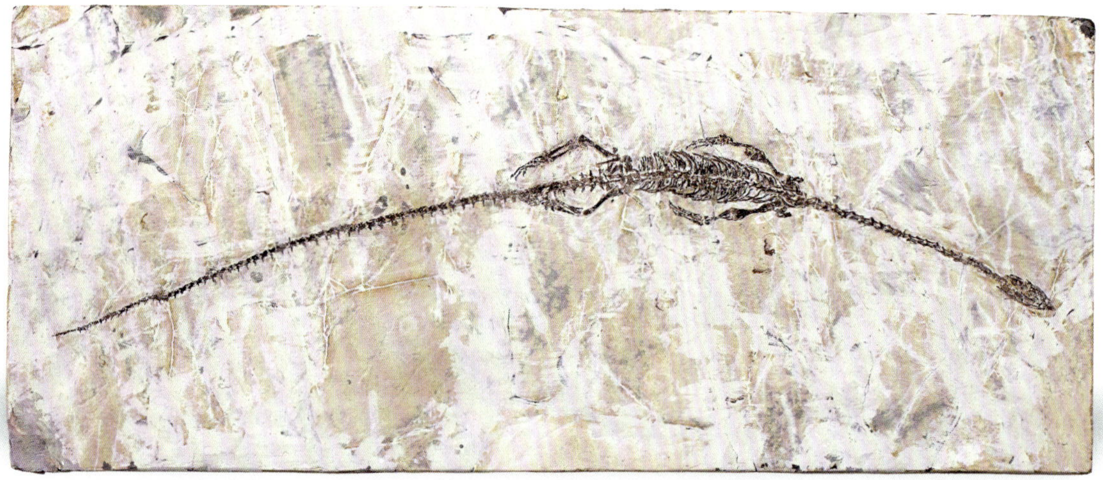

恐龙牙化石

Dinosaur Tooth Fossil

不晚于白垩纪

中国海关缉私成果。恐龙的骨骼和牙齿等坚硬部分是由矿物质构成的，在地下往往会分解和重新结晶，变得更为坚硬，这一过程被称为"石化过程"。随着上面沉积物的不断增厚，遗体越埋越深，最终变成了化石。

东北虎皮

Manchurian Tiger Skin

2002年

中国海关缉私成果。东北虎为国家一级保护动物。2002年10月，哈尔滨海关查获正在交易东北虎虎皮、虎骨的犯罪嫌疑人。经审讯，黑龙江省密山市刘某早年在俄罗斯务工时在山上设套捕猎，误毙一只东北虎。刘某通过过境货车夹藏的方式将虎皮、虎骨运回家中，并伺机贩卖。

狐狸皮

Fox Skin

2013年

中国海关缉私成果。狐狸皮是一种制裘原料皮。主要品种有红狐皮、蓝狐皮、白狐皮、银狐皮等几个品种。2013年11月，汕头海关破获一起涉嫌以伪报贸易性质走私高档皮草的大案，案值约76亿元，查扣涉嫌走私水貂皮、狐狸皮等皮草约100万张。

玳瑁

Hawksbill Specimen

2001年

中国海关缉私成果。玳瑁为国家二级保护动物。

八灵博局镜

Bronze Mirror with Eight Gods and Bo-Ju Pattern

汉代

中国海关缉私成果。博局镜又名规矩镜，主要流行于汉代中期，包括西汉末期至王莽时期，是汉代铜镜中流行时间最长的一种。因其表面有规则的TLV形装饰，也被外国学者称为TLV镜。此铜镜四柿蒂纹钮座，上镌刻有“长宜子孙”铭文，方框四角各饰一花瓣纹。内区四乳、TLV俱全，除青龙、白虎、朱雀、玄武外，还各配一瑞兽，推测是烛照、太阴幽荧、应龙和黄龙，故称八灵；外区饰锯齿纹、弦纹。

青铜犀牛尊

Bronze Rhinoceros

清代

中国海关缉私成果。尊是商周时期用于盛放酒的器皿，其后也逐渐成为礼器，此件清代犀牛尊应该是“复古”“崇古”之风背景下的产物，并非实用器。

鎏金宗喀巴像

Gilding Figure of Tsongkhapa

清代

中国海关缉私成果。宗喀巴是藏传佛教格鲁派的创立者，整顿戒律和教风、建立学院式寺院，著有密宗论著《菩提道次第广论》。

宗喀巴坐像

Figure of Tsongkhapa

清代

中国海关缉私成果。宗喀巴本名罗桑扎巴，元至正十七年生于青海湟中（藏语称湟中为“宗喀”）。上师圆寂时将自己的衣帽传给弟子贾曹杰。藏传佛教史上将宗喀巴大师、贾曹杰、克主杰合称为“师徒三尊”。此尊上师像头戴僧帽，身披袈裟，双手于胸前结说法印，金刚坐于莲花座之上。

财神多闻天王像

God of Wealth Vaisravana Figure

清代

中国海关缉私成果。四大天王，又称护世四天王，是来源于印度教神话的护法天神，后被佛教纳入体系中，分别是东方持国天王、南方增长天王、西方广目天王和北方多闻天王。此尊佛像应是北方多闻天王，又名毗沙门，是古印度的财神，佛像头戴宝冠，右手持宝幢，左手握一银鼠，老鼠口中吐出宝珠，天王呈游戏坐姿态。

释迦牟尼唐卡

Thangka of Sakyamuni

清代

中国海关缉私成果。释迦牟尼是佛教徒对佛教创始人的尊称。早期小乘佛教将释迦牟尼看作是指导人生解脱之路的唯一导师，到了大乘佛教时期，释迦牟尼则被极度“神”化。此唐卡主佛为释迦牟尼佛结金刚坐于绘有雪白狮子的须弥座上，左手施禅定印，右手施触地印，身侧有阿难、迦叶两位尊者随侍左右。

马头明王唐卡

Thangka of Hayagriva

清代

中国海关缉私成果。马头明王，又称马头金刚，是观音的其中一种化身，密宗认为其是六观音之一，也有认为是无量寿佛的忿怒相。此唐卡绘三面六臂马头明王与佛母像，左侧手臂从下至上依次拿花、天杖、钺，右侧手臂从下至上依次拿颅碗、宝剑、绳索。

彩绘象牙马

Painted Ivory Horses

现代

中国海关缉私成果。圆雕、浮雕、镂雕、填彩、染色等牙雕技法在清代已广泛应用，特别是称为“茜色”的染色工艺在当时具有重要地位和影响。这两尊象牙马延续了圆雕、浮雕、染色等工艺，并配有如意云纹木座。

象牙镂雕云龙纹小圆盒

Ivory Hollow Carving of Small Round Box with Cloud and Dragon Pattern

清代

中国海关缉私成果。此圆盒采用镂雕技法雕刻出“一龙三现”的样式，子母口扣合，盒盖、盒身皆有纹饰。

白釉刻花牡丹纹瓷枕

White Glazed Porcelain Pillow with Peony Pattern

金代

中国海关缉私成果。瓷枕是中国古代瓷器中较为流行的造型之一，创烧于隋代，唐代以后开始大量生产，盛行于宋代。此件瓷枕枕面阴勾单线边栏，内部剔刻折枝牡丹纹，剔地部分露出化妆土，白中泛灰，此类品种在河北、河南、山西的一些瓷窑中可见。

齐白石《山水图》折扇

Folding Fan *Landscape* by Qi Baishi

近代

中国海关缉私成果。齐白石为近现代国画大师，其书工篆隶，取法于秦汉碑版，行书饶古拙之趣，篆刻自成一家。

溥心畬《山水图》

Landscape by Pu Xinyu

近代

中国海关缉私成果。溥心畬原名爱新觉罗·溥儒，为清恭亲王奕䜣之孙，初字仲衡，改字心畬，著名书画家、收藏家。绘画擅山水、人物、花卉，与张大千有“南张北溥”之誉，又与吴湖帆并称“南吴北溥”。

陶鬲

Li Pot

新石器时代晚期

中国海关缉私成果。鬲是一种饪食器，出现于新石器时代，商周时期继续流行。作为实用器皿时，在三个袋状足下燃火煮食；作为陪葬明器则会将表面磨光，甚至偶有施红彩或白彩。

白玉蝴蝶

White Jade Butterfly

明代

中国海关缉私成果。单面阴刻蝴蝶纹样，表面有少量沁色。

象牙雕荷莲观音

Ivory Carving of Avalokitesvara Sitting on the Lotus

20世纪晚期

中国海关缉私成果。其采用整根象牙抛光、雕刻，主体是观音立于盘龙之上，身后背光有莲花数朵。

象牙雕盘凤观音

Ivory Carving of Avalokitesvara with Coiling Phoenix

20世纪晚期

中国海关缉私成果。其由整根象牙雕刻而成，观音立于竹林云端，身后为凤凰飞翔于云端以及竹林的背景。

象牙雕“群仙贺寿”

Ivory Carving of “Birthday Celebration by Immortals”

20世纪晚期

中国海关缉私成果。其由整根象牙雕刻张果老、蓝采和、韩湘子、吕洞宾等八仙，降龙伏虎等众罗汉以及寿星等群仙贺寿的场景。

象牙雕月季山石盆景

Ivory Carving of Chinese Rose and Rock Bonsai

现代

中国海关缉私成果。象牙以圆雕、透雕成太湖石月季桃花小景。

象牙雕“多子多孙”

Ivory Carving of “Having Many Sons and Grandsons”

现代

中国海关缉私成果。以镂雕和圆雕相结合表现了石榴树下几个孩童正撒网捕鱼，渔网之下朵朵莲花象征“连年有余”，石榴又有着“多子多孙”的寓意。

象牙雕竹菊山石盆景

Ivory Carving of Bamboo, Chrysanthemum, and Rock Bonsai

现代

中国海关缉私成果。象牙圆雕盆景，翠竹与斧劈石相映成趣，满地菊花和水仙错落有致。

驼鹿头骨及角

Moose Skull and Horn

2002年

中国海关缉私成果。驼鹿为国家二级保护动物。

犀牛角

Rhinoceros Horn

现代

中国海关缉私成果。犀牛属国际保护的珍稀濒危动物，从1993年起，国家禁止犀牛角贸易，并取消了犀牛角用药标准，对出售、运输、携带和邮寄犀牛角的行为都要依法查处。

红珊瑚

Red Coral

现代

中国海关缉私成果。重2560克。红珊瑚由生长在温暖海域的珊瑚虫堆积而成，因生长缓慢，质地莹润，与珍珠、琥珀并列为三大有机宝石，又被列为佛教七宝之一。由于红珊瑚的稀有性与不可再生性，极具收藏价值，近年来屡遭盗采破坏，属国家一级重点保护濒危野生动物。根据《濒危野生动植物种国际贸易公约》《中华人民共和国海关法》《中华人民共和国野生动植物保护法》等法律法规的规定，邮寄、携带、托运红珊瑚等野生动植物及其制品出入国境，必须持有允许进出口证明、并向出入境海关申报。

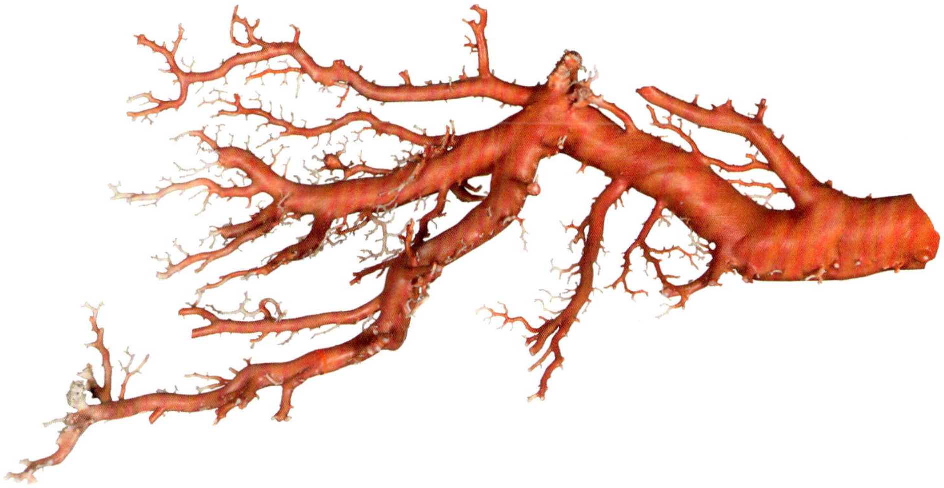

独角鲸牙

Narwhal Ivory

现代

中国海关缉私成果。长213.5厘米。独角鲸，又称一角鲸，多生活于加拿大北部和格陵兰岛西部的海湾和水湾，左上颚突出唇外犬齿，长度一般可达2米至3米，呈现螺旋状。《濒临绝种野生动植物国际贸易公约》将独角鲸列入监控，并且管制其长牙的交易。

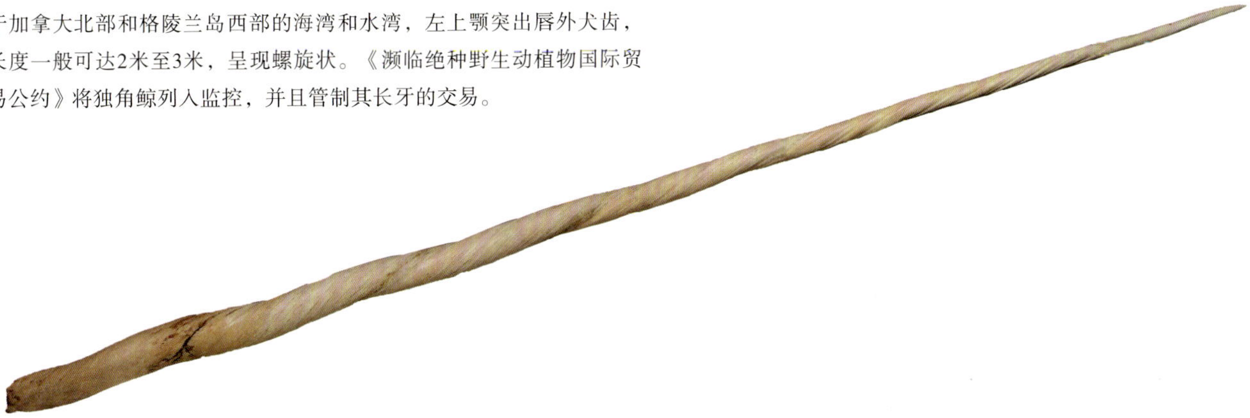

海关统计

Customs Statistics

Statistical work is one of the basic functions of the customs. Customs statistics started in 1859. In 1873, the Statistical Department was set up, which was designed to regularly compile and publish the monthly, quarterly and annual Returns and Reports of the Foreign Trade of China as well as the *Decennial Report*. Their content involved politics, economy, military affairs, society, culture, etc. Therefore, it had become an important source of information and intelligence for Western powers to loot China's strategic resources. However, it also provides systematic and reliable historical data for the study of China's modern economic and social development. After the founding of the People's Republic of China, the customs conducted the statistical work on import and export goods trade and customs affairs according to law. Starting with 1981, customs statistical data have become the data of import and export trade published by China, which is very important for national macroeconomic regulation and control, trade policy and measure formulation, and customs administration in aiding decision-making, monitoring, early warning and supervision.

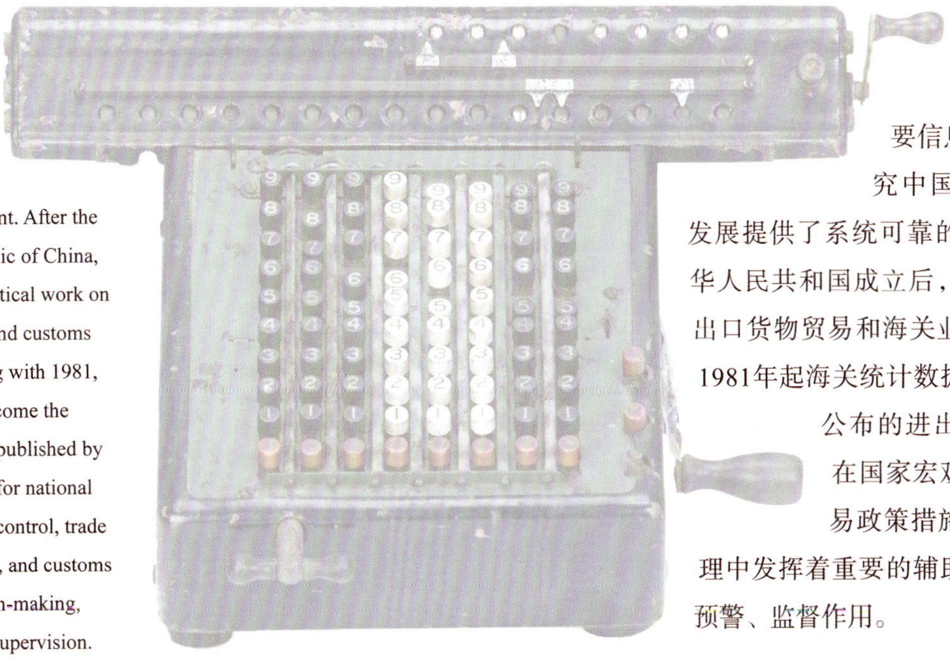

统计是海关的基本职能之一。海关统计始自1859年，1873年海关总税务司署设立造册处（1932年后改称统计科），专门负责定期汇编出版各通商口岸贸易总册、华洋贸易论略和月报、季报、年报等刊物以及《各埠海关十年报告》，其内容涉及政治、经济、军事、社会、文化等方面，成为西方列强掌控掠夺中国战略资源的重要信息情报，也为研究中国近代经济社会发展提供了系统可靠的历史资料。中华人民共和国成立后，海关依法对进出口货物贸易和海关业务进行统计。1981年起海关统计数据成为我国对外公布的进出口贸易数据，在国家宏观经济调控、贸易政策措施制定和海关管理中发挥着重要的辅助决策和监测、预警、监督作用。

《海关华洋贸易总册》

Returns of Trade and Trade Reports

20世纪初期

清末民初的中外贸易统计总册。晚清时期，海关即开始统计进出口贸易数据，各关上交总税务司署，由海关造册处汇总出版。

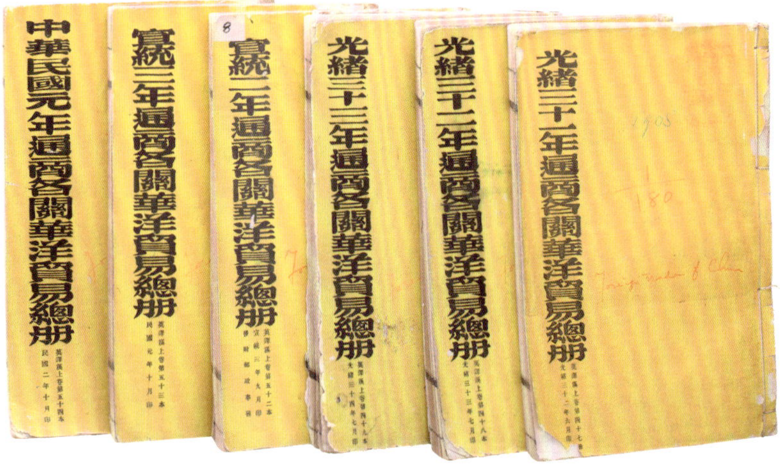

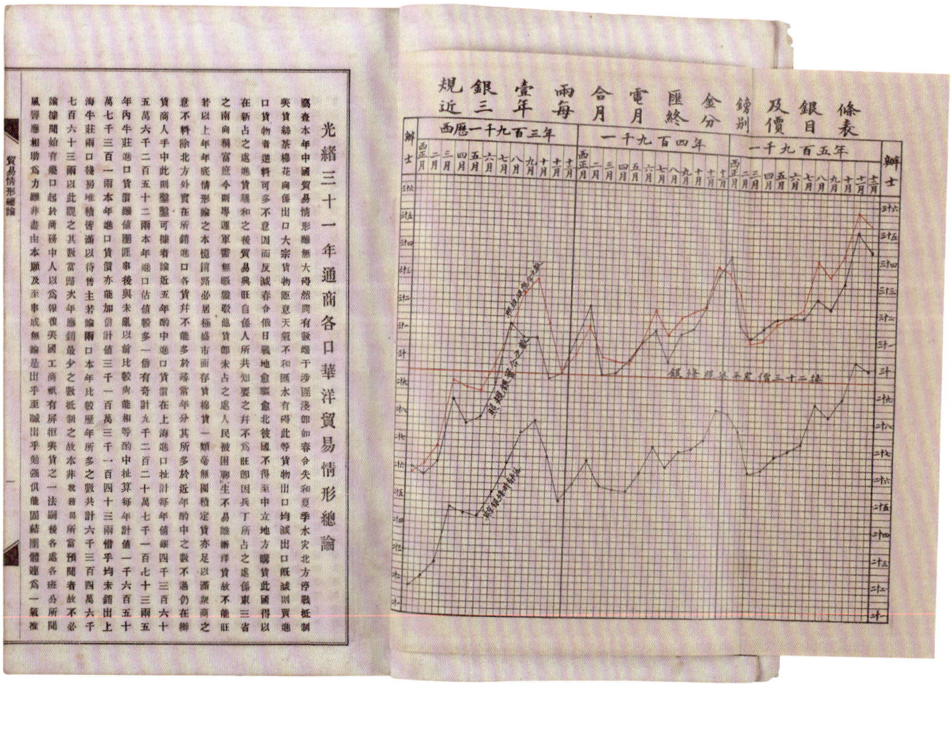

《中国药物目录》

List of Chinese Medicines

1889年

用中文、英文或拉丁文对照的形式分别列出1884年11月1日至1885年10月31日19个海关出口的中药材名称、产地、质量、价格和输出地。

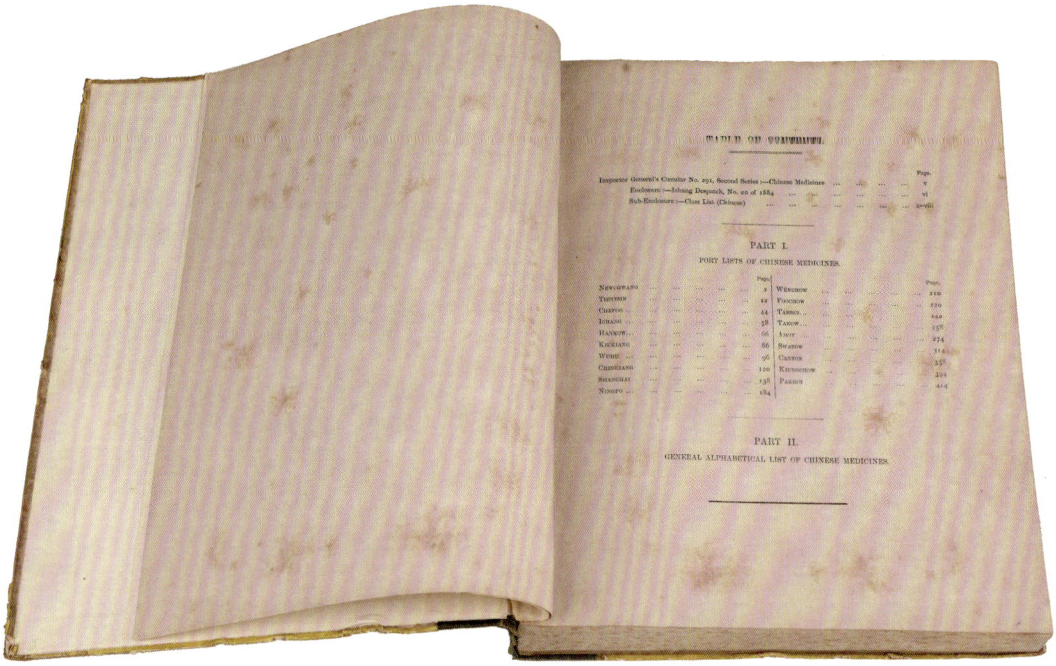

《十年报告》

Decennial Report

1882年至1931年

光绪八年（1882年），各关税务司应总税务司赫德之命编写并上报各口岸及所在地区自同治十一年（1872年）起至当年的贸易报告，并由总税务司署汇总印刷出版。自此，开始以10年为周期编印出版《各埠海关十年报告》，民国时期改为《最近十年各埠海关报告》，简称《十年报告》。报告以文字为主，贸易统计数据为附属内容，涵盖了各口岸及所在或附近省份10年来社会生活、政治经济、文化教育等方方面面的变迁，当时既为西方列强提供了重要信息情报，也为学术研究留存了系统可靠的历史资料。1941年，受战争影响，《十年报告》编制被迫中断，1947年12月停止编写《十年报告》。

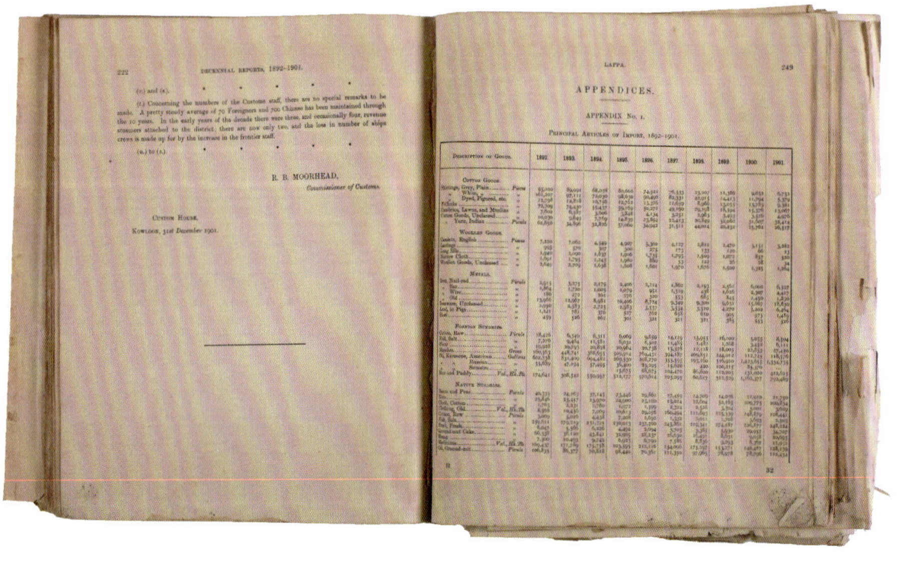

《一九四九年中国对外贸易报告》

China Foreign Trade Report in 1949

1950年

中华人民共和国中央人民政府海关总署1950年编印，为中华人民共和国海关的第一份年度对外贸易报告。

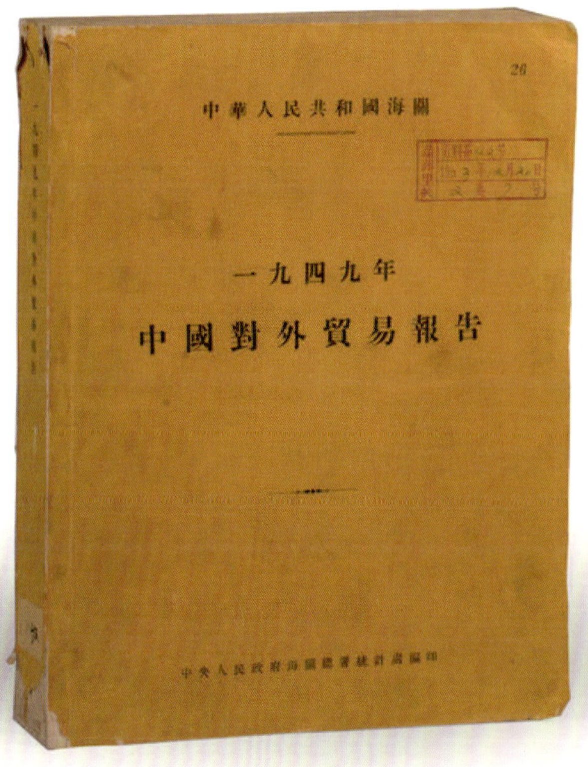

手摇计算器

Hand-powered Calculator

20世纪20年代至40年代

20世纪20年代以前，各关编制各类进出口贸易统计均以人工操作或使用算盘作为辅助。1923年，江海关首次购买手摇计算器用于海关税收等统计的编制工作。1931年，为加入国际贸易统计公约以提高统计地位，海关总税务司署决定购买国外进口的专用统计机器，在上海统一编制海关进出口贸易统计，大幅提高了工作效率和准确性。

磁带、磁盘

Tape and Disk

20世纪70年代末至80年代

用于转录各地海关统计资料的信息载体。

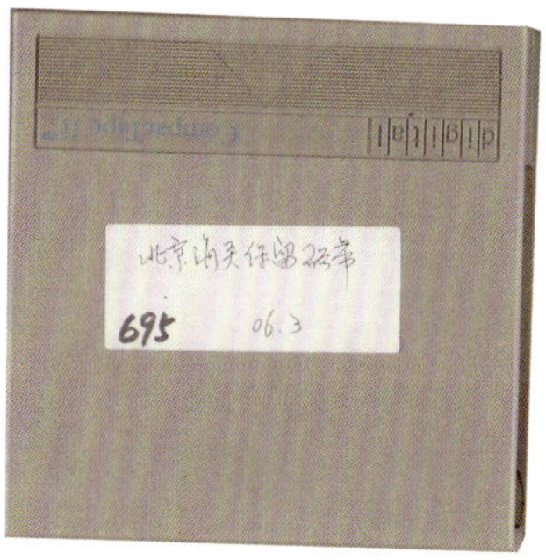

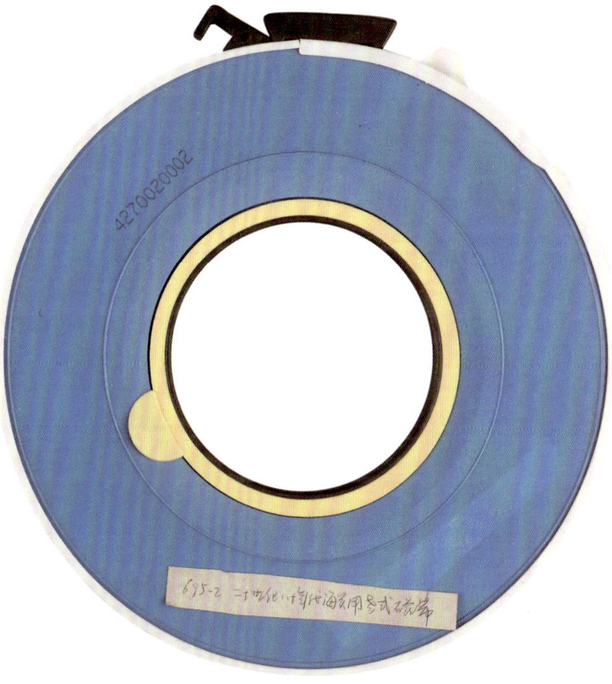

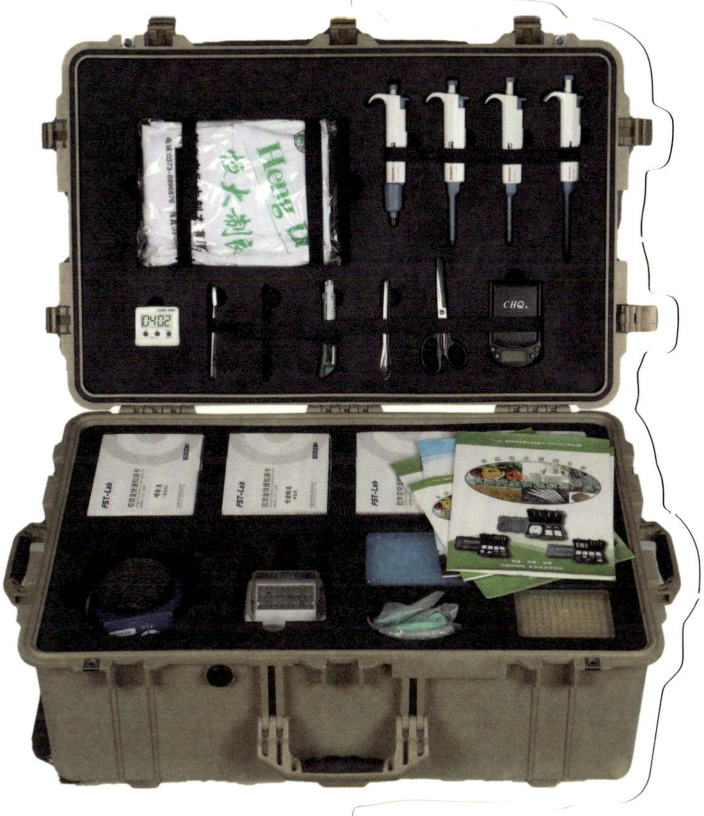

检验检疫

Inspection and Quarantine

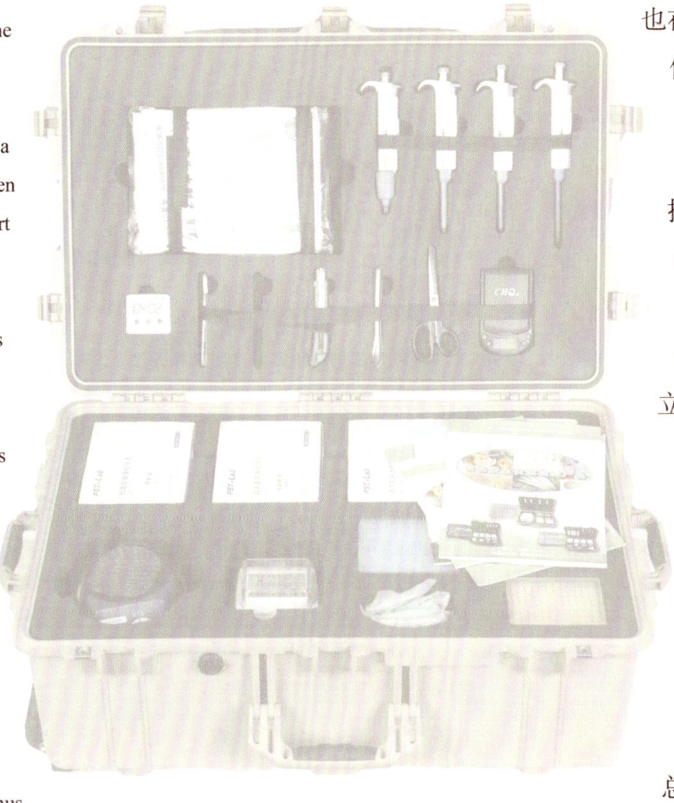

我国检验检疫历史悠久，《周礼》、秦律中就有对商品质量、入境动物等进行检验检疫的法律规定，历代边境互市、市舶贸易场所的“牙人”“驵侩”等也在一定程度上从事了相关工作，但未形成成熟的制度和管理体系。近代海关兼办海务港务期间施行了一系列海港卫生检疫措施。国民政府成立后，开始自设机构、颁布法律法规进行进出境商品、动植物和卫生检验检疫工作。中华人民共和国成立后，进出口商品检验、出入境动植物检疫、国境卫生检疫、进出口食品安全机构名称及隶属关系多次变更。1998年3月“三检合一”成立国家出入境检验检疫局，由海关总署管理；2001年4月，国家出入境检验检疫局划归国家质检总局；2018年4月，原质检总局的出入境检验检疫管理职责和队伍划归海关总署统一管理。

The inspection and quarantine processes in China have a long history. Legal provisions on the inspection and quarantine of commodity quality, entry animals, etc. appeared in the *Rites of the Zhou* Dynasty and the law of the Qin Dynasty. “Brokers” or “middlemen” of different dynasties in frontier trade and marine trade were engaged in relevant work, but no mature systems or management systems were formed. Modern customs implemented a series of port health quarantine measures when they concurrently handled the marine and port affairs. After its establishment, the National Government of the Republic of China set up organs and promulgated laws and regulations to conduct the inspection and quarantine of entry-exit commodities, animals and plants, and health. After the founding of the People’s Republic of China, the name and affiliation of the organ responsible for import and export commodity inspection, entry-exit animal and plant quarantine, frontier health quarantine, and import and export food safety have changed many times. In March 1998, “commodity inspection, animal and plant quarantine and health quarantine were integrated into one”, and thus State Administration for Entry-exit Inspection and Quarantine was set up, which was under the administration of General Administration of Customs, P.R. China. In April 2001, State Administration for Entry-exit Inspection and Quarantine was put under the administration of General Administration of Quality Supervision, Inspection and Quarantine of the People’s Republic of China (AQSIQ). In April 2018, the function and work force of inspection and quarantine of the AQSIQ were put under the unified administration of General Administration of Customs. P. R. China.

国境卫生检疫
Frontier Health Quarantine

秦律中已有我国对国境检疫和处置的记载，但至近代仍未形成成熟制度和体系。1873年为防止疫病传播，上海、厦门海关首先开始采取海港检疫措施。此后，各关逐步开展检疫业务。1930年，检疫业务移交国民政府卫生部海港检疫处。抗日战争期间，部分沿海沿江港口的检疫事务暂由该口海关接管。中华人民共和国成立后，国境卫生检疫部门承担出入境卫生检疫、疫情监测、卫生监督等工作，在维护人民群众健康和生命安全、促进对外经济贸易发展等方面发挥了重要作用。

Frontier quarantine and disposal were recorded in the law of the Qin Dynasty, but no mature institutions and systems had been formed until modern times. In 1873, in order to prevent the spread of epidemics, Shanghai and Amoy customs first began to take quarantine measures at harbors. Since then, all customs gradually conducted quarantine measures. In 1930, the quarantine affairs was handed over to the Harbor Quarantine Bureau of the Ministry of Health of the National Government. During the Anti-Japanese War, the quarantine affairs of some coastal ports and ports along rivers were temporarily taken over by the customs of these ports. After the founding of the People's Republic of China, frontier health quarantine departments were responsible for entry-exit health quarantine, epidemic monitoring and health supervision, etc., which had played an important role in safeguarding people's health and life and promoting the development of foreign economic and trade cooperation.

上海海港检疫所收入传票

Receipt of the Shanghai Harbor Quarantine Station

民国时期

江海关自1873年起开始办理检疫业务，并于1899年在吴淞口外崇宝沙（位于上海市宝山区以北、崇明岛以南，现坍没于长江中）设立华洋检疫所，以检验来自鼠疫疫区的船舶。1930年7月，南京国民政府卫生署在上海建立全国海港检疫管理处，并设立上海海港检疫所。检疫所以检疫查验为主，注重鼠疫、霍乱、天花、斑疹伤寒及黄热病5种传染病的监测，之后业务逐渐扩展，除了监测以外，还为出入境人员接种预防天花、霍乱等的疫苗。

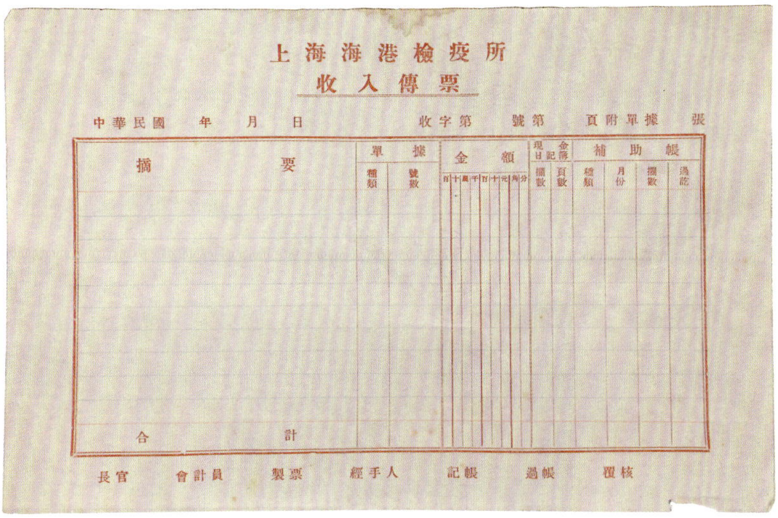
上海海港檢疫所
收入傳票
中華民國　年　月　日　收字第　號第　頁附單據　張
摘要 | 單據（種類、號數） | 金額（百、十、萬、千、百、十、元、角、分） | 現金日記簿（欄數、頁數） | 補助帳（種類、月份、欄數、過訖）
合計
長官　會計員　製票　經手人　記帳　過帳　覆核

除鼠及免予除鼠船只报告表

Report Form of Ship's Deratization and Exemption from Deratization Issued by the Harbor Quarantine Station

民国时期

民国时期海港检疫所使用的工作表。

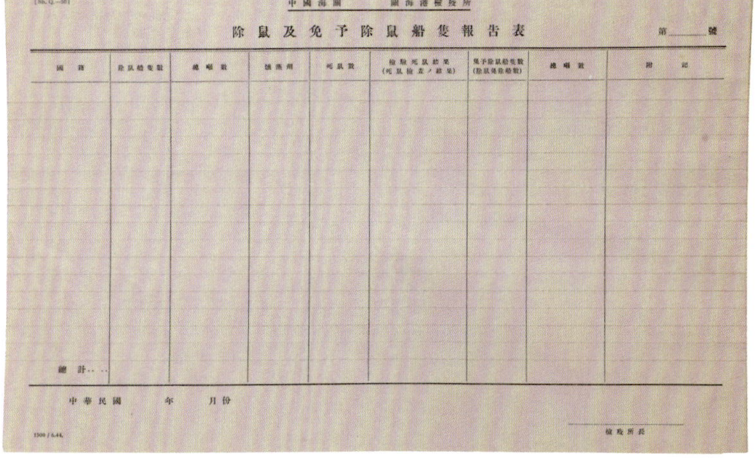
中國海關　關海港檢疫所
除鼠及免予除鼠船隻報告表　第　號
國籍 | 除鼠船隻數 | 總噸數 | 燻蒸劑 | 死鼠數 | 檢驗死鼠結果（死鼠檢查之結果） | 免予除鼠船隻數（除鼠免除船數） | 總噸數 | 附記
總計
中華民國　年　月份
檢疫所長

《上海口防护染疫章程》

Sanitary Regulations for the Port of Shanghai

1913年

鸦片战争后，我国口岸被迫相继打开，随着对外海运迅速发展，传染病传入危险日益加深。为防止印度和东南亚的霍乱传入，江海关税务司于1873年制订方案，开始对来自疫区口岸的船只采取检疫措施，在此方案上形成了《上海口防护染疫章程》。厦门关税务司也拟定了《厦门口岸保护传染瘟疫章程》，此后，其他海港也纷纷开办检疫业务，但几乎都由海关派医官办理，各港口检疫章程亦由各港海关监督会商各国领事制订，全国没有统一法规。

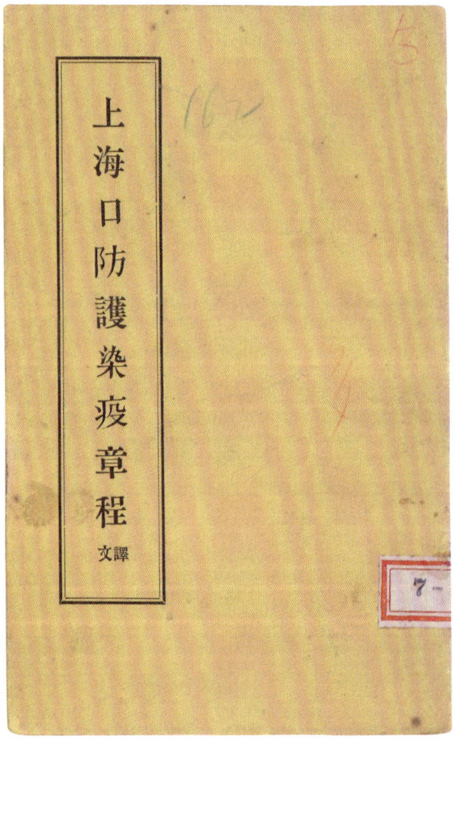

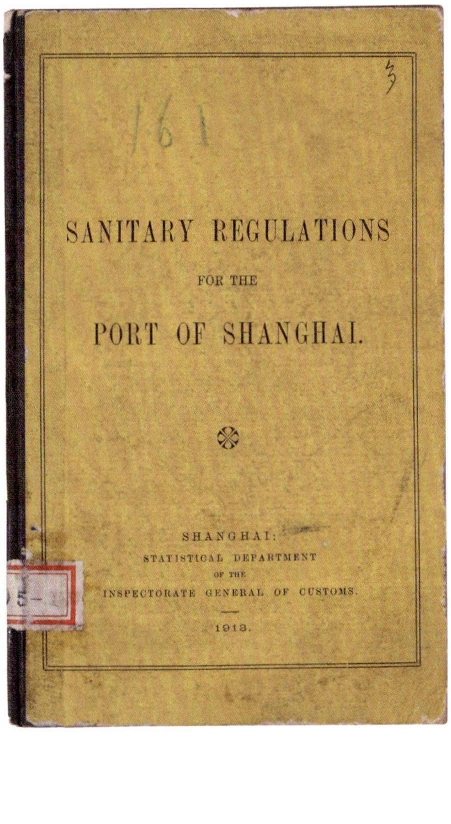

《海港检疫章程》

Harbor Quarantine Regulations

1930年

1912年，东三省防疫事务总处成立，负责领导东三省检疫工作，随后提出“中国人自己办检疫”的主张。在南京召开的第一次全国卫生会议上，东北鼠防管理处处长伍连德正式提出从海关收回检疫所的要求。1930年7月，经南京国民政府批准，全国海港检疫管理处在上海成立，收回全国各地海港检疫所，公布了《海港检疫章程》《海港检疫、消毒蒸熏及收费规则》《海港检疫标志旗帜及制服规则》。自此，各检疫机构有了统一的检疫法规，开始共同开展船舶蒸熏除鼠、消毒等其他调查研究，使全国的海港检疫事业有了进一步发展。

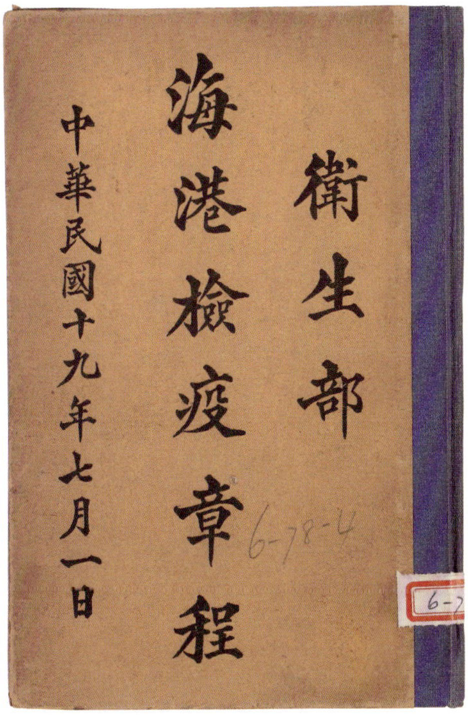

原卫生检疫制服

Old Uniform for Health Quarantine Officer

20世纪晚期

“三检合一”前，国境卫生检疫工作人员制服。该制服佩戴1990年10月国境卫生检疫系统启用的新制服标志：蛇杖肩章、领花、纽扣。

病毒模型

Virus Propagation Model

现代

裂谷热病毒（Rift Valley Fever Virus）经蚊虫传播，可感染动物和人。该病毒可引起反刍动物流产，而且患病幼崽死亡率近100%，历史上裂谷热病毒曾对畜牧业造成多次重创。人感染后通常出现发热、头痛、出血、休克等症状，严重者甚至死亡。

黄热病毒（Yellow Fever Virus）能够引起黄热病，主要通过伊蚊叮咬传播。临床以高热、头痛、黄疸、蛋白尿、相对缓脉和出血等为主要表现。由于黄热病的死亡率高且传染性强，已纳入世界卫生组织规定的检疫传染病之一。

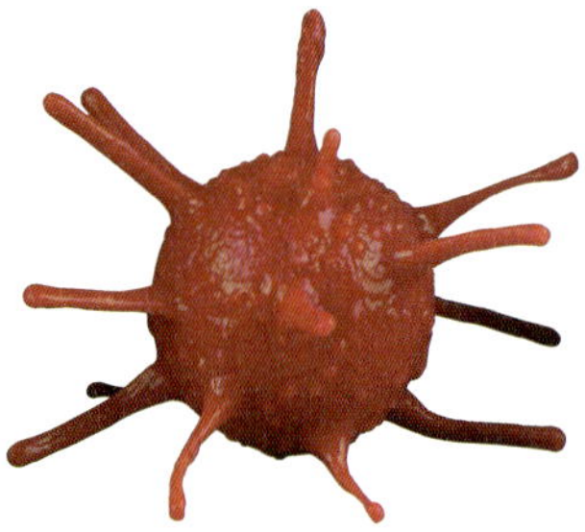

黄热病毒模型

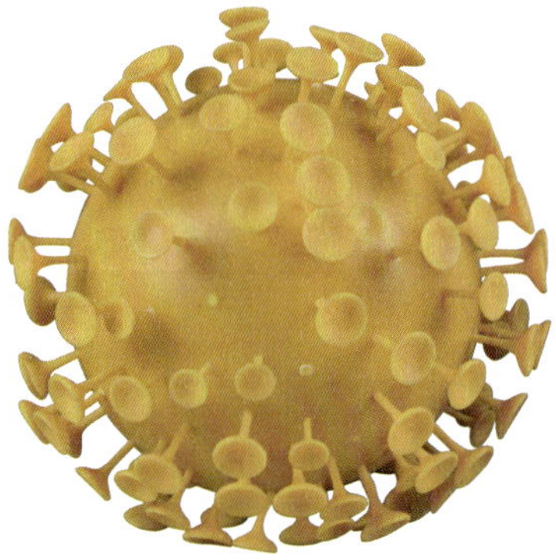

裂谷热病毒模型

防护服

Protective Suit

现代

在对口岸传染病可疑病例的排查处置中，卫生检疫人员须穿着防护服以确保健康、安全，避免受到外界传染病可疑病例、外环境的污染，从而预防感染传染病致病因子。

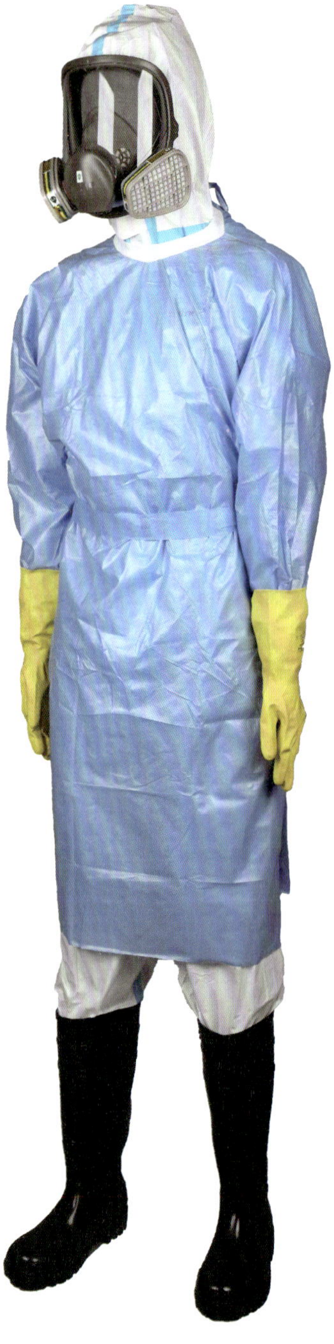

熏蒸防护工具箱

Fumigation Protection Kit

现代

熏蒸检疫工作中配备的防护工具箱，箱内包含防护面罩、3号滤毒罐等常用工具。由于熏蒸时多使用剧毒气体，因此熏蒸作业开始前应充分贴合佩戴防护面罩等，避免熏蒸作业人员中毒。

出入境动植物检疫

Entry-Exit Animal and Plant Quarantine

秦律中已有我国对入境动物检疫和处置的记载，但至近代仍未形成成熟制度和体系。1903年，近代第一处官办动物检疫场所在中东铁路局设立。20世纪20年代，南京国民政府先后自设机构、颁布条例和细则，标志着近代官方系统管理出入境动植物检疫的开端。中华人民共和国成立后，出入境动植物检疫部门依法对出入境动植物及其产品进行检验检疫、监督管理，并组织风险分析和预防，在保护国门生物安全和生态安全、保护农林牧渔业生产和人民身体健康、促进对外贸易发展等方面发挥了重要作用。

Entry-Exit animal and plant quarantine and disposal were recorded in the law of the Qin Dynasty, but no mature institutions and systems had been formed until modern times. In 1903, the first modern government-run animal quarantine site was set up in the Chinese Eastern Railway Bureau. In the 1920s, Nanjing National Government set up its own organs and promulgated regulations and detailed rules, which marked the beginning of modern official system to manage entry-exit animal and plant quarantine. After the founding of the People's Republic of China, the entry-exit animal and plant quarantine departments conducted inspection, quarantine, supervision and administration of entry-exit animals and plants and their products in accordance with the law. Risk analysis and prevention was also organized. All those have played an important role in safeguarding the biosecurity and ecological safety of our country, protecting the production of agriculture, forestry, animal husbandry and fishery and people's health, and promoting the development of foreign trade.

南方菟丝子标本

Specimen of Cuscuta Australis R.Br

现代

菟丝子是一种生理构造特殊的寄生植物，它所寄生的植物范围很广，其他植物和作物被寄生后，不仅产量减少、品质降低，而且增加了感染植物病毒的风险。

假臭草标本

Specimen of Eupatorium Catarium Veldk

现代

一种入侵植物，原产于南美洲，中国境内首次发现是在20世纪80年代的中国香港，20世纪90年代之后陆续在深圳、广州被发现。假臭草所到之处导致其他低矮草类迅速死亡，严重影响当地植物多样性分布，并且因其吸收肥料能力强，严重消耗了土壤养分，致使农作物缺乏养分。此外，它还分泌有毒恶臭气体，影响家畜觅食。

毒麦标本

Specimen of Lolium Temulentum L.

现代

入侵植物，原产于欧洲，外形酷似小麦，经常和小麦混生，但它的种子中含有能麻痹中枢神经、致使人畜昏迷的毒麦碱，并且影响小麦的产量和质量，被认为是恶性杂草。

检出转基因成分的美国苜蓿草

American Alfalfa Detected with Transgenic Ingredients

现代

苜蓿草作为一种优质饲料，素有“牧草之王”之称，主要用于奶牛养殖业。目前我国苜蓿草市场缺口较大，已成为苜蓿草进口大国，但进口仅限于非转基因苜蓿草。近年来，出入境动植物检疫部门多次从进口美国苜蓿草中检出未经准入的品系特异性基因J101和J163，不合格货物均已作退运或销毁处理。

检疫动物标本

Specimen of Quarantined Animals

现代

根据《中华人民共和国进出境动植物检疫法》《中华人民共和国进出境动植物检疫法实施条例》，动植物进境前应由申请人向直属海关提交申请材料，直属海关进行审核并提出审核意见，或将初审意见提交海关总署，由海关总署提出审核意见，最后由海关总署或直属海关向申请人制发批准文件。未获批准文件的，不得运输或携带动植物入境。

（图依次为：①龟壳标本、②杨家鼠标本、③狐猴标本、④穿山甲标本、⑤锦鸡标本、⑥小毛足鼠标本、⑦梅花鹿标本、⑧火烈鸟标本）

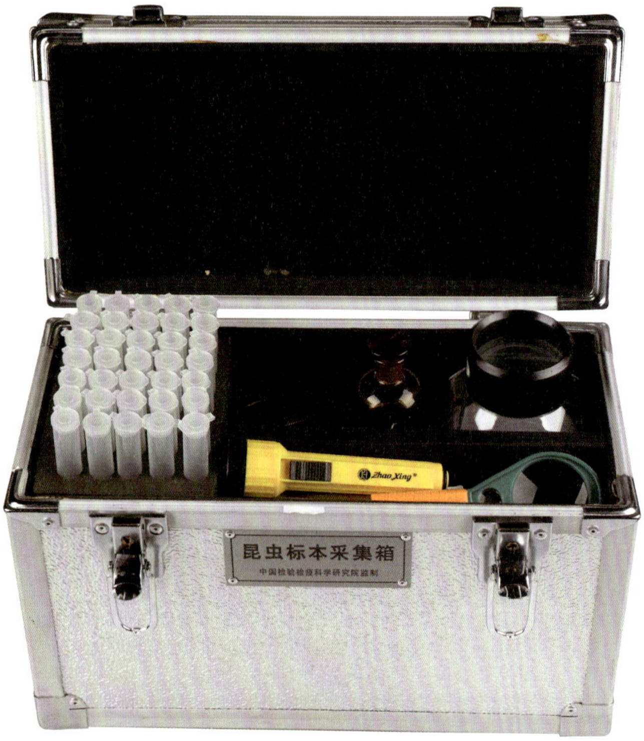

昆虫标本采集箱

Insect Specimen Collection Box

现代

海关、林业部门工作过程中配备的工具箱，配有各种常用标准工具。

原动植物检疫制服

Old Uniform for Animal and Plant Quarantine Officer

20世纪晚期

“三检合一”前，出入境动植物检疫工作人员所配发、穿着的制服。

进出口食品安全
Import and Export Food Safety

古代至近代，我国未实行系统有效的进出口食品卫生安全监督检验。中华人民共和国成立后，进出口食品安全部门依法承担进口食品、化妆品检验检疫、监督管理及境外生产企业注册管理，组织评估审查境内出口食品安全管理体系和状况，开展安全风险分析和预防，拟定出口检疫要求等职责，在维护人民群众健康和生命安全、促进贸易便利化等方面发挥了重要作用。

China did not carry out systematic and effective supervision and inspection on the health and safety of import and export food until modern times. After the founding of the People's Republic of China, the departments in charge of import and export food safety undertook the inspection and quarantine, supervision and administration of import foods and cosmetics, as well as the registration of overseas enterprises according to law. They also conducted risk analysis and prevention, and formulated export quarantine requirements, playing an important role in safeguarding people's health and safety and promoting trade facilitation.

原检验检疫制服

Old Uniform for Inspection and Quarantine Officer

现代

1998年3月"三检合一"后至2018年4月出入境检验检疫管理职责和队伍划归海关总署管理前，出入境检验检疫工作人员均穿着1999式制服并佩戴标志。

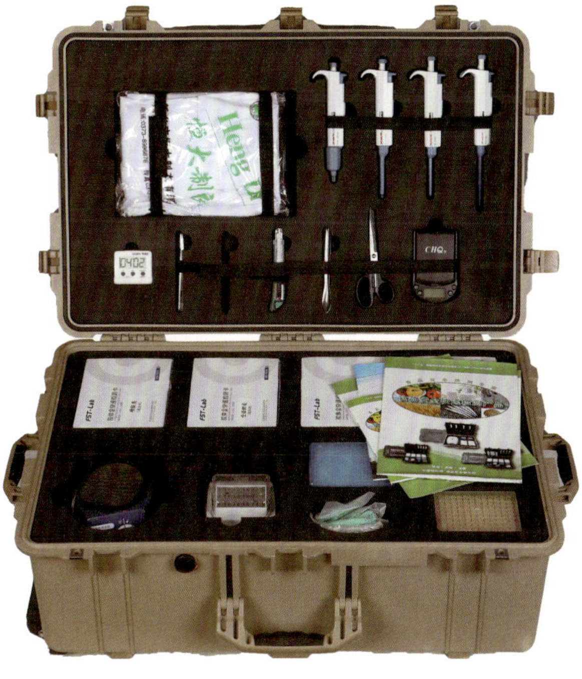

乳品安全检测箱

Milk Product Safety Test Kit

现代

这是中国检验检疫科学研究院根据国家对乳制品加强口岸检验、确保食品安全的监管要求，自主研发的运用于口岸工作的手提式乳品安全检测箱。

进出口食品、化妆品

Import and Export Foods and Cosmetics

现代

2018年4月，“关检融合”后，海关依法检验检疫、监督管理进口的婴幼儿奶粉等食品和化妆品，依照多边及双边协议检验检疫和监督管理出口食品。

荷莱蕊
PRIMAVITA
较大婴儿配方奶粉
6-12月龄 2段
Older Infant
Milk Powder Formula
净含量 900g

Primavita
康维多
康维多佑儿
无乳糖婴儿配方奶粉
原装进口
净含量 400克e

荷莱蕊
PRIMAVITA
幼儿配方羊奶粉
12-36月龄 3段
Young Children Goat
Milk Powder Formula
净含量 900g

STENDERS
SUGAR SCRUB
Apricot

STENDERS
24 Carat Gold
Silk for face and decollete

KOREA NO.1 BRAND
PEPERO
White Chocolate

Lindt
LINDOR
IRRESISTIBLY SMOOTH
ASSORTED CHOCOLATES

GHIRARDELLI
CHOCOLATE
INTENSE DARK
86%
CACAO
midnight reverie

进出口商品检验

Import and Export Commodity Inspection

我国进出口商品检验起源于早期对外贸易，西周即有明确商品质量管理规定，但未形成成熟制度和体系。1928年，国民政府工商部颁布《商品出口检验暂行规则》并先后在上海、广州、汉口等地设立商品检验局，对于出口商品（后扩展到进口商品）实施检验，标志着我国自主施行进出口商品检验的发端。新中国成立后，进出口商品检验部门依法承担进口商品风险评估、预警、反应、验证以及依据协议承担出口商品检验等工作，为促进我国对外贸易和经济社会全面发展发挥了不可或缺的重要作用。

Import and export commodity inspection of our country originated from the early foreign trade. Specific provisions on commodity quality control emerged in the Western Zhou Dynasty, but no mature institutions and systems had been formed. In 1928, the Ministry of Industry and Commerce of the Nanjing National Government promulgated *Provisional Rules for Commodity Export Inspection* and established Bureau of Inspection and Testing of Commercial Commodities successively in Shanghai, Guangzhou, Hankou and other places, to inspect export commodities (later expanded to import commodities), which marked the beginning of independent administrative implementation of China's import and export commodity inspection. After the founding of the People's Republic of China, import and export commodity inspection departments undertook risk assessment, early warning, response and verification of import commodities according to law, and undertook the work of export commodity inspection, which have played an indispensable and important role in promoting China's foreign trade and all-round economic and social development.

原商品检验制服

Old Uniform for Commodity Inspection Officer

20世纪晚期

“三检合一”前，进出口商品检验工作人员所穿着的1986式制服。

奥运火炬

Olympic Torch

2007年

2007年6月，原质检总局应北京奥组委要求承担了2008年北京奥运会奥运火炬质量监控任务，原质检总局检验监管司牵头成立检测及监造小组，对火炬进行极端自然环境条件测试和抽样检测，并赴中山、东莞等零部件加工和协作单位进行质量监查和督促，为全球瞩目的奥运火炬接力奠定了基础。

检出固废的货物

Goods Detected with Solid Wastes

现代

检验检疫技术中心化矿金属材料检测实验室对申报品名为“球碎矿”“不规则非整张牛皮革”的货物进行检验、鉴别，发现货物混有大量的生活废物，推断货物属于我国禁止进口的固体废物。

经商品检验发现问题并召回的商品

Defective Commodity Recalled after Inspection

现代

该玩具进行滥用测试后，挂件脱落形成小零件，存在儿童误食窒息的风险。

该玩具所配吸盘DINP实测值200000毫克/千克，超过标准限量（DIDP+DINP + DNOP）1000毫克/千克要求，存在危害儿童健康的风险。

该玩具形状特殊，沙球手柄能穿过测试的模板，存在使儿童窒息的风险。

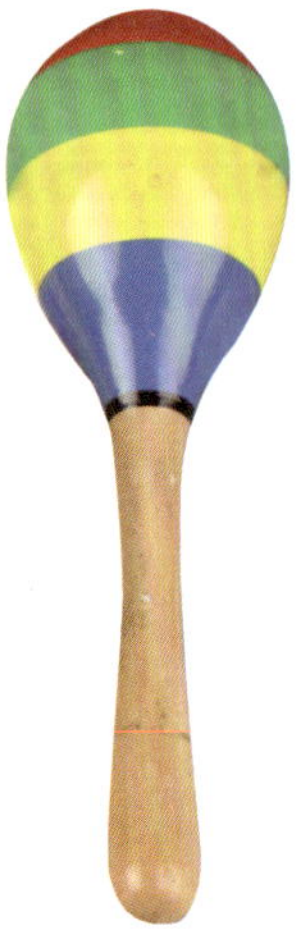

展厅实景

Photos of Exhibition Hall

“千秋古关”部分

清代十三行外国商馆区复原场景

“百年洋关”单元

近代海关查验复原场景

九龙关滞港缉私舰艇返穗半景画

“时光之镜”海关查验场景

海关罚没财物处置互动展项

打击走私濒危动植物及其制品展项

打击走私固体废物互动展项

海关实验室建设展项

红其拉甫海关建关初期复原场景

"关服集萃"展柜

“国盛关兴”单元

“海关902”艇专题展厅

后记

中国海关博物馆面向社会正式开放以来，积极践行文化自信，立足于行业博物馆实际，以展览为龙头、以藏品为依托、以研究为支撑、以社教和宣传为两翼、以制度为根本，逐步建立健全了具有中国海关博物馆特色的业务运行体系和管理模式，并主动围绕中心、服务大局，不断完善基本陈列、推出系列临时展览和巡展外展、充实馆藏文物，努力当好中华传统文化的弘扬者、行业文化的传播者、海关知识的普及者。2018年国务院机构改革，原质检总局的出入境检验检疫管理职责和管理队伍划入海关总署，中国海关博物馆按照海关总署领导“将检验检疫内容纳入博物馆基本陈列”的指示要求，在保持对外开放的同时对基本陈列“新中国海关”部分进行全面改造，增加了政治建关、国境卫生检疫、进出境动植物检疫、进出口食品安全、进出口商品检验、国盛关兴——海关改革等单元，并对原有单元进行全面优化，重点充实了党的十八大以来中国海关大力推进“五关”建设，打造让党中央放心、让人民群众满意的新时代中国特色社会主义新海关的新举措、新业绩、新成果、新风貌。

本书作为中国海关博物馆学术研究丛书之一，及时吸收、补充本馆最新业务建设成果，力争向读者提供最丰厚的海关精神文化滋养。近年来，中国海关博物馆相继出版《雄关漫道》《烽火硝烟守国门》《中国近代海关建筑图释》《币海关踪》等系列书籍，对于每本出版物，从内容到文字、从纸张到图片、从版式到设计，我们无不精益求精、力求止于至善，期望以最完美的面目呈现给读者。在此谨对那些曾为本馆建设发展做出贡献的人士致以崇高的敬意，并向参与本书编撰的同志们表示衷心感谢。同时也希望社会各界一如既往地关心支持中国海关博物馆，并积极参与海关历史、海关文物的研究，共同为繁荣海关文化、建设社会主义文化强国贡献力量。

本书收录的非馆藏文物均为授权复仿制件，并已注明其原件所在地。海关历史博大精深、海关业务专业复杂，因编著者学识、时间所限，本书内容难免存在错漏之处，敬请专家学者、广大读者批评指正。

中国海关博物馆馆长

2020年11月

Postscript

Since its official opening to the public, China Customs Museum has gradually established and perfected a customs-style museum business operation system and management model. Based on exhibitions, collections, research, social education and publicity functions, it actively practises cultural confidence and serves the central task as well as the overall interests of the country. By constantly improving its permanent exhibitions, launching series of temporary exhibitions, itinerant exhibitions, and outside exhibitions, and enriching collections, it strives to promote traditional Chinese culture, disseminate and popularize customs culture and knowledge.

In 2018, the State Council institutional reform was conducted, under which, the inspection and quarantine functions and work force were integrated into General Administration of Customs. China Customs Museum, at the request of the General Administration of Customs to "include the inspection and quarantine contents into the permanent exhibition of the museum", completely transformed the exhibition section of "Customs of New China" while keeping it open to the public. It increased such units as customs construction with political thinking, frontier health quarantine, entry-exit animal and plant quarantine, import and export food safety, import and export commodity inspection, customs reform, etc. Moreover, it optimized the original units, and enriched the content on the "customs construction in five aspects" by China Customs since the 18th National Congress of the CPC, as well as the new measures, new results, new achievements, and new features for the construction of the new socialist customs with Chinese characteristics in the new era that CPC Central Committee trusts and people are satisfied with.

As one of the academic research works of China Customs Museum, this book has absorbed and replenished the latest achievements of the Museum, striving to provide the most abundant customs culture for readers. In recent years, China Customs Museum has published a series of books, such as *Strong Pass Iron Wall*, *Guarding the National Gateway in the Flames and Smoke of War*, *Architecture illustration of Chinese Maritime*

Customs and *Currency and Customs*. For each published book, we strive to be perfect in content, words, paper, pictures, formats and designs, in the hopes of presenting perfect work for readers. Here we would like to pay high tribute to those who have contributed to the construction and development of the Museum and express our heartfelt thanks to those who have participated in the compilation of this book. Meanwhile, we hope that all sectors of society can, as always, care for and support China Customs Museum, and actively participate in the study of customs history and customs cultural relics, so as to make contributions to the prosperity of customs culture and the promotion of the socialist theme.

The cultural relics which are recorded in this book and are not the collections of the Museum are all authorized copies, and the sites of their originals have been noted. The customs history is extensive and profound and customs affairs are professional and complicated, but the knowledge and time of editors are limited. Therefore, this book probably has errors and omissions, and your comments and criticism are highly appreciated.

Fan Kun

Director of China Customs Museum

November 2020